Building a Godly Home

VOLUME TWO:
A Holy Vision for a Happy Marriage

Building a Godly Home

VOLUME TWO:
A Holy Vision for a Happy Marriage

William Gouge

edited and modernized
by Scott Brown and Joel R. Beeke

REFORMATION HERITAGE BOOKS
Grand Rapids, Michigan

Building a Godly Home, Volume 2
© 2013 Reformation Heritage Books

Reformation Heritage Books
2965 Leonard St. NE
Grand Rapids, MI 49525
616-977-0889 / Fax 616-285-3246
e-mail: orders@heritagebooks.org
website: www.heritagebooks.org

Printed in the United States of America
13 14 15 16 17 18/10 9 8 7 6 5 4 3 2 1

Library of Congress Cataloging-in-Publication Data

Gouge, William, 1578-1653.
   [Of domesticall duties]
   Building a Godly home / William Gouge ; edited and modernized by Scott Brown and Joel R. Beeke.
      pages cm
   Includes bibliographical references and index.
   ISBN 978-1-60178-226-7 (hardcover, v. 1 : alk. paper) 1. Christian ethics—Early works to 1800. 2. Families—Religious life—Early works to 1800. I. Brown, Scott. II. Beeke, Joel R., 1952- III. Title.
   BJ1241.G6 2013
   248.4'859—dc23
                                                    2013000372

For additional Reformed literature, request a free book list from Reformation Heritage Books at the above address.

Contents

Preface

Have you ever needed some detailed, practical counsel for your marriage? Have you ever wished someone would speak to the everyday matters that pop up in your marriage and family life? Have you ever heard sound teaching, but wished for more than broad theological principles? You needed someone to speak frankly. You wanted someone to show you exactly how the biblical principles applied in the real situations you were experiencing.

In this second volume of the series, *Building a Godly Home*, William Gouge (1575–1653) does just that. His marriage counsel is focused on the everyday matters that husbands and wives experience while living together. The basis for his counsel to married couples is his exposition of Ephesians 5:21–33, already presented in volume 1.

Gouge delivers very detailed explanations of the various parts of the husband-wife relationship. He analyzes nearly every possible aspect of married life. You will be amazed at the probing detail with which he examines these matters. He exposes the minutest parts of marriage. Yet he does not lose sight of the big picture. He goes to the heart of the matter.

Husbands and Wives Living Together

Gouge first directs his attention to the general category of husbands and wives living together in a family. This volume begins with a discussion of who ought to be able to marry and how they should proceed from singleness to marriage. How do you choose a suitable mate? What qualities must this mate possess? How should medical conditions impact whether you should get married or not?

Gouge proceeds to the matters of daily married life. His remedies against adultery will surprise you with their practicality, simplicity, and modern feel. He even speaks to the issue of when it is right and wrong for a husband and wife to live apart from each other. He explains how to live with an unbeliever; how to pray and care for their salvation; how to edify one another in the faith; how husbands and wives can foster a bad reputation for their spouses and how to avoid it. He confronts the husband who does not help his wife, but lets the weaker vessel carry all the heavy burdens herself—especially in practicing hospitality together and relieving the poor. Then Gouge turns his attention to wives.

Wives Who Submit to and Support Their Husbands

Gouge answers practical questions such as: How does a wife respect her husband? How should a wife think about submission? What are the particular sins of women? How does a wife deny honor to her husband? How does a wife live with someone of higher rank? What should a wife do if she has low esteem for her husband?

He also addresses matters that might puzzle many modern people but are of great concern to godly women who desire to obey the Bible's call to respect the authority of their husbands. For example, he speaks of the gentleness a woman should show her husband, her modesty in dress, and her respectful speech towards her husband—and about him when he is not there.

As anyone who has ever had a difficult supervisor knows, honoring authority can be a trial for the best of Christians. How much more this is the case in marriage! How should a wife relate to a foolish or disobedient husband? For what things must a wife receive her husband's consent? What should a wife do if her husband sinfully forbids something? What should a wife do if she does not agree with her husband about handling the children? Gouge answers these questions in a gracious, biblical manner.

The saying goes, "When momma ain't happy, ain't nobody happy." Gouge recognizes the importance of a wife cultivating contentment instead of contention. He addresses what a wife should do if she is displeased with where she lives. He counsels her about how to respond when her husband reproves her. He gives her directions for when she feels that her husband does not make enough money for her standard of living. Most of all, Gouge calls wives to imitate Christ in humility.

Husbands Who Love and Lead Their Wives
Gouge addresses the centrality of love and compassion for a good husband, and discusses how love must fill and shape his use of authority. How does a husband stir up his wife's love in the same way Christ wooed His church? How should a husband respond when he sees sin in his wife? How can he set her free to fulfill her responsibilities towards God and their family?

Gouge shows concern that husbands not misuse their authority. They must not be harsh. They must not become too demanding in hospitality and the labors that go with it. They should make sure they are not being too suspicious or controlling. Their use of authority should not discourage their wives, but encourage them.

Christian leaders understand how important it is to win the consciences of people so that you are not pressuring them to act against what they believe is right, and the husband's leadership in the home is no exception to this rule. What should a husband do when his wife's conscience is against some lawful thing he wants her to do? What should a husband do when his wife feels a false fear or guilt about something good? What should a husband do if his wife is misapplying the Word of God? How should a husband correct his wife in a way that shows her love and honor? Again, Gouge's treatment gives the answers we need to the real questions we face.

Love speaks many languages, and Gouge calls the man to use them all, from a kind and cheerful facial expression to giving her special gifts. He strongly emphasizes the husband's responsibility to provide for his wife's financial needs. He urges men to show their wives tenderness and compassion when they are sick, especially when they face the travails of pregnancy and childbirth. At every turn, Gouge summons husbands to the high calling of loving their wives—as Christ did the church—with sacrificial, affectionate service.

William Gouge provides husbands and wives one of the most detailed and honest treatments of the husband and wife relationship ever written. He speaks from a solid biblical position and with a sweet spirit of love and mercy throughout. Though a bit antiquated at times, we trust that you will find this book extremely insightful and helpful. May the Lord send His Spirit with His truth, so that this book will be an effective instrument to transform many marriages, to the blessing of generations to come.

Many thanks to Jonathan Sides and Paul Smalley for their invaluable editorial assistance on this volume. Also, thanks to Linda den Hollander and Kim DeMeester for their expert typesetting, to Gary den Hollander for his able proofreading, and to Jay Collier for seeing this book through the printing process. As editors, we wish to thank our precious wives, Deborah Brown and Mary Beeke, who ably pass Gouge's "high-bar" tests in this volume! Our hearts are often filled with praise for granting them to us.

—Scott Brown and Joel Beeke

–1–

Seeking Marriage

Having in the former treatise laid down the foundation of all family duties by expounding the words of the apostle,[1] I now intend to present their distinction in order, beginning with the first and most important couple in the family, *husband and wife.*

We will first speak of the persons who are to be accounted true and lawful husbands and wives, and then of the duties which they owe to each other.

Husband and wife are those who are rightly joined together by the bond of marriage, whereby two are made one flesh. For the better clearing of this point, we will consider both the parties that may be so closely joined together, and also the manner how they are rightly joined in so firm a unity.

About the parties we are to ask who may seek a mate for marriage and what kind of mate is to be taken. All who are able, without inevitable danger to their spouse to perform the essential duties of marriage, may be married. Out of this proposition arise three questions to be discussed.

1. Who are to be counted able?
2. What danger is inevitable?
3. Whether marriage is free for all but such?

---

1. For his exposition of Ephesians 5:21–6:4, see William Gouge, *Building a Godly Home, Volume 1, A Holy Vision for Family Life* (Grand Rapids: Reformation Heritage Books, 2013).

Physical Maturity in Them That Are to Be Married

They are to be counted able who have passed puberty, and are not made impotent by defect of nature or any other occasion. Physical maturity is absolutely necessary for consummating a just and lawful marriage. Because God at first made Adam of full age, so when He sought out a wife for him, He made her of full age too. He made her a "woman," not a child (Gen. 2:22). Where the apostle advises parents to take care for the marriage of their children, he adds this condition, "if she pass the flower of her age" (1 Cor. 7:36). Childhood is counted the flower of age. While the flower of the plant sprouts, the seed is green, unfit to be sown.

Question: How long does the flower of age last?

Answer: The civil law, and common law also, set down twelve years for the flower of a female's age, and fourteen, of a male's, which is the minimum. Before those years they can have no need of marriage, nor yet are well fit for marriage. If they wait some years longer, it will be much better for the parties themselves that marry, for the children which they bring forth, for the family of which they are the head, and for the nation of which they are members. Note the ages of the kings of Israel and Judah when they were first married, and we shall find few of them to be under twenty, and those few, not above one or two years under, and yet of all sorts of people the kings used to marry earliest, that so they might have heirs quickly.

Objection: Solomon was but a child when he came to the crown (1 Chron. 22:5; 29:1), and yet he had a child of a year old at least (2 Chron. 12:13).

Answer: He was said to be a child not simply, but comparatively, in relation to his other brothers which were older than he was (1 Kings 2:22), and in regard of that great work he was to undertake (1 Kings 3:7). In the time of his reign he is said to be old (1 Kings 11:4), which could not be if he had been a child in age when he began to reign, for he reigned but forty years.[2]

Against this principle of fitness of age is the practice of such parents, or other friends of children, who make matches for them in their childhood and move them to consent, and so cause them to be married. Such marriages are mock marriages, and mere nullities. For children cannot know what pertains to marriage, much less can they perform that which is required of married persons. Their consent, therefore, is justly accounted no consent unless they ratify it after they come to years.

Impotent Persons that Should Not Seek after Marriage

They are to be accounted *impotent* and in that respect unable to perform the essential duties of marriage, who (to use the scriptural phrase) were born eunuchs from their mother's womb (Matt. 19:12), or by any accidental occasion are so made, likewise those who are defective, or closed in their secret parts, or taken with an incurable palsy, or possessed with frigidity,[3] or any other similar obstacle.

These ought not to seek after marriage, for by those signs of impotency God shows that He calls them to live single.

Contrary to this manifestation of God's will do they sin who conceal their impotency and join themselves in marriage, whereby they frustrate one main end of marriage, which is procreation of children, and do such a wrong to the party whom they marry, that sufficient satisfaction can never be made.

---

2. We omit Gouge's brief chronological digression about the age of other Israelite kings.

3. *Impotent...palsy...frigidity*: Gouge does not refer to temporary sexual problems or emotional difficulties, but long-term physical disabilities like paralysis or deformity that prevent sexual relations.

Barrenness Does Not Hinder Marriage

Question: Are those who are barren to be ranked among those impotent persons?

Answer: No, there is great difference between impotency and barrenness.

Impotency may be known and discerned by outward visible signs; barrenness cannot. It is not discerned except by lack of child-bearing.

Impotent persons cannot yield due benevolence,[4] but those who are barren may.

Impotency is incurable, but barrenness is not simply so. Many after they have been a long while barren have become fruitful, and that not only by an extraordinary work of God above the course of nature, as Sarah (Gen. 18:11) and Elizabeth (Luke 1:7), with whom by reason of age it ceased to be after the manner of women, but also by such a blessing as might stand with the course of nature, being obtained by prayer, as Rebekah (Gen. 25:21) and Hannah (1 Sam. 1:5–20), of which daily experience gives good evidence. Many after ten, fifteen, twenty, and more years of barrenness have brought forth children.

On these grounds many saints who have been barren have married, and their practice not forbidden, nor their marriage dissolved. Though procreation of children is one end of marriage, yet it is not the only end. So sacred is the marriage bond, that though it is made for children's sake, yet it may not be broken for lack of children.

That Inevitable Danger which Hinders Marriage

Those who are infected with contagious diseases that spread themselves into those who have company with them, and infect them also, should not seek after marriage. That cannot

---

4. *Due benevolence*: sexual intercourse (1 Cor. 7:3, KJV).

but endanger the party whom they marry. It was for mutual good of one another that God ordained the law of marriage (Gen. 2:18). To use it to the hurt and danger of one another, is against the main end of the first institution.

The law of shutting out a leper from all company with men proves as much (2 Chron. 26:21), for if lepers might not have mutual companionship with any man, much less might they have matrimonial companionship with a wife or a husband.

By contagious diseases, not only will both parties which fellowship together be infected, but also their offspring. Their disease, which otherwise might die with them, is propagated to their posterity. A similar restraint may be applied to such foul and loathsome diseases that make the company and society of that person who is infected wearisome and offensive to their companion.

They sin against the end and use of marriage who conceal such diseases, and join themselves in marriage, to the inexcusable harm of the party whom they marry.

The Lawfulness of Marriage to All Sorts of Persons
Where there is no such just obstacle as has been mentioned, it is lawful for all sorts of people of whatever calling or condition to marry. "Marriage is honourable in all," or among all, namely in, or among all sorts of people (Heb. 13:4). It is counted a doctrine of devils to forbid to marry (1 Tim. 4:1–3). It is a doctrine contrary to God's Word, and a doctrine that causes much inward burning and outward contamination, and so makes their bodies, which should be temples of the Holy Spirit, to be pig-pens of the devils.

The disease which marriage is set apart to cure is a common disease which has infected all sorts of people. Why then shall not the remedy be as common? In this case the apostle says of all, without exception of any, "to avoid fornication, let every man have his own wife, and let every woman have her own husband." And again, "If they cannot contain [control themselves], let them marry: for it is better to marry than to burn" (1 Cor. 7:2, 9).

Objection: There are eunuchs which have made themselves eunuchs (that is, have abstained from marriage and lived in a single life with chastity) for the kingdom of heaven's sake (Matt. 19:12).

Answer: That is spoken of some particular persons to whom the gift of chastity was given, not of any distinct conditions and callings, as if everyone of this or that calling had so done or were able so to do. Christ added this clause, "He that is able to receive it, let him receive it" (Matt. 19:12), and the apostle to the same purpose says, "every man hath his proper gift of God" (1 Cor. 7:7).

Against this necessary and legitimate liberty is the impure and tyrannical restraint of the Church of Rome, by which all that enter into any of their holy orders are kept from marriage. Do they not tempt God by putting a yoke upon men's necks, which neither our fathers nor we are able to bear (Acts 15:10)? No such restraint was ever placed by God's Word upon any of those holy functions which He ordained. Under the law it was lawful for high priests, ordinary priests, all sorts of Levites, and extraordinary prophets, to marry, and under the gospel, for apostles, bishops, deacons, and all ministers of the Word.

The effects of this diabolical doctrine have been horrible, such as fornication, adultery, incest, homosexuality, etc. Many wives were put away from their husbands because their husbands were ministers, and many ministers put from their calling because they had wives. Many children were by this means born illegitimately, and among them many in their infancy cruelly murdered. Six thousand heads of infants were found in the ponds of a religious house. How many more thousands have been from time to time cast into other ponds, or buried in gardens, or other places, or in other ways carried out of sight? Devilish must that doctrine be which has such devilish effects. Well did he wish, who wished that all they who cannot control themselves would realize how rashly they profess perfection, and vow virginity.[5]

The Things Absolutely Necessary to Make a Person Fit for Marriage

They who have the ability to marry must be careful in choosing a "help meet"[6] for them, for this was God's care when first He instituted marriage (Gen. 2:18). To make a help meet for marriage, some things are absolutely necessary for the very essence or being of marriage; others, necessary for the comfort and happiness of marriage.

In regard of the former sort, there must be chosen:

1. *One of the same kind* or nature, for among all the creatures which were made, "there was not found an help meet" for man (Gen. 2:20). Therefore, out of man's bone and flesh God made a woman of his own nature and kind.

Contrary to this is the detestable sin of sexual perversion with beasts, explicitly forbidden by the law (Lev. 18:23). This is a sin more than beastly, for the brute beasts content themselves with their own kind. This is unnatural.

2. *One of the contrary sex.* The male must choose a female, the female a male, because God made Adam a male, made Eve a female, and joined them in marriage. A conjunction of these different sexes is only fit for increase of mankind, and other marriage duties.

Against this are those unnatural minglings of parties of the same sex, which the apostle counts as judgments inflicted

---

5. Gouge cites Bernard of Clairvaux (1090–1153), *On the Conversion of Clerics,* book 29.

6. *Help meet*: a helper suitable for a person (Gen. 2:20).

on the pagans, because "they changed the truth of God into a lie, and worshipped, and served the creature more than the Creator" (Rom. 1:25–26).

3. *One not with relatives by blood or marriage which are forbidden by the law of God.* These forbidden marriages are expressed by Moses (Lev. 18:6–16) and explained in a table of relatives by blood or marriage which none may marry, appointed to be hung up in every church.

Against this is incest, a sin not only forbidden by God's Word, but so horrible even to the pagans as, to use the apostle's words, "is not so much as named among the Gentiles" (1 Cor. 5:1). That rebuke is well confirmed by the pagan orator's moving exclamation against one Sassia, who married her son-in-law, in these words, "O incredible wickedness of a woman, not heard of in any age but this! O unbridled and untamed lust! O singular boldness! Not to fear the power of God and shame of men!... Lust, impudence, madness, overcame shame, fear and reason."[7]

What may we now think of the dispensations which the Pope gives for incestuous marriage, granted to great princes even by the Council of Trent? Does he not show himself by this to be that man of sin, "who opposeth and exalteth himself above all that is called God" (2 Thess. 2:4)?

4. *One that is free, not married, nor betrothed to another.* The law of marriage notes thus much in this clause, "They twain [two] shall be one flesh" (Matt. 19:5). In that the law inflicts the same punishment upon the person which being betrothed[8] commits immorality (Deut. 22:22–24), that it does upon a married person, it is evident that it is unlawful to marry one betrothed to another, as well as one married to another. So firm is this betrothal that the law called a betrothed young

---

7. Gouge quotes the Roman orator, Cicero (103–43 B.C.), *Pro Cluentio.*

8. *Betrothed*: solemnly promised for marriage to a specific person in a manner more binding than engagement.

woman a *wife*, and a betrothed young woman might not be put away without a bill of divorce.

Against this is bigamy and polygamy, which we have already discussed,[9] to which head may be referred marriages with those who have been betrothed to others beforehand. These are utterly unlawful.

The Lawfulness of Other Marriages after One of the Married Couple Is Dead

Question: Are those who have buried their husband or wife free to marry again?

Answer: Yes, as free as those who were never married. The law of Moses does not only permit a widow to marry again, but if her husband died before he had any children, it commanded the next kinsman that was living and free to marry her, that he might raise up seed to his deceased brother (Deut. 25:5–9). If he refused to do this, a penalty of shame was inflicted on him; the rejected widow was to "loose his shoe from off his foot, and spit in his face" in the presence of the elders. The apostle explicitly says that a woman, when her husband is dead, is at liberty to be married (1 Cor. 7:8–9). Speaking of young widows he further says, "I will therefore that the younger women marry" (1 Tim. 5:14).

This liberty which the prophet of God and apostle of Christ grant to a wife, can by no argument be denied to a husband: for the bond of marriage gives them a similar power over another's body (1 Cor. 7:4), and knits one as unbreakably as the other (Matt. 19:6). Husbands, therefore, as well as wives have used this liberty, as Abraham (Gen. 25:1).

The apostle that gives this liberty gives a reason for it taken from the limitation of that time during which married persons have power one over another, and that is the time

---

9. See Gouge, *Building a Godly Home*, 1:138.

of this life only. "For the woman which hath an husband is bound by the law to her husband, so long as he liveth; but if the husband be dead she is loosed" (Rom. 7:2). On this ground, all the reasons which authorize or move those who never were married to marry may be applied to them that by death have their spouse taken from them.

Question: May this liberty be extended any further than to a second marriage?

Answer: We find no restraint from a third, or fourth, or more marriages, if by the divine providence so many wives, or husbands one after another be taken away while there is need for the surviving party to use the benefit of marriage. The woman of Samaria that had five husbands one after another, is not blamed for being married to so many, but for living with one (after the others were dead) that was not her husband (John 4:18). Neither did the Lord condemn that woman who was said to have seven husbands one after another (Matt. 22:23–32).

Against this is the opinion of Montanists and Cataphrygians,[10] ancient heretics that counted those marriages which the survivor made after the death of a spouse to be adulterous. Tertullian,[11] an ancient and learned father, was so far infected with this heresy that he wrote a treatise in defense of it. It seems by their arguments that one main ground of their error was a misinterpretation of those Scriptures which forbid men to have two wives at once, and women to have two husbands at once, like, "They (two) shall be one flesh" (Gen. 2:24). A bishop or a deacon must be "the husband of one wife" (1 Tim. 3:2, 12). "Let not a widow be

---

10. *Montanists and Cataphrygians*: sectarian second-century movement originating in Phrygia, Asia Minor, that claimed direct revelations from God through prophecy and taught rigorous morality and asceticism.

11. *Tertullian*: Christian theologian Quintus Septimius Florens Tertullianus (died c. 220), from North Africa.

taken into the number under threescore years old, having been the wife of one man" (1 Tim. 5:9).

These are indeed explicit texts against such digamists[12] and polygamists who we described earlier, but they make no more against second (or more) marriages after one mate being dead, than against first marriages. Those who deny such later marriages to any kind of ministers belong to the same category as these heretics. So do our adversaries. They exclude those who are married again after one wife is dead from such functions of inferior orders,[13] into which they admit those who are but once married. They cite many of those Scriptures which Montanists do (1 Tim. 3:2, 12; 5:9) which shows that they are infected with the same heresy, though they pretend to renounce it.

Equality in Years Between Husband and Wife

That matrimonial companionship may prove to be a comfort, it is necessary that there should be some equality between the parties that are married in *age, estate, condition, and piety.*

For age, as the party that seeks a mate must be old enough, fit to give consent, and able to perform marriage duties, so the mate which is taken must be somewhat suitable in age, if one young, both young, if one of middle age, both so, if one grown to years, the other also. It is noted of Zacharias and Elizabeth, that "both were well stricken[14] in years" (Luke 1:7). If both were old together, then both also were young together. Equality in years makes married people more fit for procreation of children, for a mutual performance of

---

12. *Digamists*: people married to two other people at the same time.

13. *Inferior orders*: or minor orders; acolytes, exorcists, lectors (readers), and porters (doorkeepers); positions lower than the priests in the church hierarchy of the Roman Catholic Church. See Council of Trent, session 23.

14. *Stricken*: advanced, far ahead.

marriage duties to each other, and for making their company and fellowship happier in every way.

This equality is not to be taken too strictly, as if the married couple were to be just of the same age, but only for some correspondence in years, which may be though there be a disparity of five or ten, or somewhat more years, especially if the excess of years be on the husband's part. In addition to the fact that according to the ordinary course of nature a man's strength and vigor lasts longer than a woman's,[15] it is very fit that the husband should be somewhat older than his wife, because he is a head, a governor, a protector of his wife. The Scripture notes many husbands to be older than their wives, as Abraham was ten years older than Sarah (Gen. 17:17). And if we carefully observe the circumstances of the histories of Isaac and Jacob and their wives, we shall find that the husbands were older than their wives. To my remembrance an approved example of a husband younger than his wife cannot be found in Scripture.

Contrary to this equality in years is the practice of many men and women who, being aged, to satisfy their lust or for some other interest, marry those who are but in the flower of their age. They do many times largely fail of their expectation, for those young ones, finding the society of aged folks to be burdensome and wearisome to them, soon begin to be disgusted with them, and cause more grief and irritation than they ever gave comfort and contentment.

On the other side, there are others in the prime and strength of their age, for wealth, honor, or such similar respects, who marry those that with age begin to be decrepit and unfit to be married, hoping that they will not live long, but that with a little trouble they shall purchase much dignity or riches, and after a while be free again. But God

15. In the seventeenth century women often died in childbirth or suffered from its medical aftereffects.

often deals with such in their kind by prolonging the life of those aged persons, and so making the burden to be much more grievous and tedious than was imagined, and by taking away those young ones sooner than they looked for, by which it comes to pass that all their hopes perish. The pagans observed inequality in years to be occasions of much trouble, and therefore prescribed rules against it.[16]

Equality in Estate and Condition between Those to Be Married

Some equality in outward estate and wealth is also appropriate for the parties that are to be married together, lest the disparity (especially if it be too great) make the one look down on the other. If a man of great wealth is married to a poor woman, he will think to make her as his maidservant, and expect that she should carry herself towards him as inappropriate for one with whom he shares his life and bed. Such a one may rather be said to be brought into slavery than marriage. And if a rich woman marry a poor man, she will expect to be the master, and to rule him, so as the order which God has established will be clearly distorted, and the honor of marriage laid in the dust. For where no order is, there can be no honor.

Likewise we might speak of social status, that there also should be some equality, that princes, nobles, and gentlemen marry those who are of their own rank, and the commoner sort those who are of their degree. Note what sort of wives Abraham, Isaac, and Jacob married, and it will appear that they had respect to this parity. Disparity in condition as well as in estate is a means to make men and women get puffed up and arrogant towards one another, even to twit one another in the teeth[17] with their former estate and condition.

---

16. Gouge cites Aristotle (384–322 B.C.), *Politics*, book 7.
17. *Twit…in the teeth*: mock them to their face.

Contrary on the one side are the practices of those who attempt to marry above their own estate and status, thinking by such marriages to advance themselves. This is the only thing which many seek after in seeking wives and husbands. But by this it comes to pass that they often meet with the worst matches, and make their marriage a kind of slavery for them. Great portions make many women proud, picky, spendy, lazy, and careless. A man would do much better, even for help of his outward estate, to marry a prudent, sober, thrifty, careful, diligent wife, though with a small portion, than such a one. A proud back, a picky tooth, and a spendy hand will soon consume a great portion, but a "wise woman buildeth her house" (Prov. 14:1), and "a virtuous woman is a crown to her husband" (Prov. 12:4). Also, many wives that are married to very rich husbands are more confined and limited in their allowance, than those married to men of lower estate. It is not the means which a man has, but his mind and disposition that makes him free and bountiful to his wife.

Against this are the marriages which men of great authority and ability make with common women, even their own maids many times, and those of the lowest rank, their kitchen-maids, and the marriages which women of noble blood, and great estate, make with their serving-men. Do they not betray much worthlessness of mind and unrestrained power of lust?

If it is said that such marriages are not simply unlawful, the rule of the civil law gives a good answer, "Always in marriages not only what is lawful, but what is honest and suitable, is to be considered."[18]

---

18. Gouge quotes from book 23 of the *Digest*, a collection of Roman laws made by the order of the emperor Justinian (c. 482–565) and still influential in early modern Europe.

Equality in Piety and Religion between Those
to Be Married Together

The parity which is of greatest consequence between parties to be married is in *piety*.[19] In this respect it is good that as a Christian be married to a Christian, so one that truly fears God to one of the same mind and disposition, as it is noted of Zacharias and Elizabeth, "they were both righteous before God" (Luke 1:6). A worthy couple, one worthy of another, being both alike in such excellent qualities, they could not but reap from each other much comfort and profit every way.

This is one of the most principal points that are included under that condition given by the Holy Spirit in choosing a spouse, in these words, "in the Lord" (1 Cor. 7:39).

There is no better way to increase love, preserve peace, motivate to all duty, be helpful to one another in all things and at all times, as this parity. By this they shall be made both able to do more good to one another, and capable to receive more good from one another: especially in the best things, even in those which concern their spiritual edification in this world, and eternal salvation in the world to come.

For Christ is the fountain and head of all spiritual life and grace. "It pleased the Father that in him should all fulness dwell" (Col. 1:19), so that it is He that fills all in all things (Eph. 1:23). Now Christ shares that life and grace which are in Him with the members of His body. If then I, being a member of that mystical body, am linked by that near and sacred bond of marriage to one of the members of that body, what hope there is of mutual sharing with one another, and mutual receiving from one another of those gifts and graces which either of us receive from Christ our head! If an unbelieving wife may be saved by a believing husband, and an

---

19. *Piety*: godliness, which Calvin defined as a mixture of the fear of the Lord and love for God.

unbelieving husband by a believing wife, much more will one believer be more and more edified by another.

Happy is that family where both the husband and wife are mutual members of Christ's body. There the house will be made God's church, as the house of Aquila and Priscilla was (Rom. 16:5). God's worship will be maintained there. Children will be trained up there in the nurture of the Lord, and servants also taught the fear of God. They that are indeed of Christ's kingdom, will be as leaven which seasons the whole lump (Matt. 13:33). Note the profession which Joshua makes to this purpose (Josh. 24:15), and the effect which is noted of the ruler whose son Christ cured, "he himself believed, and his whole house" (John 4:53).

Let me exhort parents and other governors of children both to train up their own children in true piety and fear of God, and also to seek such matches for them, as they may have some assurance that they are of the same faith, and of the same mind and heart: thus shall they obtain for their children much happiness in their marriage as Abraham did to Isaac (Gen. 24).

Against this teaching are marriages with atheists, infidels, and similar persons (Gen. 6:4; Deut. 7:3; Ezra 9:2; Neh. 10:30; Mal. 2:11; 2 Cor. 6:14).

Getting Married

Having shown what *persons* are fit to be joined in marriage, it remains to show after what *manner* they are to be joined. There are in Scripture three steps or degrees commended to us by which marriageable parties are in order to proceed to marriage.

1. A mutual liking.
2. An actual betrothal.
3. A public ceremony of marriage.

The first liking is sometimes on the parents' or other friends' part, and then made known to the party to be married, as the friends of Rebekah, liking the offer of Isaac which was made by Abraham's servant, made it known to Rebekah herself (Gen. 24:58). Sometimes again the first liking is on the party's part that is to be married, and then if that party be under the authority of parents, the matter must be proposed to them, before there be any further proceeding, as Samson who, seeing and liking a daughter of the Philistines, told his father and his mother (Judg. 14:2). Even if the party is not under the authority of any, it is very fitting that counsel be taken of wise and understanding friends, that in a matter as weighty as marriage, there may be advice of more heads than one, for the preventing of what might happen through rashness.

After a liking is thus taken by one party for a good mate, that liking must be proposed to the other party so liked, to know whether there is a reciprocal affection of one towards another. Thus Samson went and talked with that woman whom he liked to be his wife (Judg. 14:7).

If at first there is a good liking mutually and thoroughly settled in both their hearts for one another, love is likely to continue in them forever, as things which are well-glued and settled before being shaken up and down will never be torn apart, but if they are joined together without glue, or shaken while the glue is moist, they cannot remain firm. Mutual love and good liking of each other is as glue. Let the parties to be married be well settled before they come to meet with trials through cohabitation, and that love will not easily be loosened by any trials.

Against this is the adulterous and irrational practice of those who so soon as they cast their eye on any whom they like, never advise or consult about a right and due process toward marriage, but instantly with all eagerness and speed, like irrational beasts, seek to have their desire and lust satisfied. Though to keep themselves free from the penalty of the laws under which they live they obtain means to be married, yet they show a lustful and adulterous mind. And their practice is too similar to the practice of the Benjamites, who caught wives from among the daughters of Shiloh as they were dancing (Judg. 21:23), or else to the practice of the ancient world, which so grieved the Spirit of God that He repented that He had made man, and was moved to bring a general deluge on the whole world. Their practice was this, that "they took them wives of all that they chose" (Gen. 6:2), that is, they rashly and suddenly married whomsoever they liked, without any consideration of their condition.

What Is Betrothal?
When both parties have shown a mutual liking to each other, and upon mature deliberation and good advice do think one

to be a fit match for another, it is necessary that a joint consent and absolute promise of marrying one another before sufficient witnesses be made. Rightly made, this is a betrothal, which is the first step of a marriage.[1]

Many good and weighty reasons may be proposed to show how necessary it is that a betrothal should go before marriage. For:

1. It adds much to the honor of marriage, that it should be deliberately and advisedly step after step, by one degree after another consummated and made up.

2. It puts a difference between those who intend marriage in the fear of the Lord, for such holy ends as are warranted in the Word, and those who intend it only to satisfy their lust, or for other similar carnal ends. For these cannot stand to wait, as was noted before. But they that use this solemn preparation by a betrothal before marriage, show that they desire to have all things fit for so sacred a matter duly performed; and therefore they are content to wait so that they can make a better marriage.

3. It is a means of knitting the hearts of the two parties to be married more firmly and unbreakably together before they come to dwell together. For a betrothal being the first step of a marriage, it is an evident demonstration of God's counsel concerning the betrothed parties, that God has

---

1. We omit here much of Gouge's section on a "contract" of marriage because it applies to the now obsolete practice of espousal (from Latin *sponsalia*, "betrothal"). In this contract a man and woman became legally betrothed before marriage. Rather than attempt to rewrite Gouge's material for our modern cultural practice of engagement, which Gouge did not foresee, we have chosen to omit it except for those portions we deemed relevant.

We have changed Gouge's word "contract" to "betrothal" to avoid confusing modern readers with the terminology of a legal contract, although such was very appropriate for Gouge's day. The words betroth and espouse remain familiar to some modern English speakers because of the Bible, especially the King James Version (Ex. 21:8–9; 22:16; Lev. 19:20; Deut. 20:7; 22:23–30; Hos. 2:19–20; cf. Matt. 1:18; Luke 1:27; 2:5; 2 Cor. 11:2).

prepared them for each other to be husband and wife, so that after the betrothal is made, they may simply and absolutely pray for each other, that God would bless them one to another, to live comfortably and happily together.

Before a betrothal is made, they can pray for one another only with the desire that God has appointed them to be husband and wife. Often it happens that after many great hopes and probability of proceeding in such or such a match, by some occasion or other it is completely broken off, but a lawful betrothal ties so firm a knot as cannot be broken. Such a man may conclude that being betrothed to a woman she shall be his wife, and so may a woman conclude of a man. This consideration will further move them to observe more carefully what good qualities or what other things are in each other which may make them lovelier to one another.

4. It is a means to make them prepare themselves beforehand to perform such marriage duties as God's Word requires of husband and wife. A betrothal gives them assurance of marriage if they live long enough to see it, so that they cannot but know that it is high time for them to think how they are to carry themselves when they come to live at home together, and to consider what crosses ordinarily accompany the married state, that they may be prepared beforehand wisely to pass them over, or patiently to endure them.

5. It may be a means of discovering many hidden inconveniences, which otherwise would never come to light. For many friends, fearing to speak of private matters lest they hurt the relationship between themselves and their friends, will not make them known till they see some urgent necessity to move them so to do. Though the evil be such, as being known would hinder marriage, yet till they see some sure evidence that they shall indeed be married (if no just objection be put in) they will hope that some other occasion may arise to hinder the marriage, and in that respect conceal their objection.

But because a betrothal is the beginning of marriage, after they have notice of it they will not refrain to disclose what they know. It is for this end that the betrothal is openly proclaimed in the church three times, that if any do know any just cause why those betrothed may not lawfully proceed to marriage, they make it known. It is a commendable custom, and great pity, that it is so much neglected as it is.

6. It is a means to stir up the parties which are to be married, more carefully and diligently to provide all things fit for their dwelling together, and well ordering their household beforehand, that they lack not necessities when they need them. Being betrothed, they know that it cannot be long before they must come to dwell together.

The Time Between the Betrothal and Marriage

Question: How much time must pass between the making of a betrothal and consummating of marriage?

Answer: This must be left to the wise consideration of the parties betrothed, and of their friends, for the same time cannot precisely be prescribed to all. Occasions may arise either to hasten or put off the marriage. Only extremes on both sides must be avoided. The wedding should not be performed too suddenly after the betrothal, for then the goals and reasons of a betrothal, before mentioned, are made void. Nor should it yet be put off too long, for then Satan may take the opportunity to tempt them by their disadvantage.

The praiseworthy custom of our and other churches shows that at least three weeks must pass between betrothal and marriage. The betrothal is to be proclaimed three times, and that but once a week, before the wedding be celebrated. And we read that the virgin Mary was at least three months betrothed before Joseph took her as a wife (Luke 1:27, 56). When the angel first came to her she was betrothed; after that she went to her cousin Elizabeth with whom she lived three months. Being returned home, Joseph was warned by an angel to take her as his wife (Matt. 1:20). I note this not as a rule for every one precisely to follow, for the virgin Mary had a just occasion to tarry three months with her old cousin Elizabeth, and others may have occasions to put off their marriages, which may be lawful, as long as the marriage is not put off too long, and that there is a mutual and joint consent of both parties. For after the betrothal is made, neither the man nor the woman have power over their own body.

Against this is that illegitimate course which many take, to be pledged to marry and made sure of a wife, and then to travel beyond sea, or to any other place, and be absent from their spouse a year, or two, or three, or it may be more years. If a man might not go to war, not be charged with any business that should draw him from his wife the first year of his marriage, much less may he absent himself for any long time after he is betrothed but not married (Deut. 24:5). This may be a means to alienate the heart of his spouse from him forever.

Religious Consecration of Marriage

The last degree of consummating a marriage is the open and public ceremony which consists of a religious *consecration* and a civil *celebration*. A religious consecration of marriage is performed by the blessing of a public minister of the Word openly in church in the day time. This has been used of old by Christians, and still is continued among us. Though we have neither explicit precept, nor particular pattern in God's Word for this manner of performing a wedding (for there is no particular rule set down in the Scripture), being agreeable to the general rules, we ought in conscience to subject ourselves to it.

The general rules are these, "Let all things be done decently, and in order" (1 Cor. 14:40). The churches of God have such a custom (1 Cor. 11:16). "Submit yourselves to every ordinance of man for the Lord's sake" (1 Peter 2:13), with similar verses. But this manner of consecrating marriage is very decent and in good order, a praiseworthy custom of the churches, and an ordinance of those governors under whom we live, therefore legitimate, and to be observed. Neither is this order, custom, and ordinance appointed without just and weighty reasons. For:

1. Marriage is a kind of public action. The well or ill ordering of it much tends to the good or hurt of family, church, and nation. By marriage families are started, and church and nation increased and continued.

2. "Marriage is honorable" (Heb. 13:4), the most sacred bond that knits any two persons together.

3. Marriage is God's covenant (Prov. 2:17), in which He Himself has a main and principal part. God is the chief agent in joining man and woman in marriage.

On these grounds it has been thought very necessary that weddings should be performed in the day time (as a work of light that need not be covertly done) and in a public place, so that any that will may have free access, either to object against it, and hinder it (if there be just cause) or to be a witness and to add his blessing. Among public places the church is thought the fittest, because it is the house of prayer where people and actions are most solemnly blessed. Of all people, a public minister is thought to be the best to celebrate marriage, and to join the parties to be married, together, because he stands in God's place, and in and by his ministry God joins them together, and blesses them, so that after the minister has rightly joined husband and wife together in matrimony, it may be well said, "Those whom God hath joined together, let no man put asunder."

The form of consecrating marriage which is prescribed in our liturgy or common prayer-book,[2] distinctly, clearly, and

---

2. *Common prayer-book*: the Book of Common Prayer, containing the liturgical forms for the worship of the Church of England of which

fully sets down whatever is to be observed and done by the parties to be married, their parents, or other governors, and the minister that joins them together, that I can add nothing to it. It declares the grounds, ends, and uses of marriage. There open proclamation is made whether any can object against the intended marriage. There each party is solemnly charged, that if either of them know any obstacle why they may not lawfully be married, to disclose it.

There also each party is openly demanded if freely and willingly they will take one another for husband and wife. There the duties of married persons are declared, and they are each asked whether they will subject themselves to it or not. All this being openly professed, the parent or someone in his place is called forth to give the bride to the bridegroom. Then they two actually taking each other to be husband and wife, and testifying the same by express words, and by mutual pledges, the minister in God's name joins them together, pronounces them to be lawful husband and wife, and by prayer seeks God's blessing upon the action, and upon their persons. Thus the marriage is consecrated, and the two made one flesh, that is, lawfully joined together by the sacred bond of marriage.

Clandestine Marriages

Against this are clandestine marriages, those who are made in private houses, or other secret places, or in churches without a sufficient number of witnesses, or at night, or without a lawful minister of the word, etc. As those seeking of secrecy take much from the honor and dignity of marriage, so it implies some evil clinging to it, "For every one that doeth evil hateth the light" (John 3:20). There is little hope that such

---

Gouge was a part. Originally compiled by Thomas Cranmer in 1549, it was revised under Queen Elizabeth in 1559, replaced by the Westminster Directory of Public Worship in 1645, then restored in 1662.

marriages should have any good success. For where such means as are sanctified for obtaining a blessing on marriage are neglected, what blessing can be expected?

Civil Celebration of Marriage

Though we may regard the consecrating of marriage fully consummate, yet for the greater ceremony of so honorable a thing, it is very necessary that further there be added *a civil celebration* of it. Under this I include all those lawful customs that are used for the setting forth of the outward ceremony, as meeting of friends, accompanying the bridegroom and bride both to and from the church, putting on best clothing, seating, with other signs of rejoicing, for which we have express warrant from God's Word.

In general, a wedding is a time of rejoicing; some deduce it from the definition of the word, as if "marriage" meant "merry age." But to let that pass, the Scripture sets forth a time of rejoicing by the joy of the bridegroom over his bride (Isa. 62:5), and says "the voice of joy, and the voice of gladness, the voice of the bridegroom, and the voice of the bride" (Jer. 33:11). On the contrary, it is counted a judgment, when joy is taken away from the bridegroom and the bride (Jer. 7:34; Joel 2:16).

For meeting of friends at the time of marriage, it is noted that "Laban gathered together all the men of the place," when his daughter was married (Gen. 29:22). When Samson was married, "they brought thirty companions to him" (Judg. 14:11). When a friend of the virgin Mary was married, Jesus and His disciples, besides many others, were invited (John 2:2). In the parable of the marriage of the king's son, it is noted that many guests were "bidden to the wedding" (Matt. 22:3). In all which histories it is further noted, that feasts were made at the wedding ceremonies. And the phrases which the prophet uses of a bridegroom's decking himself with ornaments, and a bride's adorning herself with jewels, give warrant for putting on the best apparel at that time (Isa. 61:10; Jer. 2:32).

Here, by the way, let us be careful that the things which may lawfully be used be not unlawfully abused, as commonly marriage festivities, and that especially in feastings, are.

Ordering Marriage Feasts Well or Poorly

Marriage feasts are abused:

1. When they are made at an unseasonable time, as on the Lord's Day, or in a time of mourning (Isa. 22:12–13).

2. When they exceed the financial ability of him that makes the feast (Luke 15:13).

3. When the abundance prepared is immoderately taken, even to gluttony and drunkenness. The wicked practice of drinking health to the bridegroom and bride, often causes much excess drunkenness (Luke 21:34).

4. When too much time is spent there (Isa. 5:11).

5. When God is completely forgotten there, and the company poisoned with corrupt talk, unchaste songs, and similar evils (Isa. 5:12).

6. When the needy and distressed are not remembered there (Amos 6:6).

For preventing of these abuses, a seasonable time for celebrating marriage must be chosen out, and moderation used both by him that makes the feast, and also by them that partake of it. Moderation must be had, I say, in the measure of eating and drinking, and in the time spent there, which time must be sanctified with such talk "which is good to the use of edifying, that it may minister grace to the hearers" (Eph. 4:29). And for the more cheerfulness there, witty questions and doubtful riddles may be propounded (as Samson did) to exercise the wit and judgment of the guests (Judg. 14:12).

There may be also "singing psalms and hymns and spiritual songs, making melody in their hearts to the Lord" (Eph. 5:19). Furthermore, in order that the marriage meeting, fun, and feasting may be better sanctified, good choice is to be made of the guests that are invited to it. We have a worthy pattern in those who were married in Cana of Galilee, and invited to their feast Jesus, His mother, and His disciples (John 2:1–2). Those like Jesus will offer opportunities for pleasing and holy conversations, by which all the guests may be much edified. Those like Mary will be a good example of modesty, sobriety, and other Christian graces. Those like the disciples will be far from scorning and mocking wholesome and good instructions, but rather pay careful attention to them, and treasure them in their hearts.

Above all, that the fun and joy of marriage be not dampened, as Belshazzar's was, let those that are married and all that come to rejoice with them, be sure that they have true assurance of their spiritual marriage with Christ, and of a good right in Him to His creations which they use. Otherwise their sins will be as that handwriting which appeared to Belshazzar on the wall (Dan. 5:5).

Finally, with respect to that liberty which God gives with plenty and abundance to eat of the best foods, and drink of the sweet, let the poor that barely have enough be remembered (Neh. 8:10).

Thus by a right celebrating of marriage, is it much honored, and husband and wife are brought together with much honor.

The Honor of Marriage Regarding Its First Establishment

There is great reason why marriage should be formally celebrated with such honor, for it is a most honorable thing in its establishment, ends, privileges, and mystery. No ordinance was more honorable in the first establishment of it, as is evident by the *Author*, the *place* where it was instituted, the *time* when it was instituted, the *persons* who were first married, and the *manner* of joining them together.

1. The Author who first instituted marriage was the Lord God (Gen. 2:18–22). Could there have been a greater, or any way a more excellent Author?

2. The place was Paradise; the most beautiful, glorious, pleasant, honorable, useful, and in every way most excellent place that ever was in this world. Place, though it is but a circumstance, adds much to the honor of a thing. Solemn ordinances are made in honorable places. Thus with us wedding ceremonies are done in churches, not in private houses.

3. The time was the most pure and perfect time that ever was in the world, when no sin or pollution of man had stained it, even the time of man's innocence. Purity adds much to the honor of a thing.

4. The persons were the most honorable that ever were, even the first father and mother of all mankind, they who had absolute power and dominion over all creatures, and to whom all were subject. None but they ever had a true monarchy over the whole world.

5. The manner was with as great deliberation as ever was used in establishing any ordinance. For first the three glorious persons in the Trinity met to consult about it. For "the LORD God said" (Gen. 2:18), and to whom should He speak? Not to any created power, but to Him that was begotten of Himself, that Wonderful, Counselor, etc. In this consultation this ordinance, "It is not good for man to be alone," is found to be very necessary, therefore a determination is set down, to "make an help meet" for man. To cause a better effect, the Lord proceeded very deliberately, by various steps and degrees.

1. All creatures that lived on the earth, or breathed in the air, are brought before man, to see if a help meet for him might be found among them.

2. Each of them being thoroughly viewed, and found unfit, another creature is made out of man's substance and side, and after his image.

3. This excellent creature thus made is presented to man by the Maker to see how he would like it.

4. Man, manifesting a good liking of her, she is given to him to be his wife.

5. The sacred law of the near and firm union of husband and wife together is enacted.

Let all the just mentioned branches concerning the first institution of marriage expressly recorded by the Holy Spirit be well weighed, and we shall easily see that there is no ordinance now in force among the sons of men so honorable in its institution as this.

The Ends of Marriage

The *ends*[3] for which marriage was ordained add much to the honor of it. They are especially three:

1. That the world might be increased, and not simply increased, but with a legitimate brood, and distinct families, which are the seminaries[4] of cities and nations, also that the church might be preserved and propagated in the world by a holy seed (Mal. 2:15).

2. That men might avoid fornication and possess their vessels in holiness and honor (1 Cor. 7:2). Regarding that tendency which is in man's corrupt nature to lust, this end adds much to the honor of marriage. It shows that marriage is a haven to those who are in jeopardy of their salvation through the gusts of temptations to lust. No sin is more hereditary, there is none of which more children of Adam do partake, than this. Well might Christ say "all men receive not this saying" (Matt. 19:11).

---

3. *Ends*: goals or purposes.
4. *Seminaries*: not in the modern sense of schools for pastors, but nurseries to grow seeds into plants later to be transplanted into other locations.

Of all the children of Adam that ever were, not one in a million of those that have come to maturity of years have been true eunuchs all their life time. Against this hereditary disease no remedy is so effective as this. For those that have not the gift of continence,[5] this is the only authorized and sanctified remedy.

3. That husband and wife might be a mutual help to one another (Gen. 2:18), a help as for bringing forth, so for bringing up children, and as for starting, so for well governing their family. A spouse is a help also for managing prosperity well, and bearing adversity well; a help in health and sickness; a help while both live together, and when one is by death taken from the other. In this respect it is said "who so findeth a wife, findeth a good thing" (Prov. 18:22), which, by the rule of relation, is also true of a husband.

Man can have no such help from any other creature as from a wife, or a woman as from a husband.

The Privileges of Marriage

If, as once it was of circumcision (Rom. 3:1), it be demanded what is the privilege, advantage, and profit of marriage, I answer, much every way.

1. By it men and women are made husbands and wives.

2. It is the only lawful means to make them fathers and mothers.

3. It is the ordinary means to make them masters and mistresses. All these are great dignities, in which the image and glory of God consists.

4. It is the most effectual means of continuing a man's name and memory in this world that can be. Children are living monuments, and lively representations of their parents.

---

5. *Continence*: sexual self-control for a life of celibacy.

5. Many privileges have of old been granted to those who were married. In pleading causes, or giving sentence, they had the first place; and in choice of offices they were preferred. In meetings they had the upper hand. And if they had many children they were exempted from watchings, and other similar burdensome functions. Among us, if the younger sister becomes married before the elder, the preeminence and precedence is given to the younger.

The privileges and honors which are given to married persons, were without question the ground of that custom which Laban mentioned of his country, that the younger was not to be married before the elder (Gen. 29:26).

The Mystery of Marriage

Great is that mystery which is set forth by marriage, namely, the sacred, spiritual, real, and sacred union between Christ and His church, which is excellently explained in Solomon's Song, and in Psalm 45, and expressly noted in Ephesians 5:32.

By this, husband and wife, who entirely love one another as they ought, have an evident demonstration of Christ's love to them. For as parents by that affection which they bear to their children, may better discern the mind and meaning of God towards them, better than those who never had a child, so may married persons better know the disposition of Jesus Christ, the spouse of every faithful soul, than single persons.

Marriage and Single Life Compared Together

Let now the admirers and praisers of a single state bring forth all their reasons, and put them in the other scale against marriage. If these two be duly poised and rightly weighed, we shall find single life too light to be compared with honest marriage. All that can be said for the single state is grounded upon accidental occasions. Paul, who of all the writers of Holy Scripture has spoken most for it, draws all his commendations to the head of *expediency*, and restrains all to *present necessity* (1 Cor. 7:26).

Objection: He uses these words, "good" (1 Cor. 7:1) and "better" (v. 38).

Answer: Those words relate not to virtue, but to expediency; neither are they spoken in opposition to vice and sin, for then would it follow that to marry (which is God's ordinance, and honorable in all) were evil and sinful. This is to revive that ancient heresy, that marriage is of the devil. Of old they who have called lawful marriage a defilement, have been said to have the apostate dragon dwelling in them. But the apostle calls that *good*, which is profitable, and that *better* which is more expedient, and yet not more expedient simply, but to some persons at some times. If any have not the gift of continence, it is not only profitable or more expedient that they marry, but also absolutely necessary. They are commanded so to do (1 Cor. 7:9). Yet on the other side, if any have the gift of continence, they are not simply bound from marriage; there are other occasions besides avoiding fornication, to move them to marry. It is therefore truly said that "virginity is not commanded, but advised."[6] Also, "We have no precept for it, but leave it to the power of them that have the power."[7] As far as men and women see a good reason for abstaining from marriage (being at least able so to do) they are persuaded by the apostle to use their liberty and keep themselves free. But all the occasions which move them to remain single arise from the weakness and wickedness of men. Their wickedness who raise troubles against others, their weakness who suffer themselves to be disturbed and too much distracted with affairs of the family, care for wife, children, etc. Were it not for the wickedness of some, and

---

6. Gouge cites Bernard of Clairvaux, *De Modo Bene Viu*, sermon 21.

7. Gouge cites the *Apostolic Constitutions*, book 4, ch. 14. This book was written in the late fourth century.

weakness of others, to please a husband or a wife, would be no hindrance to pleasing the Lord. If therefore man had stood in his state of wholeness and innocence, no such wickedness or weakness would have seized upon him, and then in no respect could the single state have been preferred before the married. But since the fall, virginity (where it is given) may be of good use, and therefore the church gives due honor both to virginity and marriage (1 Cor. 7:32–34).

Celebrating Marriage with Sorrow

Against the previously mentioned joyful celebrating of marriage are all those indirect courses which bring much grief, trouble and vexation to it, such as forced, stolen, unequal, or any other way unlawful marriages, marriages without parents' or other governors' and friends' consent, or huddled up to avoid the danger of law for former uncleanness committed, and similar cases. Many, by their disorderly and undue performing of so weighty a matter, do not only cause great trouble and disturbance on the marriage day, but also much sorrow all the days of their life. If such find no joy, comfort, or help in marriage, but rather the contrary, let them not blame God's ordinance, but their own folly and perverseness.

3

Marital Unity and Sexual Faithfulness

In the first part of this treatise it has been declared who are to be so counted as husband and wife; in this second part the *mutual duties that they share in common* are to be laid forth (chapters 3–7). These are either absolutely necessary for the marriage to really exist and remain (chapter 3), or needed and required for the marriage to go well (chapters 4–7), that is, for the good state of marriage, and for a commendable and comfortable living together.

There are two kinds of duties necessary for marriage to really exist: *matrimonial unity*, and *matrimonial chastity*. The duties necessary for marriage to go well also may be drawn to two heads, for they are either such as the married couple are mutually to perform *to each other* (chapters 4–6), or such as both of them are jointly to perform to *others* (chapter 7).

Those mutual duties done toward each other are *a loving affection to one another*, and *a provident care*[1] *for one another*. Under that provident care I include both the *means* whereby it may be best done, which is cohabitation, and the *matter* in which it consists, respecting the soul, the body, the good reputation, and the possessions of each other.

The joint duties which are to be performed to others respect those who are *in the house*, and those who are *out of*

---

1. *Provident care*: meeting immediate needs and preparing for future needs.

the house. Those who are in the house are *members* of the family, and *guests* which come to the family.

Many more particulars are included under these general heads, which I plan to deliver distinctly, as I come to them in their various proper places.

Matrimonial Unity

The first, highest, chief, and most absolutely necessary mutual duty shared between husband and wife, is *matrimonial unity*, by which husband and wife count one another to be *one flesh*, and accordingly preserve the sacred union by which they are knit together. This is that duty which the apostle requires of husbands and wives, in these words, "Let not the wife depart from her husband…and let not the husband put away his wife" (1 Cor. 7:10, 11). He speaks of renouncing each other, and nullifying the matrimonial bond, which he would have to be kept firm and sacred. By this bond the *two* are made *one*, and should constantly remain *one*, and not make themselves *two* again. This matrimonial unity is so necessary that it may not be broken or dissolved though one is a Christian, and the other a pagan. "If any brother," says the apostle, "hath a wife that believeth not…let him not put her away. And the woman which hath an husband that believeth not…let her not leave him" (1 Cor. 7:12–13).

The reasons of this sacred union are especially two: one taken from the *Author* of marriage, the other from the *nature* of it.

The Author of marriage is God. It is His ordinance, and it is He who by His ordinance has made of two, one flesh. Now notice how Christ deduces an undeniable principle from this truth: "What therefore God hath joined together, let not man put asunder" (Matt. 19:6). If man should not do it, then not wife, nor husband himself.

Such is the nature of the matrimonial bond that it makes of two one, and more firmly binds them together than any other bond can bind any other two together. How then should they be two again?

Desertion

The vice contrary to matrimonial unity is *desertion*, when one of the married couple, through offense at the true religion, and utter detestation of it, or some other similar cause, shall apparently renounce all matrimonial unity, and withdraw him or herself from all company with the other, and live among infidels, idolaters, heretics, or other such persecutors as a faithful Christian with safety of life, or a good conscience, cannot abide among. Though all good means that can be thought of are used to reclaim the party that departed in this way, yet nothing will prevail, but he obstinately persists in renouncing all matrimonial fellowship.

This desertion is in the case of marriage such a serious crime, that it frees the innocent party from any further seeking after the other. In this respect the apostle says, "If the unbelieving depart, let him depart. A brother or a sister is not under bondage in such cases" (1 Cor. 7:15). By bondage he means matrimonial submission because of which neither of the married persons has power of his or her own body, but one of the other's. Now they that are not under this bondage are not bound to seek after it. That desertion therefore on the guilty one's part is such dissolution of marriage, as frees the innocent party from the bondage of it.

In many Reformed churches beyond the seas desertion is accounted so far to dissolve the very bond of marriage, as liberty is given to the party forsaken to marry another. It is also applied to other cases than that which is above mentioned, such as when an infidel, idolater, or heretic shall depart from one of the true religion for other causes than hatred of religion, or when both husband and wife having lived as idolaters among idolaters, one of them being converted to the true faith, leaves his abode among idolaters, and goes to the professors of the true faith, but can by no means get the other party to remove, or when one of the true religion shall depart from another of the same profession, and will by no means be brought to live with the party so left, but openly manifests settled obstinacy. The matter being heard and judged by the magistrate, the marriage bond may be broken, and liberty given to the party forsaken to marry another. But because our church has no such custom, nor has our law determined such cases, I leave them to the custom of other churches.

Matrimonial Chastity
The second necessary mutual duty shared by both spouses in marriage is *matrimonial chastity*. Chastity in a large extent is taken for all manner of purity in soul or body, in which respect the apostle calls the church of God "a chaste virgin" (2 Cor. 11:2). But in the sense we use it, it especially pertains to the body, which is that virtue whereby we possess our vessels in holiness and honor, to use the apostle's phrase (1 Thess. 4:4). More plainly to our purpose, it is that purity by which we keep our bodies undefiled.

Chastity thus restrained to the body is of *single life* and *wedlock*. That of single life is opposed to fornication and it is either of those who never were married, such as Paul, in which respect he wished that all were as he (1 Cor. 7:7), or of those who are lawfully freed from the bond of marriage, such as the one the apostle calls "a widow indeed" (1 Tim. 5:3–10). Chastity of wedlock is that virtue by which the married parties, observing the lawful and honest use of marriage, keep their bodies from being defiled with strange flesh. Thus the apostle commands wives to be chaste (Titus 2:5). So as those who keep the laws of wedlock are as chaste as they that stay celibate.

Here by the way note the stupidity of our adversaries, who think there is no chastity except of single persons, for which cause in their speeches and writings they oppose chastity and matrimony as contrary to one another.

Some of their holy fathers and popes, and those not the least educated, nor of worst reputation among them, have inferred by their arguments against priests' marriage, that *marriage is a living in the flesh, a sowing to the flesh, a pollution of the flesh*.[2] To that purpose Paul's advice to husband and wife to abstain, that they may give themselves to fasting and prayer, is urged, but directly contrary to the intent of the apostle.

First, he speaks of extraordinary humiliation. Secondly, he inserts this limitation, "for a time." Thirdly, he says not simply, "that ye may pray," but "that ye may give your selves (or have extra time) to prayer," as if it did only hinder, but not corrupt prayer.

But how can the spots and blots these men cast on marriage stand with that beauty and glory in which the apostle sets it forth in these words, "Marriage is honorable in all" (Heb. 13:4)? If marriage were as papists set it forth to be, the marriage bed was very inappropriately called "a bed undefiled." Behold how contrary the points of Paul and of their popes were. I know things far more contrary than chastity and matrimony.

But to return to our matter, it is clear, that married persons may be chaste, and accordingly they ought to be chaste. To which purpose the apostle, counseling men and women to have wives and husbands in order to avoid fornication, inserts

---

2. On the points in this and the preceding paragraph, Gouge cites session 24 of the Council of Trent (1563), Pope Siricius (334–399), Pope Innocent III (1160–1216), and "Gratian," probably Pope Gregory VI (d. 1048).

this particle "own" (let every man have his *own* wife, and every woman have her *own* husband) by which he implies that they should not have to do with any other. That which Solomon expresses of a husband, by the rule of relation must be applied to a wife. As the man must be satisfied at all times in his wife, and even ravished with her love, so must the woman be satisfied at all times in her husband, and even ravished with his love (Prov. 5:19). By the similar rule the precept given to wives, to be chaste, must husbands take as directed to themselves also, and be chaste (Titus 2:5). This duty Isaac and Rebekah faithfully and mutually performed to each other.

1. It was one main end, why marriage, especially since the fall of man, was ordained, to live chastely. The apostle implies this where he says, "to avoid fornication," let every man have his own wife, and let every woman have her own husband (1 Cor. 7:2). And again, "If they cannot contain [control themselves] let them marry" (1 Cor. 7:9).

2. By chastity is a godly seed preserved on earth. By this reason the prophet Malachi enforces this duty. For after he had said, that the Lord *made one,* meaning of two one flesh by marriage, he infers this exhortation, "Therefore take heed to your spirit, and let none deal treacherously against the wife of his youth" (Mal. 2:15).

3. A special part of the honor of marriage consists in chastity, whereupon the apostle, having given this high commendation of marriage, that it is "honorable in all," adds this clause, "and the bed undefiled," to show the reason of that honor. It is as if he had said, "Because the marriage bed is in itself a bed undefiled, marriage is therefore in itself honorable, and so far remains honorable, as the bed remains undefiled."

Adultery

The vice contrary to matrimonial chastity is *adultery,* one of the worst crimes in that state, a vice by which a way is made for *divorce*, as is clear and evident by the judgment of Christ Himself, concerning that point, first propounded in His Sermon on the Mount, and again repeated in His conference with the Pharisees, where condemning unjust divorces, He excepts the divorce made for adultery (Matt. 5:32; 19:9).

Great reason there is for this. The adulterer makes himself one flesh with his prostitute (1 Cor. 6:16). Why then should he remain to be one flesh with his wife? Two, says the law, shall be one flesh, not three. The same may be said of a wife committing adultery.

Pardoning Adultery upon Repentance

Question: Seeing by adultery just cause of divorce is given, may this fault upon the repentance of the guilty person be so forgiven, as no divorce be sought by the innocent person, but both continue to live together in wedlock as before?

Answer: Though it is not fitting in this case to impose it as a sacred law upon the innocent party, to retain the guilty party, because of repentance (for we have direct and strict warrant for it) yet I doubt not but they may so do, if they will, and that without just exception to the contrary, they ought so to do. For the law of divorce did not necessarily require anyone to file for divorce, but only granted them liberty to use that punishment if they saw cause. I do not doubt but for the right to this liberty to stay married, we may take God's pattern, in retaining churches and people after they have committed spiritual adultery, and Christ's forgiving the woman that had committed adultery. For, seeing Christ said to an adulteress, "Neither do I condemn thee: go, and sin no more" (John 8:11) who cannot conceive that a husband ought to forgive that which he sees the Lord has forgiven both of husband and wife, and that he ought not to account her an adulteress, whose fault he believeth to be blotted out, by the mercy of God, upon her repentance?

The Difference of Adultery in a Man and in a Wife

Question: Is the bond of marriage as much violated on the man's part when he commits adultery as on the woman's part when she does?

Answer: Though the ancient Romans and canonists[3] have aggravated the woman's fault in this kind of sin far above the man's, and given the man more privileges than the woman, yet I do not see how that difference in the sin can stand with the general teachings of God's Word. I do not deny that more inconveniences may follow upon the woman's default than upon the man's, as, greater infamy before men, worse disturbance of the family, more mistaking of legitimate or illegitimate children, etc. The man cannot so well know which be his own children, as the woman; he may take illegitimate children to be his own, and so give the inheritance to them; and suspect his own to be dishonorably born, and so deprive them of their inheritance. But the woman is freed from all such mistakes.

Yet in regard of the violation of wedlock, and transgression against God, the sin of either party is alike. God's Word makes no difference between them. At the beginning God said of them both, "they two shall be one flesh," not the woman only with the man, but the man also with the woman is made one flesh. Their power also over one another in this respect is alike. If for good reason they abstain, it must be with mutual consent. If the husband leaves his wife, she is free, as he should be if she left him. Accordingly the punishment which by God's law was to be inflicted on adulterers is the same, whether the man or the woman be the guilty party (Deut. 22:22). If difference is made, it is fitting that adulterous husbands be so much the more severely punished, by how much the more it pertains to them to excel in virtue, and to govern their wives by example.

---

3. *Canonists*: experts in the laws of the church.

The Heinousness of Adultery

But to return to the uncovering of the heinousness of adultery, I find no sin throughout the whole Scripture so notoriously in the several colors of it set forth, as it is. For besides that it is by name forbidden in the Ten Commandments (Ex. 20:14), it is further expressly branded to be committed,

1. Against *each person of the holy Trinity*: the Father whose covenant is broken (Prov. 2:17), the Son whose members are made the members of an harlot (1 Cor. 6:16), and the Holy Spirit whose temple is made dirty (1 Cor. 6:19).

2. Against one's *neighbor*, as the party with whom the sin is committed (for this sin cannot be committed singly by one alone), the *husband* or *wife* of each party (who cannot rest contented with any satisfaction), the *children* born in adultery (whom they brand with lasting shame, and deprive of many privileges that otherwise they might enjoy), the *friends* of each party (to whom the grief and disgrace of this foul sin reaches), the *whole family* belonging to either of them (for this is as a fire in an house), the *town, city,* and *nation* where such unclean birds roost (for all they lie open to the vengeance of God for this sin), and the very *church of God* (the holy seed of which is hindered by this sin).

3. Against the *parties* themselves that commit this sin, and that against their souls, bodies, name, goods, and all that pertains to them.

As this sin is in itself a sinful sin, so by the bitter and cursed fruits which proceed from it, it is made extremely sinful. For:

1. By it husbands' and wives' affection (which of all other ought to be the most sacred) is so alienated, as seldom it is reconciled again.

2. By it the goods of the family are much wasted, the adulterous husband spending on his prostitute what he

should provide for his family, and the adulterous wife stealing what she can from her husband.

3. By it husbands and wives are stirred up to wish, and long after one another's death, and not only inwardly in heart to wish it, but outwardly also in deed to practice it.

4. If from this sin there does not arise a painful and terrifying conscience (as often there does) then (which is worse) a seared conscience, a hard heart, a mind given over to sin, and a shameless face.

Therefore, God deals accordingly with such sins. In His soul He hates them (Prov. 22:14); by His Word He has threatened many fearful judgments against them, both in this world (Hos. 4:2–3), and in the world to come (Rev. 21:8). No sin has more judgments pronounced against it than this. This sin is reckoned to be one of the most principal causes of the greatest judgments that ever were inflicted in the world, as of the general flood, of that fire and brimstone which destroyed Sodom and Gomorrah, of Canaan's vomiting out her inhabitants, of that plague which destroyed in one day 24,000, and of the Israelites' captivity, etc. By all this we see that fearful doom verified, "whoremongers and adulterers God will judge" (Heb. 13:4). Now consider what a fearful thing it is to fall into the hands of the living God.

Remedies against Adultery and Due Benevolence

God's Word has prescribed many remedies to prevent this heinous sin, such as a diligent keeping of:

- the *heart* (that lustful thoughts not proceed from it)
- the *eyes* (that they not wander on the beauty or lovely shape of anyone's body, or on sexually provocative pictures, or any other similar temptations)
- the *ears* (that they not listen to any temptations from others)

- the *tongue* (that it speak no impure and corrupt talk)
- the *lips* (that they not delight in immoral kisses)
- the *hands* (that they not do any immoral touching)
- the *feet* (that they do not carry you too near to the place where adultery may be committed)
- your *friends* (that you not be corrupted with others' immorality and uncleanness)
- your *diet* (that it not be immoderate)
- your *clothing* (that it not be too showy and immodest)
- your *time* (that it not be wasted or spent in laziness)

Above all is the remedy of the fear and awe of God, and a continual setting of Him before you, wherever you may be.

One of the best remedies that can be prescribed to married persons is that husband and wife mutually delight in each other, and maintain a pure and fervent love between themselves, yielding that due benevolence[4] to one another which is authorized and sanctified by God's Word, and ordained of God for this particular purpose. This "due benevolence" (as the apostle calls it in 1 Corinthians 7:3) is one of the most proper and essential acts of marriage. It is necessary for the main and principal ends of it: as for preservation of chastity in those who have not the gift of sexual self-control for celibacy, for increasing the world with legitimate offspring, and for linking the affections of the married couple more firmly together. These ends of marriage, at least the two former, are made void without this duty being performed.

As it is called "benevolence" because it must be performed with good will and delight, willingly, readily, and cheerfully; so it is said to be "due" because it is a debt which the wife owes to her husband, and he to her. "For the wife

---

4. *Due benevolence*: a euphemism for sexual intercourse based on 1 Cor. 7:3.

hath not the power of her own body, but the husband; and likewise also the husband hath not the power of his own body, but the wife" (1 Cor. 7:4).

I have authority from the apostle to prescribe this duty as a remedy against adultery. For to avoid fornication, he advises husband and wife to render due benevolence to one another. If then this question be asked, "How will marriage keep men and women from adultery?" this answer out of the apostle's words may be given, "by rendering due benevolence." This he further presses upon us by declaring the trouble that may follow upon the neglect of this duty, namely a casting of themselves into the snares of Satan (1 Cor. 7:5). Well might he press this duty to that end, because no other means is of similar force, neither fasting, nor watching,[5] nor uncomfortable beds, nor long travel, nor much labor, nor cold, nor solitariness, nor anything else. Some that have by these means worked hard to conquer their bodies, and subdue lust (but neglected the remedy I just mentioned) have despite them all felt lust boiling in them.

There are two extremes contrary to this duty, one in not making love enough, another in too much. There is not enough when someone who needs it does not ask for it, or being asked for by the one, it is not yielded by the other. Modesty is pretended by some for not asking it, but in a duty so right and needed, putting on a show of modesty is (to speak the least) a sign of great weakness, and a cause of much sin. To deny this duty when it is justly asked is to deny a due debt, and to give Satan great advantage. The punishment inflicted on Onan (Gen. 38:9–10) shows how great a wrong this is. From that punishment the Hebrews gather that this sin is a kind of murder. It is so much the more heinous when hatred, stubborness, delicacy, fear of having too

---

5. *Fasting…watching*: the disciplines of denying yourself food or sleep in order to seek God.

many children, or any other similar concerns are the cause of it.

Too much is either in the *measure*, or in the *time*. In the measure, when husband or wife is insatiable; provoking, rather than lessening lust, and weakening their natural strength more than suppressing their unnatural desire. Many husbands and wives are greatly oppressed by the insatiable desires of their mate in this way.

In the time, when it is against *piety, mercy,* or *modesty*.

1. Against piety, when no day, nor duty of religion, no not extraordinary days, and duties of humiliation, will make them restrain themselves. The prophet calling the bridegroom and bride go out of their bedroom in the day of a fast (Joel 2:16), and the apostle making an exception of prayer and fasting (1 Cor. 7:5), where he commands this duty of due benevolence, show that in the time of a fast it must be set aside.

2. Against mercy, when one of the married couple being weak by sickness, pain, labor, travel, or any other similar causes, and through that weakness not well able to perform this duty, the other notwithstanding will have it performed. "I will have mercy, and not sacrifice," says the Lord (Matt. 9:13). Shall God's sacrifice give place to mercy, but not man's or woman's lust (for so I may well term this unreasonable desire)?

Question: What if a husband or wife continue so long sick or otherwise weak, that the other cannot control himself?

Answer: In such cases of necessity the body must be conquered, and earnest prayer made for the gift of self-control, for surely the Lord who has brought you to that necessity will give you sufficient grace.

3. Against modesty, when husbands require this duty in that time, which under the law was called the time of a wife's separation for her disease (Lev. 15:19, etc.). For what can be expected from such dirty copulation, but a leprous and loathsome generation? This kind of lack of proper restraint

is expressly forbidden (Lev. 18:19) and a capital punishment inflicted on those who offend (Lev. 20:18). Abstinence in this time is set in the catalog of those notes which declare a man to be righteous[6] and the contrary lack of self-restraint is put in the roll of such abominations as provoked God to vomit out the Canaanites (Lev. 18:28) and to forsake His own inheritance (Ezek. 22:10).

Some include in this kind of lack of self-restraint a man's knowing of his wife after she has conceived a child.[7] But I find no such matter condemned in God's Word; neither dare I make that a sin which is not there condemned. Certain sects among the Jews are branded for this error.[8]

Objection: No other creature will so do, so it may seem to be against nature.

Answer: First, I deny the argument: though some refrain, yet all do not. Secondly, I deny the consequence, for other creatures are not so tied one male to one female, as a husband to his own wife. Besides, that to which beasts are tied by nature must be left to man's discretion.

Objection: After a woman has once conceived, no more conceptions can be expected till she has delivered.

Answer: Conception is not the only end of this duty, for it is to be rendered to those who are barren.

Question: What if the wife breastfeeds her child, should not her husband then refrain?

Answer: Because breastfeeding is a mother's duty, man ought to do what he can to control himself.

---

6. Gouge cites an incorrect reference here; the correct reference is not clear.

7. Gouge cites Augustine and Ambrose.

8. The Essenes, according to Josephus.

4

Living Together in Love

To this point we have covered those common mutual duties which tend to the preservation of the very being of marriage, and are in that respect absolutely necessary. The other mutual duties shared in marriage (though they are not of as absolute necessity as the former) are necessary in their kind for the good state of marriage, and for the better preserving of that knot: so as, if they be not performed, the end and right use of marriage will be perverted, and that state made uncomfortable, and very burdensome.

The first of these is *love*. A loving mutual affection must pass between husband and wife, or else no duty will be well performed. This is the ground of all the rest. In some respects love is proper and particular to a husband, as I propose to show when I come to speak of a husband's particular duties. But love is also required of wives, and they are commanded to be "lovers of their husbands," as well as husbands "to love their wives," so that it is a common mutual duty belonging to both husband and wife (Titus 2:4; Eph. 5:25). That is true wedlock, when husband and wife are linked together by the bond of love.

Under love all other duties are included, for without it no duty can be well performed. "Love is the fulfilling of the law," that is, the very life of all those duties which the law requires (Rom. 13:10). It is the "bond of perfectness," which binds together all those duties that pass between party and party (Col. 3:14). Where love abounds, there all duties will readily and cheerfully be performed. Where love is lacking, there every duty will either be altogether neglected, or so carelessly performed, that it might as well not be performed at all. In this respect the apostle wills that all things be done in love (1 Cor. 16:14). Love as it provokes the party in whom it rules to do all the good it can; so it stirs up the party loved to repay good for good. It is like fire, which is not only hot in itself, but also conveys heat from one to another. Note how admirably this is set forth between Christ and His spouse in the Song of Solomon; and it is further manifested in the examples of all good husbands and wives noted in the Scripture. They did mutually bear a very loving affection to one another.

Though love is a general duty which everyone owes to another, even to his enemy (Matt. 5:44), yet the closer that God has linked any together, the more are they bound to this duty, and the more must they abound in it. But of all others husband and wife are most closely and firmly linked together. Of all others therefore they are most bound here, and that in the highest degree that may be, even similar to Jonathan's love, who loved David as his own soul (1 Sam. 18:3). Solomon says, "Whoso findeth a wife findeth a good thing, and obtaineth favour of the LORD" (Prov. 18:22), which, by the rule of relation is also true of a husband: she that finds a husband finds a good thing, and obtains favor of the Lord. Husband and wife therefore are to each other a special pledge of God's favor, and in this respect above all others under God to be loved. If this be the ground (as it ought to be) of their mutual love, their love will be fervent and constant. Neither will the lack, or withering of any outward attractiveness, as beauty, status, parentage, friends, riches, honors, or similar things, withhold or withdraw, extinguish or lessen their love. Neither will any excellency of nature or grace in other husbands and wives draw their hearts from their own to those other.

Nor yet will the love of a former mate dead and gone, lessen in the least bit the love of the living mate. I mention this particular case because in many, who are far from setting their affection on strange flesh, their love of a departed former husband or wife is so fast fixed in their heart, as they can never again so entirely love any other. They who are so minded are not fit to be joined with another mate after they are released from one. If they marry again, and manifest such a mind, they plainly show that they respect this or that person more than God's ordinance. By God's ordinance husband and wife are no longer bound to one another than they live together. Death is an absolute separation, and makes an utter dissolution of the marriage bond. If the man is dead, the wife is delivered from the law of the man, so as she may take another man (Rom. 7:2–3). This liberty is also given to the man. Being now free, if they marry another (that other being now a true husband or wife) their love must be as complete to that other as it was to the former, yes, and more complete, if there was any defect in the former. For as children married out of their parents' house must not retain such a love of their parents as shall swallow up their love of the party to whom they are married, but must according to the law, leave father and mother, and cleave to their mate, so neither must the love of a former husband or wife be predominant when they are married to another. This other must be as close clung to, as if they have never been joined to a former. The living husband or wife is the present pledge of God's favor. He is now your *own* husband, and she is now your *own* wife, and not the party that is dead. I deny not but the memory of a virtuous husband or wife ought to be precious to the surviving party, for the memorial of the just is blessed (Prov. 10:7). But as the virtue of a person deceased may not be buried with the dead corpse, so neither may the person be kept above ground with the memory of his or her virtue, which after a sort is done, when love of the party deceased either takes away or lessens the love of the living. This is to give dominion to the dead over the living, which is more than the law commands.

Husbands' and Wives' Mutual Hatred Contrary to Love

There is a generation of so sour and crooked a disposition that they cannot love, but rather hate one another because they are husband and wife: for many husbands having wives, and wives husbands every way worthy to be loved, will still say to the astonishment of the hearers, "I have indeed a good husband," or "I have a good wife, but I cannot love him," or "I cannot love her." Being demanded for a reason, they do not hesitate to openly and shamelessly reply, "I think I could love him if he were not my husband," or "I think I could love her if she were not my wife."

What horrible shamelessness! Is not this directly to oppose God's ordinance and that order which He has set between man and woman? Is it not to trample under foot God's favor? Though there was nothing else to motivate love but this, that such a one is your husband, or such a one is your wife, yet this should be motive enough. Shall this be the ground of your hatred? Surely such a spirit is a plain diabolical spirit, contrary to that spirit which is from above; and if it is not cast out, it will cast those whom it possesses into the fire of hell.

Mutual Peace between Husband and Wife

Among other means of maintaining an inward loving affection between husband and wife, *outward mutual peace*, concord, and agreement is one of the principal. The apostle exhorts to "keep the unity of the Spirit in the bond of peace" (Eph. 4:3), for peace is a bond that ties one to another, and makes them to be as one, even one in spirit, as on the contrary outward discord separates men's spirits. We are commanded to "follow peace with all men" (Heb. 12:14). How much more of all persons ought husbands to have peace with their wives, and wives with their husbands? They are nearer than brothers and sisters. Behold then how good and pleasant a thing it is for them to dwell together in unity. Dwell together they must, but without peace there is no dwelling together. "It is better to dwell in a corner of the housetop, than with a brawling woman in a wide house" (Prov. 21:9; 25:24). Persons in conflict are far better out of sight and place than present together. Out of sight and place husband and wife must not be. Therefore, they must be at peace. Mutual peace between them is a great refreshing to their minds, being beaten with the conflicts of others. It is said that a wife is in this respect a haven to man (how much more man to his wife?). If the haven be calm, and free from storms and tempests, what a refreshment it will be to the sailor that has been tossed in the sea with winds and waves?

For maintaining peace:

1. All offences must be avoided as much as possible. The husband must be watchful over himself that he give no offence to his wife, and so the wife on the other side. Offences cause contentions.

2. When an offence is given by the one party, it must not be taken by the other; but rather passed by, and then will not peace be broken. The second blow makes a fight.

3. If both be angered together, the fire is likely to be the greater. With the greater speed therefore must they both labor to put it out. Wrath must not lie in bed with two who share a bed; neither may they go to separate beds for wrath's sake. That this fire may be more quickly quenched, they must both

strive first to offer reconciliation. Theirs is the glory who first begin, for they are most properly the blessed peacemakers. Not to accept peace when it is offered is worse than the pagans, but when wrath is provoked, to seek reconciliation is the duty of a Christian, and a grace that cometh from above.

4. One must not take the side of children, servants, nor any other in the family against the other. The man's partaking with any of the household against his wife, or the wife against her husband, is a usual cause of contention between husband and wife.

5. They must refrain to insult each other by the comparison of husbands or wives of other persons or with their own former husbands or wives (if they have had any before). Comparisons in this kind are very offensive. They stir up much passion, and cause big fights.

6. Above all they must beware of rash and unjust jealousy, which is the bane of marriage, and the greatest cause of discontent that can be given between husband and wife. Jealous persons are ready to pick quarrels, and to seek occasions of discord. They will take every word, look, action, and motion in the worse way, and so take offence where none is given. When jealousy is once kindled, it is as a flaming fire that can hardly be put out. It makes the party whom it possesses impossible to please.

7. In all things that may stand with a good conscience they must work to please one another, and either of them allow their own will to be crossed rather than displease the other. Paul notes this as a mutual duty belonging to them both (1 Cor. 7:33–34), and expresses their care of it under a word that signifies more than ordinary care, and implies a *dividing of the mind* into diverse thoughts, casting this way, and that way, and every way how best to please.

Fights between Husband and Wife

Against mutual peace are *fights* between husband and wife, which are too frequent in most families, and by which the common good is much hindered. Discord between husband and wife in a house is as a fight between the master and pilot in a ship. May not great danger, and much trouble be rightly feared?

We wrote before that man to his wife, and she to him, is as a haven. Now by experience we find that if the haven be full of storms it is much more troublesome and dangerous to the sailor than the open sea. Therefore, let husband and wife be of the same mind to one another as Abraham was to Lot, and when occasions of discord are offered, say, "Let there be no strife between you and me, for we are husband and wife, no more two, but one flesh."

Husbands and Wives Dwelling Together

From a mutual affection of love proceeds *a mutual provident care*[1] in husband and wife one for another. In handling this we will first note the *means* whereby their mutual care may be better performed and shown, and then the *matter* about which it must be concerned.

The means, in one word, is *cohabitation*. It is a duty that husband and wife dwell together. The phrase used in setting out the woman's creation (he *built* a woman, whereby the starting of a new home for a family is suggested) implies as much (Gen. 2:22),[2] as does the law of marriage whereby man is commanded to leave father and mother, and to cleave to his wife, that is, to go out of his father's house, and to dwell with his wife, and so does this phrase,

---

1. *Provident care*: protecting and giving to each other not just with respect to immediate needs, but future needs.

2. Gouge refers to the Hebrew term *banah*, citing Reformed scholar Wolfgang Musculus (1497–1563) on Gen. 2:22.

"forget thy father's house" (Ps. 45:10) taken from the duty of a wife, and mystically applied to the church. Peter expressly charges husbands to dwell with their wives (1 Peter 3:7), and Paul exhorts both husbands and wives not to leave one another, but to dwell together, even though one be an unbeliever (1 Cor. 7:12–13). Surely it was conscience of this duty which made the Levite to go after his wife that went away from him, to bring her home again (Judg. 19:3), and which made Jacob's wives to leave their father's house and go with their husband (Gen. 31:14). The word under which Peter includes this duty is a title appropriated to a husband, and an answerable title is appropriate to a wife, from which the notation of our two usual English words ("husband," "housewife") does not differ much.[3]

The authority which the one has of the other's body, and the advantage which by living apart, they give to Satan, (both of which are explicitly noted, 1 Cor. 7:4–5) show the necessity of this duty, and the many benefits arising from it do further press the justice of it. By husbands and wives dwelling together all marriage duties are better performed: mutual love is better bred, preserved, and increased; the good gifts of either of them are better observed by the other; better help and assistance is mutually given by each to the other; and in time they are made more capable of doing good to one another, and of receiving good one from another. Why then should they have any thought of living apart, unless they are forced by extraordinary occasions, as captivity, close imprisonment, contagious disease, and such similar matters, which are no faults of theirs, but crosses to be carried with grief and urgent prayer, together with all other good means to be used to bring them together again? Yes, if the imprisonment,

---

3. Gouge notes in the margin the Greek word *sunoikeo* from 1 Peter 3:7, literally "house with." The English word *husband* is derived from "house-band," meaning master of the house.

banishment, or other similar kind of absence, be such as one may if they choose come to the other, the party that is free ought to come to the other, if at least that other require it.

The Reasons for which Husband and Wife May for a Time Live Apart

Question: May there be any just causes for husband and wife willingly to live apart?

Answer: There cannot be any cause of utterly relinquishing one another, which is a kind of desertion, but for living apart for a time there may be just causes, as:

1. *Weighty and urgent affairs* which concern the good of the church, or nation, as when a man is sent forth to war, or as an ambassador (in which case though he may take his wife with him, yet is he not necessarily bound to, especially if the place to which he is sent is far off, the travel there difficult and dangerous, and his stay there not long). When Reuben, Gad, and half the tribe of Manasseh passed over Jordan to help their brethren in their battles against the Canaanites, they left their wives behind them in their families (Num. 32:26–27). When Uriah went to war, he left his wife at home (2 Sam. 11:3, 6), and when Moses was to bring Israel out of Egypt, his wife remained at her father's house (Ex. 18:2).

2. *Main duties of their particular calling*, as of sailors who are often on the sea, merchants who trade in other countries, lawyers who attend public places of justice, courtiers[4] who in their months, or quarters, attend their prince, keepers of women in child-bed[5] and sick persons, and other nurses.

Provided always that in these, and other cases, there is a joint and mutual consent of both parties, for if husband and wife may not defraud one another for a time to give themselves to fasting and prayer *without consent* (1 Cor. 7:5), much

---

4. *Courtiers*: Various persons who served in the royal court.
5. *Keepers of women in child-bed*: perhaps mid-wives.

less may they for lighter occasions live any time apart without consent. Provided also that they take no delight to live apart, but rather be grieved that they are forced so to do, and in testimony of it to take all occasions that they can to show their longing desire after one another by letters, messages, tokens, and other similar kindnesses, and to return with all the speed they can. No distance or absence should in the least bit diminish their mutual love.

The Error of Papists about Husband and Wife's Separation

Contrary to the duty of cohabitation is the doctrine of papists, whereby they teach, that separation may be made between husband and wife for many causes from bed, or cohabitation, for a certain or uncertain time. The Council of Trent is bold to denounce *anathema*[6] against those who say the church errs there. If the many causes which they allege, besides adultery, be carefully weighed, we shall find them all without warrant of God's Word.[7] They draw them to two heads, both *mutual consent* and *demerit*.

By consent (they say) of both married parties to attain a greater and more perfect state, consummated marriage may be released from bed and cohabitation.

Answer: 1. In marriage there is *a covenant of God* (Prov. 2:17) as well as of the two parties. The consent therefore of parties is not sufficient to break it.

2. No state in this world can be greater or more perfect than is fitting for married persons. Adam and Eve in their best state were married, and now is marriage honorable in all (Heb. 13:4).

---

6. *Anathema*: cursed by God (Acts 23:14; Rom. 9:3; 1 Cor. 12:3; 16:22; Gal. 1:8–9).

7. Gouge cites the session 24 of the Council of Trent and the Jesuit Cardinal Robert Bellarmine (1542–1621).

3. The states which they count more perfect, are either those which are not in man's power (as perpetual celibacy) or those which may be as well performed by married persons as by single persons (as functions in the church) if at least they be those which are warranted by God's Word. High Priests, and other priests, all sorts of Levites, extraordinary prophets and apostles were married. What are greater functions than these?

The causes which for *demerit,* they say, make a separation, are adultery, departing from the catholic faith, enticing or driving them to sin.

Concerning *adultery,* we deny not, but that it gives just cause of divorce, but besides we say (as we have good warrant from Christ's words in Matthew 5:32) that it is the only cause of just divorce. To make a separation for departing from the catholic faith[8] is directly contrary to Paul's and Peter's doctrine (1 Cor. 7:12–14; 1 Peter 3:1).

As for *enticing or driving to sin,* though it may be cause to move a husband or a wife to walk more cautiously and wisely, and in extremity to avoid their company for a time, or to complain to the magistrate for release (who may see it fitting to put the guilty person in prison, or else otherwise keep them apart till that guilty one be reclaimed and brought to a better mind), yet it is no sufficient cause finally to dissolve marriage in regard of bed and cohabitation.

They urge that if the right eye cause to offend, it must be plucked out (Matt. 5:29).

Answer: First, that is but a metaphor, and may be applied in various other ways. Secondly, the words are not simply, but by way of comparison to be taken, rather pluck it out than to be made to stumble thereby. Thirdly, plucking out, applied to the point in hand, may be by many other ways

---

8. *Catholic faith:* the beliefs shared by all true Christians; not Roman Catholicism in particular.

than by dissolving marriage. Fourthly, that general inhibition ("whosoever shall put away his wife, causeth her to commit adultery") restrained only with the exception of fornication, allows neither this nor any other such cause of dissolving marriage.

Husbands' and Wives' Unlawful Absenting Themselves from One Another

Also against the duty of *cohabitation*, is the practice of many men, who living themselves in one place (suppose at London) send their wives to some country house, and there even cage them up, as hawks, never caring to come to them, but are then most happy, when their wives are farthest off. If their wives live at home they will be abroad, dining and lodging where their wives shall not know. Their own house is as a prison to them. They are not well except when they are out of it. Likewise is the wicked idea and practice of many wives, who for no other reason than mere whim, being eager in pursuing their pleasures, and satisfying their lusts, ramble out of their own houses in the day, sleep out of them in the night, and remain in other company days and nights, or at least are glad when their husbands have reason to be away from home—not unlike the immoral housewife which Solomon describes (Prov. 7:10, etc.). I speak of matters too famous, or rather infamous. I would there were no just cause to tax this lightness. But let those who desire to approve themselves to God or man, take heed of these heinous and more than heathen vices. Though Israel play the harlot, yet let not Judah offend (Hos. 4:15).

Too near to the kind of unlawful separation do they come, who though they live both in one house, yet make that house by their estranging themselves one from another as two houses, the man abiding in one end of it, his wife in another, and so have their different rooms, different tables, different servants—all is different. If the smallness of their house will not allow them to live separately, yet they will have different bedrooms, or at least different beds so that they that shall call them bed-fellows, shall only nick-name them. Thus they rob each other of that due benevolence which they mutually owe to one another, they expose themselves to the devil's snares, they more and more estrange their hearts one from another, and deprive themselves of such mutual comforts and helps, as by matrimonial fellowship they might grant to, and receive from one another.

5

Caring for
Each Other's Souls

The *matter* about which husbands and wives should be concerned to provide care for each other, is in general the good of one another; that each of them do that for the other, which Solomon in particular applies to a wife, that is, good and not evil all the days of their life (Prov. 31:12). Now the good of man extends to his *soul, body, good reputation, and possessions.*

A general duty tending to the good of all these is *prayer.* Peter requires such a conduct of husband and wife one towards another, that their prayers not be hindered (1 Peter 3:7), by which he takes it for granted that prayer is a mutual duty which one owes to the other, which Isaac performed for his wife (Gen. 25:21). Here husband and wife may be helpful to each other in all things needed by either of them, for it is the means which God in wisdom has sanctified for the obtaining of every blessing needed by ourselves or others. By many it is counted but an unimportant duty and of little use; but the truth is, that to perform it rightly, in truth and faith, is both difficult in the deed, and powerful in the effect. It is the best duty that one can perform for another and the least to be neglected.

We heard before, that Isaac prayed for his wife. To show the good he did to her it is noted that he prayed to the Lord, so that she, being barren before, by that means conceived. All the medicine in the world could not have done her so much good. Always, therefore, without ceasing is this duty to be performed. Whenever husband and wife offer any prayer, they must remember one another. Often they must purposefully make time to pray especially for one another, and that both in the absence, and also in the presence of one another.

This latter especially concerns the husband, who is as a priest to his wife, and ought to be her mouth to God when they two are together; yet I doubt not, but that the wife may pray in the husband's presence when they two are alone, either for *trial* (that he may have knowledge of her ability and gift in that kind) or for *help* (if the wife is much more able to perform that duty than the man is, as many wives are). Not without cause therefore have I reckoned this among common mutual duties.

The Things for which Husbands and Wives Are to Pray Alone

There are various needed blessings which husbands and wives are to pray for that pertain only to themselves, and are most fitting to be mentioned in private prayer between themselves, as:

1. That as they two are *one flesh*, so they may be also *one spirit*, that their hearts may be as one, knit together by a true, spiritual, matrimonial love, always delighting in one another, ever helpful to one another, and ready with all willingness and cheerfulness to perform all those duties which they owe to one another.

2. That their marriage bed may be sanctified, and as it is by God's ordinance, so it may remain to them by their using it well, a bed undefiled. There is no other thing, for which mutual prayer in private between husband and wife is more needed, and that so much the rather, because of the natural heat of lust which is in most. If it is not by prayer (the best means for that purpose) lessened, it may prove a defilement

of the undefiled bed, and husband and wife become adulterers to one another. As other things, so this also is sanctified by the word and prayer. The *word* gives an authorization and direction for the use of it; *prayer* both seasons it, and procures a blessing upon it.

3. That they may have children, and those may be heirs of salvation, and live in this world to their own and others' good. That they may be handsome and well-proportioned children, neither mentally handicapped in understanding, nor physically handicapped in bodily shape, nor yet wicked and infamous in their lives, which could not but be a grief to their parents, and might also open the mouths of the wicked against them.

4. That God would give them what they need of this world's goods, and other good means to nourish, nurture, and send out their children well, and enough for the support of their family, and of that state where God sets them.

5. That such necessary gifts and graces as are lacking in either of them may be given: and such vices and weaknesses as they are subject to may be helped.

These and many other similar things give occasion to husband and wife in special manner to pray for one another, and with one another.

Husbands' and Wives' Hateful Curses and Wishes against One Another

Against that holy and heavenly duty of prayer are those horrible and hellish curses which too often pass out of the mouths of many husbands and wives against one another (and that many times for very small reasons) cursing the day that ever they knew one another, and wishing that one of them had been under the ground before they came together. These curses are offensive in any man's mouth, but more than most offensive in the mouth of husband and wife against one another.

Many, who for outward shame refrain to belch forth such rotten, stinking speech, feel little guilt for wishing the same in their hearts. If a husband be a bit harsh, and a wife complaining, or if through sickness, or any other occasion they seem burdensome to each other, or if any dislike of one arise in the heart of the other, or if their hearts be set upon others, or if the survivor is to carry away the goods and lands, their hearts will be filled with a thousand wishes of another's death. Yes, many times those who have very good husbands or wives, without any show of reason (only through an inward corruption of their heart, and malicious instigation of Satan, not taking notice of their own good) are ready to wish they were in heaven, claiming to desire their eternal bliss when in fact their only desire is to be released and freed from them.

God often meets with such wicked wishers (by which He shows how hateful such wishes are to Him) for sometimes according to their wish He takes away good husbands and wives from those that are evil. When they are gone He makes their loss to be so painfully felt, as those ungodly wishers do (as we speak) in every vein of their heart regret their rash wishes. Yes, to aggravate their misery the more, He gives them such sour and perverse husbands and wives in place of those good ones (for seldom comes one better) as they are forced with many deep sighs and groans to wish (but all in vain) their former wives and husbands alive again, and so to verify the proverb, "A good thing is not so well discerned by enjoying, as by lacking it." Sometimes again God in anger crosses their wishes, and first takes away the wishers of others' death, or else prolongs the life of both to their greater irritation.

Husbands' and Wives' Neglect of Mutual Prayer

The very neglect of mutual prayer in husbands and wives for each other is also a sin contrary to the just-mentioned duty of prayer. If all that are guilty were as well known to man as to God, how many unkind husbands and wives, careless of one another's good, would be noted more than they are? Rare are those husbands and wives that have their seasons to pray alone together with one another, if ever they pray for one another. Though in outward compliments they may seem very kind, and in the outward things of this world, very generous, yet if they pray not for one another, they are neither kind, nor generous. Hearty, fervent, frequent prayer is the greatest token of kindness and best part of giving to each other that can be.

Husbands' and Wives' Mutual Care for One Another's Salvation

From the general duty of prayer which is profitable to all things, I come to the particular branches of husband and wife's mutual provident care, and will first begin with that which is first to be sought, the good of one another's soul, which the apostle intimates to be a thing to be sought after, where he says, "What knowest thou, O wife, whether thou shalt save thine husband? or how knowest thou, O man, whether thou shalt save thy wife?" (1 Cor. 7:16). Peter commands wives to do their best to *win* their husbands (1 Peter 3:1) and Paul sets before husbands the pattern of Christ's love, which had special respect to the soul and the salvation of it (Eph. 5:25–26), so that this is a mutual duty pertaining to them both, which Peter further implies where he calls them "heirs together of the grace of life" (1 Peter 3:7).

It is the greatest good that one can possibly do for another, to be a means of helping the advance of his salvation. And there is nothing that can more soundly and firmly knit the heart of one to another, than to be a means of it.

Husbands' and Wives' Care to Win One Another, When One of Them is Not Called

That the salvation of the soul may be gained, we must consider the present and particular state of husband or wife. If one is a believer but the other not, the believer must use all the means that may be, to draw on the other also to believe. If both be believers, their mutual care must be to edify one another in their most holy faith.

For the first, it is the main drift of Peter's exhortation to believing wives, about their conduct, to draw on their unbelieving husbands to the true faith (1 Peter 3:1). His phrase "that they may be won" or gained, as it generally concerns their soul's salvation, so in particular to their first conversion. Now if this duty pertains to a wife, much more to a husband, who is appointed a head to his wife, and a savior (Eph. 5:23). To this end Paul advises believing husbands and wives that are married to unbelievers to dwell with them (1 Cor. 7:12–13).

For what a sad thing is it, that two which in this world are so nearly linked together as to make one flesh, should in the world to come be as far separated from one another, as heaven is from hell. This indeed shall happen in many, for Christ has plainly foretold it, that of two that were in one bed together (who are more fitly set forth under this phrase than husband and wife, who most usually are called bedfellows?), one shall be taken to mercy and glory, and the other shall be forsaken or left to endless and difficult torture and torment (Luke 17:34). But though it is foretold that thus it shall happen with many a couple, yet our care must be, with our utmost power to prevent it, as in ourselves, so in our bedfellow.

If it pleases the Lord to give such a blessing to the endeavor of a husband or wife, as to be a means of the conversion of their bedfellow, then will the converted party both entirely love the other, and also heartily bless God (as there is just cause) that ever they were so nearly linked together.

This duty of winning one another, is to be applied to those who are married not only to plain unbelievers, but also to papists or other idolaters, to atheists, or any other profane persons, to heretics, separatists, schismatics, or any that believe falsely.

Husbands and Wives Edifying One Another

The second duty tending to the soul's salvation is that two believers being married together, they work together to build up one another more and more (1 Thess. 5:11). One Christian owes this duty to another, much more husband and wife. The apostle writes, "Looking diligently lest any man fail of the grace of God" (Heb. 12:15). If no man, then neither wife nor husband.

A spiritual edifying of one another is the best use which we can make (and ought to make) of those joints and bonds whereby we are knit to one another. By virtue of them the body (namely, the mystical body of Christ) receives increase to the edifying of itself and increases with the increase of God. Now the bond of marriage being of all the firmest by which we are nearest knit together, by virtue of what bond should we edify one another, if not by virtue of the marriage bond?

Husbands and Wives Hindering Sin in One Another

Two things are required for spiritual edification. One respects the *hindrances* of growth in grace. The other the *helps* of it.

The *hindrances* of grace are all kinds of sins. Sin to grace is as water to fire; it quenches the heat of it, and if without stop it be poured on it, it will completely put it out. Regarding this, there ought to be a mutual care in husbands and wives, both to *prevent* sin before it is committed, and also to give what *cure* they can after it is committed.

That it is a mutual duty for husbands and wives so much as they can, to prevent sin in one another is evident by that reason which the apostle uses, to keep them from defrauding one another, in these words, "that Satan tempt you not" (1 Cor. 7:5). For out of the purpose and matter of those words, this general doctrine may be gathered: *husbands and wives ought to be careful to keep one another from the temptations of Satan*, that is, from sin, to which all his temptations tend. Rebekah performed the duty of a good wife in keeping Isaac from blessing Esau (Gen. 27:6), which, if he had, he would have sinned against God's clear Word (Gen. 25:23). Though she failed in the manner of doing it, yet her end was good.

As that love they owe to one another, so that care which they ought to have of themselves requires as much, for sin provokes God's wrath, His wrath sends down vengeance, that vengeance which falls on the husband can hardly miss the wife, or miss the husband which falls on the wife, by reason of their near union. Though it falls not on both their heads, yet it cannot fail to seriously affect and even afflict the party that escapes. The wives of those rebels who were swallowed up alive in the wilderness, perished in similar manner with their husbands. For they who are so near as husbands and wives, and do not what they can to prevent one another's sins, make themselves accessory to them.

For the better doing of this duty, husbands and wives must be watchful over one another, and observe what sins either of them are given to, or what occasions are offered to draw either of them into sin. If either of them be prone to get angry suddenly, the other must work to take away all causes of offence. If both should be testy and hasty to wrath, when the one sees the other first moved, the party whose passion is not yet stirred ought to be settled and composed

to all meekness and patience, lest, if both together be provoked, the whole household be set on fire. If either of them
be given to drunkenness, covetousness, or any other sin, the
other ought by wise and gentle persuasions to keep them (as
much as they can) from those sins. Yes, they may also get
others that are discreet and able to warn them, or use what
other good means they can to that purpose.

Husbands and Wives Curing Sin in One Another

When either husband or wife is fallen into any sin, a mutual
duty it is for the other, to use what cure may be of that sin,
as if one of them were wounded, the other must take care
for the healing of that wound. Abigail performed her duty in
this kind (1 Sam. 25), when, after she had heard what a rude
welcome her husband gave to David's servants, she quickly
went to carry a large quantity of food to David, and humbled herself before him, and so moved David to lessen his
anger. She waited for the right time also to tell her husband
his fault, and the danger into which he brought himself by it.

More directly, and with better success did Jacob cure the
superstition, or rather idolatry of his wife Rachel, as may be
gathered by comparing Genesis 31:29–34 and Genesis 35:2–4.

A brother in general must not allow sin to remain in his
brother—much less may husband or wife the one upon the
other. "Thou shalt not hate thy brother in thine heart," says
the law, "thou shalt in any wise rebuke thy neighbour, and
not suffer sin upon him" (Lev. 19:17). To do this then is a sign
and fruit of hatred. If a husband should see his wife, or a wife
her husband, lying in the fire, or water, ready to be burnt or
drowned, and not do their best help to pull them out, might
they not justly be thought to hate them? But sin is as fire
and water, which will burn and drown men in damnation.
This duty may be performed by meek instructions, forceful

persuasions, gentle reproofs, and by the help of some good minister or other discreet and faithful friend.

Husbands and Wives Helping Forward the Growth of Grace in Each Other

Till now we have discussed preventing and curing hindrances of grace. To this must be added helping to advance the growth of grace, which husband and wife must mutually work to bring about in one another. The care which Elkanah had to carry his wives along with himself to the tabernacle of the Lord year by year, shows that his desire was to uphold them in the fear of God (1 Sam. 1:4). The gifts and portions, which at that time he used to bestow on them, imply the care that he had to encourage them to hold on in serving the Lord. It was without question the main end which the Shunammite aimed at in providing lodging for the prophet, that both she and her husband might be built up in grace (2 Kings 4:10).

This duty may be the better done by the following means:

1. By taking notice of the beginning, and least measure of grace, and approving it.

2. By frequent discussions about such things as concern growing in grace, mutually asking questions to one another, and answering them.

3. By their mutual practice and example, making themselves patterns of piety to each other.

4. By performing exercises of religion, such as praying, singing psalms, reading the Word, and similar things together.

5. By maintaining holy and religious exercises in the family. Though this duty especially pertains to the husband, the wife must remind her husband of it if he forgets it; and stir him up, if he is slow; thus did the good Shunammite (2 Kings 4:9–10). No man's persuasion in this kind can so much prevail with a man as his wife's.

6. By stirring up one another to go to the house of God, to hear the Word, partake of the sacrament, and conscientiously perform all the parts of God's public worship.

There is great need that husbands and wives should work to help advance the growth of grace in each other, because we are all so prone to fall away and grow cold, even as water if the fire goes out, and more fuel not be put under it. And of all others, husbands and wives may be most helpful because they can soonest see the beginning of decay by reason of their close and continual familiarity together.

The Sins of Husbands and Wives against the Mutual Care of One Another's Salvation

The vices contrary to that general mutual duty of husbands and wives in obtaining the salvation of one another, and to the particular branches included under it, are many:

1. *A careless neglect of it* when husbands and wives are so attentive to earthly things, that they think it enough if they provide one another with the things of this life. Of this most that live in this earth are guilty, and among others, even many of them who have the reputation of very good and kind husbands and wives. But whatever the opinion of others be of them, the truth is, that if they fail in this point, they go no further than the very pagans have done, and their kindness may be as the apes' kindness, which causes death.

2. *The unworthy walking and unchristian conduct of a believer that is married to one who does not believe.* The unbeliever is kept from embracing the gospel and made more to dislike and detest it. If a popish or profane husband be married to a wife that makes profession of the truth of the gospel, and she be stubborn, proud, loose, irritable, wasteful, or given to any other similar vices, will he not be ready to scoff against the religion she professes and utterly protest against it? So also a popish or profane wife, if she be married to such a husband.

3. *Negligence in observing one another's disposition or conduct.* It comes to pass that they keep not back, nor restrain one another from running into any sin, but prove such husbands and wives to one another as Eli proved a father to his sons, whence it happened that God's severe vengeance fell upon the neck of the one and of the other. Pilate's wife, though a pagan woman, shall rise up in judgment against many such wives, for she did what she could to keep her husband from shedding innocent blood (Matt. 27:19).

4. *A soothing of one another's spirit,* and seeking mutually to please one another in all things, without respect of good or evil. Such as these the Scripture calls "menpleasers" (Eph. 6:6). From this it comes to pass that husbands and wives are so far from drawing one another from sin, that the better rather yields to the worse, and both run into evil, as Adam was persuaded by his wife to transgress against God's clear command, and wise Solomon was drawn by his wives to idolatry (1 Kings 11:4), and Sapphira consented to the sacrilege of Ananias her husband (Acts 5:2).

5. *An undue fear of offending one another* by Christian instruction, admonition, reproof, and similar things. Many who are often moved in conscience to make known to their husbands and wives the sins in which they live, and the danger in which they lie, do nevertheless through careless and causeless fear, refrain from doing so.

6. *An ungodly and envious disposition,* by which many husbands and wives are moved to mock and scoff at that holy zeal and eagerness which they observe in their mates, as Michal, who compared David to a fool, or vain fellow, because he showed his zeal by dancing before the ark (2 Sam. 6:20). Thus many nip the work of the Spirit in the very bud, and cause grace soon to wither. But cursed be that husband, or wife, that thus perverts the main purpose of their close relationship.

6

Guarding Each Other's Health, Reputation, and Property

After the good of the soul follows the good of the body, where husband and wife must show their provident care[1] over each other, and do what they can to do good to one another's position in society, and to nourish and cherish one another's body. This duty the apostle lays down under the comparison of a body which he calls flesh, saying, "No man hateth his own flesh, but nourisheth and cherisheth it" (Eph. 5:29). Now husband and wife are "one flesh" (Eph. 5:31). This duty the apostle applies in particular to husbands. At the first institution of marriage it was applied in particular to the wife, whom God made to be a help meet for man (Gen. 2:18), so it is a mutual duty pertaining to both. It seems that Rebekah was so careful of Isaac in this respect, that she could readily make savory meat for him, such as he loved (Gen. 27:14).

This duty extends itself to all states, both of prosperity and adversity, of health and sickness—for so much do they mutually covenant and promise when they are first joined together in marriage. "I take thee," says each to the other, "for better or worse, for richer or poorer, in sickness and in health to love and to cherish." Therefore they ought mutually to rejoice in the wellbeing of one another, and also in all distress to help and comfort each other, putting their

---

1. *Provident care*: meeting immediate needs and preparing for future needs.

shoulders under one another's burden, and helping to relieve one another as much as they can.

What Solomon said of a friend and a brother, may appropriately be applied in this case to a husband and wife, "a friend loveth at all times, and a brother is born for adversity" (Prov. 17:17), that is, a trustworthy and faithful friend is constant in his goodwill, and ready to perform all duties of kindness at any time, whether it be prosperity or adversity. The change of outward state makes no alteration in his loving affection and friendly conduct. He seems to be as it were born and brought forth against the time of trouble and affliction, because then his provident care and tender affection is most shown. Of all friends, none ought to be more careful, none more faithful to one another than husband and wife. How then ought they to love at all times, and if any trial come to either of them, the other so to conduct himself, as it may be truly said they were joined together for adversity?

Thus shall they verify the truth of that by which God was moved to create mankind male and female, namely, that "it was not good for man to be alone" (Gen. 2:18), but that it was rather *good*, that is, necessary, profitable, and comfortable for man and woman to be together. In this respect the wise man says, "He that findeth a wife findeth a good thing" (Prov. 18:22), and by the rule of relation we may infer, "she that findeth a husband findeth a good thing."

Husbands' and Wives' Slowness to Help One Another in Time of Need

Contrary to this duty is a certain unnatural affection in some husbands and wives, who greatly resent to provide the things that are needed for one another. The man commonly thinks the command too great, the woman thinks the effort too much. Their affections toward each other are as if they were mere strangers. Nay, many strangers will be more ready to perform, and more cheerful in performing needed duties (as occasion is offered) than such unnatural husbands and wives. If a little sickness, or other similar cross fall on one of them, the other thinks, "no one has ever had such a burden," and by their dissatisfaction make the burden much more heavy than otherwise it would be, as when two oxen are in one yoke and one holds back, making it much harder for the other to pull.

Thus they pervert one of the principal ends of marriage, which is to be a continual comfort and help to each other (Gen. 2:18), and to ease the burdens of one another. In this respect they are made coworkers. Job's wife, by her unnatural conduct towards him in his affliction, greatly aggravated his misery (Job 2:9). When he stood in most need of her help, she gave least to him. It appears by Job's complaint of her in these words, "My breath is strange to my wife" (Job 19:17), that she altogether neglected him in his misery. The common speech of many after their husband or wife having long lain sick is departed, betrays their unnatural affection. Their speech is this, "If my husband (or wife) had died so much sooner I would have saved so much money." What does this imply but that they wished that their husband (or wife) should have died sooner that they might have spared more.

Husbands' and Wives' Mutual Respect for One Another's Reputation

The provident care of husbands and wives should extend itself further to the honor and good reputation of one another. As dear ought the good reputation of the wife be to the husband, and of the husband to the wife, as their own. The great regard that Joseph had of the honor of Mary, his espoused wife, made him think of putting her away privately when he observed her to be with child and knew not of whom, for he was not willing to make her a public example (Matt. 1:19).

The same respect moved Bathsheba to send secretly to David, and tell him that she was with child (2 Sam. 11:5). The commendation approved by the Holy Spirit which the good husband (noted by Solomon in Proverbs 31:28) gives of his wife, shows how husband and wife ought in that respect to honor each other on good grounds. For:

1. A good name is a most precious thing, better than precious ointment (Eccl. 7:1), which gives a sweet fragrance, and is to be chosen above great riches.

2. So closely are husbands and wives joined together that the good name of the one cannot but tend to the honor of the other; so that they seek their own honor also.

Husbands and Wives Preventing Each Other's Discredit

For direction here, we consider how this duty may be *performed*, and how it may be *manifested*. To perform it well, care must be taken both to *prevent and cure a bad reputation*, and also to *obtain and preserve a good reputation*. To prevent a bad reputation respect must be had of these three things: what one says about another, how they listen to things related by others, and what judgment they give of one another.

For the first, husbands and wives may in no case delight to tell to others, and spread abroad the weaknesses and imperfections of one another, or anything that may tend to discredit either of them, but rather cover and conceal them as much as they may with a good conscience. It is expressed that "Joseph being a just man" labored to conceal that moral blemish which he imagined to be in his wife (Matt. 1:19), so this is consistent with justice. It is also a part of love, for love covers a multitude of sins (1 Peter 4:8).

For the second, husbands and wives must not have their ears wide open to hear every story and report that shall be brought to one against the other, but rather show themselves displeased and offended with them that are ready to relate a bad report. If a husband or wife shows a willingness to listen to stories and reports of the another, the devil will stir up instruments enough to fill their heads with stories, and those for the most part both frivolous and forged. Not only strangers, but children, servants, and they which are of the same family will ever be telling some story or other, to curry favor,[2] as we speak. But an utter dislike of such flattering gossips, will take away their reasons for telling untrue or empty reports.

For the third, the judgment which husbands and wives give of one another must either be very charitable, or very sparing. If one hear reported any notorious crime of the other, they may not be quick to judge and condemn, even if they think they see some evidence of it, but rather suspend their judgment. This seems to be the mind of Joseph. Though he observed Mary to be with child, he would not presently judge her to be a notorious adulteress, or condemn her as a hypocrite, unworthy to live, and therefore would not make her a public example.

In brief, that husbands and wives may be the more sparing in judging one another, they must not rashly believe any evil report of one another, but rather suppress all groundless suspicions as much as they can. That the judgment which they give of one another may be charitable, they must well observe the properties of love when judging. These are, first, to interpret doubtful things in the better part. Secondly, to moderate, as far as truth and justice will suffer, the faults which are evident. Michal offended against the first to a high degree, and was cursed (2 Sam. 6:20). Abigail observed the latter, and was blessed (1 Sam. 25:25).

---

2. *Curry favor*: win someone's affection by flattering them and talking down others.

The Wisdom of Husbands and Wives in Curing
One Another's Bad Reputation

To *cure a bad reputation*, husbands and wives must first give one another notice of the report that goes of them, and seek to work in them both a sight and also a sense of those evils which are in the mouths of others. After giving notice, they must labor to bring them to repentance of those sins, for which they obtained a bad reputation, and to a manifestation of repentance, by doing things fitting for repentance, which is by a zealous and conscientious practice of such virtues as are completely contrary to the vices for which they were evil spoken of. It may, with good probability, be gathered out of the histories of the Levite, whose wife played the whore, that thus he dealt with her (Judg. 19:1–3). And thus Abigail endeavored to deal with her husband (1 Sam. 25:37).

Husbands' and Wives' Care in Obtaining
One Another's Good Reputation

To *obtain a good reputation*, husbands and wives must first take notice of the good qualities which are in one another, and as one has occasion to speak of the other, to make those good qualities the subject of their speech. Secondly, they must lend a willing and joyful ear to those who shall (so far as they can conceive) truly and genuinely, without flattery or hypocrisy, speak anything in commendation of the one or of the other, not thinking themselves dishonored (which is the conceit of many) when their mate is praised, but rather having their hearts the more enlarged to praise God, for giving to them such an excellent sign and pledge of His favor. Thirdly, they must imitate those good things which they behold, or hear to be in one another, and so imitate them as they which have known both husband and wife in times past, may say, this she learned of him, or this he learned of her.

Husbands' and Wives' Wisdom in Preserving Each Other's Good Reputation

To *preserve a good reputation*, it will be fitting for a husband or wife wisely and seasonably to give one another notice of the good things people are saying about them, to provoke them both to give glory to God (as the apostle thanks God for that report which was spread abroad of the faith and love of the Colossians in Colossians 1:3–4) and also to walk worthy of that good report (as the apostle who had given a great testimony of the bounty of the Corinthians), earnestly exhorts them to finish their benevolence, "lest," he says, "we…should be ashamed in this same confident boasting" (2 Cor. 9:4). For if they of whom there is once a good report raised, grow weak, get cold, backslide, or fall into notorious and scandalous sins, they will extinguish and put out their good name among men, and turn it into an evil report, according to that which Solomon says, "Dead flies cause the ointment of the apothecary[3] to send forth a stinking savour: so doth a little folly him that is in reputation for wisdom and honour" (Eccl. 10:1).

Husbands' and Wives' Affection towards One Another's Honor

In the last place, to show a mutual provident care of one another's good reputation, husbands and wives must be so affected with the report that goes of either of them, as if the report were of their own selves. If the report be good, to be glad of it, and to rejoice; if it be evil, to be grieved, and irritated at it after a holy manner. Thus shall they show a true sympathy and fellow-feeling of one another's credit, according to that general rule of the apostle's, "Rejoice with them that do rejoice, and weep with them that weep" (Rom. 12:15).

---

3. *Apothecary*: pharmacist or chemist, in this case a maker of perfumes.

The Vices Against Mutual Care of One Another's Honor

Vices contrary to these duties concerning the good reputation of a husband and wife are generally two. One is a readiness to disgrace and discredit one another, like Michal the wife of David, of whom we heard before (2 Sam. 6:20). This is a hateful and detestable vice, which cannot stand with true matrimonial love, but rather argues an utter dislike, and a plain hatred of one another.

Husbands and wives discredit one another, either by obtaining a bad reputation, or hindering a good reputation. A bad reputation is obtained by the following means.

1. By broadcasting one another's weaknesses, as when tattling gossips meet, their usual prattle is about their husbands, complaining of some vice or other in them. "My husband," says one, "is covetous. I cannot get anything of him. He makes me go as nobody goes." "And my husband," replies another, "is so furious that none can tell how to speak to him." So one after another goes on in this track, some relaying such weaknesses as should be concealed; others (which is worse) plainly telling lies about their husbands. In similar manner also, husbands when they meet with their good friends, make their wives the common subject of all their talk, one accusing his wife of one vice, another his wife of another vice. There are two respects for which this vice (most detestable in itself) is made more offensive in a husband or a wife. First, because they know more than any other of one another's weaknesses, so as if they be so evil minded, they may much more discredit one another, than any other can. Secondly, because of their near union, they are most bound to conceal and cover each other's nakedness, but a more horrible curse do husbands and wives deserve, that so do.

2. By opening their ears, and paying attention to every little report that any shall raise. More secret heart-burning of one against the other, and more open quarrels and fights

between them, ordinarily arise from this than from any other thing.

3. By perverting and misinterpreting one another's actions, words, and even thoughts also, taking everything in the worst way.

4. By concealing from one another the common evil rumors which are raised of them, and are in every man's mouth. Intimate companions are most fit to disclose such things to one another, and most bound to do it—most fit, because of their mutual familiarity; most bound, because of their close union.

Many husbands and wives hinder one another's good name by envying one at the good report that is made of the other, and arguing against the same, as if the honor of the one must turn to the dishonor of the other. Thus as water quenches hot iron, so this envious disposition is a means to extinguish the heat of the iron, and to put out the glorious light of a good reputation. As they impair the honor of one another, so they horribly discredit and dishonor themselves.

The other general vice of this kind is a careless regard or plain neglect of one another's reputation. When the husband is no way affected with any report about his wife, nor the wife with any report of the husband, but act as if they were mere strangers to one another, they pass by all reports made of one another. What mutual love can there be in such? However their hands have been joined together, surely their hearts were never united, so as it had been better they had never known one another, unless the Lord do afterwards knit their hearts, and unite their affections more nearly and firmly together.

Husbands' and Wives' Managing Together the Possessions of the Family

Yet there remains one thing more about which husbands and wives ought to manifest a mutual provident care over each other, and that is about the goods of this world. Though the husband, while he lives with his wife, has the truest property in them, and the greatest title to them, yet I refer this to those mutual duties which husband and wife owe to each other, in three respects. First, because in conscience they pertain to the use of the wife, as well as of the husband. Secondly, because the wife is appointed by God's providence a joint governor with the husband of the family, and in that respect ought to be a help in providing such a sufficiency of the goods of this world, as are needed for that state where God has set them, and for that responsibility which God has committed to them. Thirdly, because the wife, if she survives the husband, ought to have such a portion of those goods, as are fitting for her status and responsibility.

In these respects we see it required, even a binding duty, that husband and wife, in a mutual regard for one another, be as thoughtful and diligent as they can be with a good conscience in getting, keeping, and using sufficient goods and riches for the mutual good of one another. Concerning the husband's duty in this respect no question is made. The practice of all good husbands mentioned in Scripture, the care of providing for their own required of them (1 Tim. 5:2), their position and office to be their wife's head, with many other similar arguments, of which we shall more distinctly speak when we come to declare the particular duties of husbands, do prove as much.

The greatest question is concerning the wife, whether she is bound to take any care about the possessions. But if the Scripture be thoroughly searched, we shall find proof enough to show that she also is bound here. For first, the general end which God aimed at in making the woman (namely to be a help to man) implies as much (Gen. 2:18), for here may she be a very great help, as we shall see in various particulars. Secondly, that general property attributed to a wife to be "a good thing" confirms as much (Prov. 18:22), for that which is profitable is called good, and it is one respect where a wife is termed "a good thing," that she may by her planning and diligence bring much profit to her husband. Therefore, in this, among other respects, the good wife which Solomon describes, is said to do good to her husband all the days of her life (Prov. 31:12), for by her hard work and planning she did preserve and increase his possessions, that the heart of her husband trusted in her, and he had no lack of gain (Prov. 31:11). If the particular actions by which that good wife is described are well noted, we may easily observe that she was a special help to her husband, even in his outward state.

We may infer these two points. First, that this provident care about outward temporal goods is lawful, not unbecoming a Christian man or woman. Secondly, that it is a mutual duty pertaining both to husband and wife.

For the first, how needful the goods of this world are for preservation of life and health, state of the family, good of the church and nation, relief of the poor, with such uses, no man can be ignorant. God has given them as blessings to His children, often times in great abundance, and His children have accordingly been thankful for them. Thus, a provident care about them is not unlawful, but very expedient and necessary.

For the second, if there should not be a joint care here, the care and pains of the one might be altogether in vain. For suppose a husband is hard-working, as Jacob was (Gen. 31:40), and makes a good profit, if the wife either by her spending, idleness, negligence, or similar vices, allows that which is brought home to be embezzled and wasted, or consume it herself by her extravagance, putting on a show, or love of entertaining worthless friends, where will be the profit of the husband's hard work? Or on the other side, if a wife should be as hard-working and successful in getting, as the good housewife before mentioned was (Prov. 31:10–24), and the husband by gambling, drinking, partying, or other means should waste it all, what fruit would remain of the wife's planning and work? In this mutual provident care of husband and wife, each of them must have an eye to their own place. Matters outside the home are most relevant to the man, and are especially to be ordered by him. That which the wife is especially to care for is the business of the house, for the apostle lays it down as a rule for wives (as we shall later more particularly declare) that they keep the home (Titus 2:5), and govern the house (1 Tim. 5:14). By this means may they be very profitable to each other.

The Vices Contrary to the Good Management of the Goods of the Family

Against that duty, are these following vices:

1. *Covetousness*, and too much care for themselves, as when a husband so rakes, and scrapes, and hoards up for himself that he neither grants to his wife so much as is fitting for her status while he lives with her, nor thinks of providing sufficient support for her, if she outlives him, but rather thinks how to cheat her of that which the law assigns to her. Or when a wife secretly hoards up whatever she can get, either by her own hard work, or else by stealing from her husband, sometimes selling corn, wares, household-stuff, or other similar commodities, so privately that the husband shall never know it, sometimes taking money out of his desk, box, wallet, chest, or similar places, so as either it shall not be missed, or if it be, it shall not be known who had it. There are many

who, not trusting their husband's provision or in dislike of them or on some other respects, commit whatever they can get to the trust and custody of others, whereby it often comes to pass that they themselves, meeting with deceitful friends, are utterly defeated, because they dare not make their fraud known. As covetousness is in itself an offensive sin, so it is made much more heinous by cheating a husband or wife, who ought to be as dear to each other as themselves.

2. *Extravagance*, and too lavish spending upon themselves, and those things which are most pleasing to their own corrupt desire, as when husbands without any restraint or measure, spend their goods abroad in hunting, hawking,[4] gambling, eating, drinking, etc., and suffer their wives to lack what they need at home, and yet took their wives to maintain them, and therefore had their portion. Or when wives bring their husbands into debt, and weaken, if not overthrow their estate, by gorgeous decorating and adorning their houses, by showy and costly clothing, by delicacies and expensive food, by gossiping abroad, etc. Many wives are so violent here, that if their desire is not satisfied, their husbands shall have no rest (they were accustomed to a lifestyle, and it matters not whether their husband's estate can bear it) in so much as many are forced wittingly, for quietness sake, to suffer their estate to sink. O foolish and wretched wives! How little do they consider that they were married to do their husbands good and not evil all the days of their life! Is this to be a help to man? Rather, is it not to thwart completely God's counsel, and pervert His purpose? Can we think that God will do nothing, and not take vengeance on them? Yet much more will God take vengeance on these husbands, because of that image of Himself which He has placed in them, and because of that place and authority where He has set them. The apostle plainly says of them,

---

4. *Hawking*: falconry; hunting with trained predatory birds; popular sport of the wealthy in early modern times.

that they are worse than unbelievers (1 Tim. 5:8), which being so, they must look for the greater judgment.

3. *Laziness*, and a careless neglect of their estate. Many men spend day after day, like a bird that flies up and down from tree to tree, from twig to twig. They go from place to place, but do not know why. When they meet with any company, they stay as long as the company stays, and then seek after other company, and are ready to go with any to bar, tavern, theater, bowling alley,[5] or other such places. Many women also spend all the morning lying in bed and dressing themselves, and the afternoon as occasion is offered in sitting doing nothing at home, or walking around for no reason, but only to pass the time, little regarding their husband's estate, whether it increase, or diminish. Thus by the laziness and carelessness of husband and wife, lovely estates many times come to ruin, and both of them brought to poverty and begging.

5. The Puritans strongly opposed plays and theater for moral reasons. In early modern England, bowling was commonly associated with drinking at taverns and gambling.

7

Serving Together in Family Ministry

Until now I have given such common duties as mutually respect the husband and wife, and are to be performed by each to the other. There are other common duties which they are both jointly bound to perform to other persons, and those either *members* of the family, or *strangers* coming to the family.

Concerning the members of the family, though there are some particular duties belonging to the master, and some to the mistress, some to the father, and some to the mother, of which we shall speak in their due place; yet in general the government of the family, and the several members of it belongs to the husband and wife both (if at least they have a family) and it is a shared duty to be helpful to one another there.

Objection: Seeing it is not necessarily required that a husband and wife should have a family to govern, for two may be married and have neither children nor servants (as many are) and yet be true husband and wife, why is this care of a family ranked among the duties of husband and wife?

Answer: First, because ordinarily when two are married they gather a family, and are the governors of it, so that though this is not true in some particular cases, yet for the most part it holds true. Secondly, because the joint government of which I speak is by virtue of the marriage bond. If a man and a woman should live together in a house, and by mutual consent have a joint authority and government, this would be very offensive to all that should know it, or hear of it. Neither are they by any ordinance of God bound to be so helpful to one another as husband and wife, nor the members of a family so bound to subject themselves to both. Thirdly, the duty of which I speak, though it is about the government of a family, concerns a husband as he is a husband, and a wife as she is a wife, that by virtue of their marriage bond, and near union, they be helpful to one another in well ordering the things of the family.

Whether the man ought to look to the good government of his house is a question beyond all doubt. He is the highest in the family, and has both authority over all, and the responsibility of all is committed to him. He is as a king in his own house; as a king is to see that land well-governed where he is king, so he that is the chief ruler in a house. The duty which the apostle applies in particular to elders and deacons, in general belongs to all husbands, that they rule their own house honestly; and again, that they be those who can rule their children well, and their own households (1 Tim. 3:4, 12). The care of many husbands is in this respect commended in Scripture, as of Abram, of Jacob, of Joshua, of David, the ruler at Galilee, and of many others. That the wife also ought to be a help to him there, is very evident, for the apostle makes it plainly their responsibility that they govern the house (1 Tim. 5:14). Would the wise man have so highly commended a wife for well governing her husband's house if it had not applied to her (Prov. 31)? It is very likely that Abigail had a great hand in governing Nabal's house, because the servants complained to her of Nabal's rudeness, and because she had the servants at her command, ready to do what she would have them; yes also, because she could so readily prepare such a large amount of food for David and his men, as she did. Hence is it that the wife is called mistress of the house, as well as the husband master of the house.

Objection: A woman is not to teach, nor to usurp authority over the man (1 Tim. 2:12).

Answer: First, that branch of teaching concerns public assemblies and churches, in which she may not teach, but not to private families in which she may, and ought to teach. Bathsheba taught Solomon (Prov. 31:1). When Apollos was brought to the house of Aquila, Priscilla the wife of Aquila helped to explain to Apollos the way of God more perfectly (Acts 18:26). Second, the other branch concerning authority does not refer to the subordinate members in the family, over which the wife of a household governor has authority, but only to the husband, over whom if she take any authority, she usurps it. Therefore neither this place of Scripture, nor any other, excludes the wife, being jointly considered with the husband, to rule and govern those in the family which are under them both.

Objection: This joint government of the wife greatly reduces the dignity and authority of the husband.

Answer: Not at all, for she is subordinate to her husband, and must so rule others as she be subject to her husband, and not command anything against his command (provided that his command be not against the Lord and His Word). We see that in all states the king or highest governor has other magistrates under him, who have a command over the subjects, and yet by this the king's supreme authority is not reduced a bit, but rather is better established, and he more honored. So is it in a family.

Let therefore husbands and wives assist one another, for so they may be very helpful to one another, and bring, by their mutual help in governing, much good to the family. The husband by his help aiding his wife, adds much authority to her, and so causes her not to be despised, nor thought little of. The wife by her help causes many things to be discovered, and so fixed, which otherwise might never have been found out. Two eyes see more than one, especially when one of those is more at hand, and more often present, as the wife is in the house.

Besides, there are many things in governing a family well that are more fit for one to handle than for the other, as for the husband to handle the great and weighty affairs of the family (as performing God's worship, establishing rules and order, providing convenient housing, and other necessities for the family, keeping children in awe when they get big or grow stubborn, ruling male servants, etc.). The wife best handles some lesser, but very needed matters, as nourishing and instructing children when they are young, making the house attractive, organizing the food brought into the house, ruling female servants, etc.

Furthermore, as the man especially is to perform the very actions of prayer, reading the Word, catechizing, and other similar duties in the family, so the wife may be a great help in reminding her husband both of the duty itself, and of the time of performing it, and encouraging him to do it. She should also be involved in gathering the family together, and exhorting them to be ready and eager, in making herself an example to the rest by her diligent and reverent attention, in often urging and pressing to her children and servants such points of instruction as her husband has taught, yes, in praying, reading, teaching, and performing similar exercises herself, so far as she is able, when her husband is absent, or negligent and careless, and will not himself do them, or it may be, is not able to do them, or if she performs them not herself, in getting someone else to perform them.

The Vices Contrary to a Joint Care of Governing the Family

The mind and practice of many, both husbands and wives, is against this duty. Many a husband, because the wife's office is especially to abide at home, will put off all government to the wife, leaving it to her not only to order the things in the house, but also to bring in all necessary things, to order and govern the children both young and old, yes, even to provide for them also, to take in, to put out, to use all sorts of servants as please her. If servants shall be stubborn against her, he will take no notice of it, nor endure to be told of it, much less grant her his assistance, but allow her to be disgraced and despised. As for religious duties, he will not touch them. Oh, men of low value, unworthy to be husbands of wives! Shall your wives who were made to be a help to you, have no help from you, no, not in those things which especially belong to your responsibility? Shall the weaker vessels bear all the burden? Surely as the man carries away the greatest reputation and honor when a family is well governed (though it be by the joint care and wisdom of his wife) so he lies most open to the judgment of God if the government of it is neglected, and through the neglect of it, children and servants grow ungodly. Consider Eli, and David. For as in a nation, the greatest honor of good government, victorious battles, happy peace, and prosperity, and the greatest dishonor and damage of the contrary, returns to the king, so to the man who is chief governor in a family. It is assumed that all who do any good are instruments of the highest governor, and if any evil or trouble happens, that it is through his negligence.

On the other side, because the husband is the highest authority, many wives think that the government of the family has nothing at all to do with them, and are careless of the good of it, and will not stir their least finger to order anything rightly. But, if anything is wrong, they lay all the blame on their husbands. Do not such pervert that main end for which God made them, even to be a help? Do they not carry themselves most unworthily of the position where God has set them, namely, to be joint governors with their husbands, and partakers of their dignities? As by their negligence they make themselves accomplices to all the evil which happens in the family, so surely shall they have their part in those judgments which are executed on the head of it.

Most contrary to this duty is the practice of those who are hindrances to one another in governing the family, as when wives are not only negligent themselves in coming to religious exercises, but keep back children and servants, and so are a great grief to their religious husbands, or when they use any of the children or servants to be instruments of sin, or are themselves discontent and troublesome in the house, similar to her of whom Solomon speaks in this proverb, "It is better to dwell in a corner of the housetop, than with a brawling woman in a wide house" (Prov. 21:9).

Husbands also are often a hindrance to that good government which their wives would help advance, when they scoff and scorn at that good counsel which their wives give them for that purpose, or when they will not allow their wives to handle anything at all, nor endure that they should find any fault, much less take in hand to fix anything that is wrong. These and such similar perverse dispositions are in husbands and wives, by which it comes to pass that they who were joined together to be a mutual help to each other, prove heavy, intolerable burdens.

Husbands' and Wives' Mutual Help in Hospitality

The next shared duty of husband and wife concerns those who come to their house, but are not members of it, whether they are family, friends, acquaintances, or strangers, especially if they be saints, to whom hospitality, that is, a kind and courteous welcome and care for guests, is due (Heb. 13:2; Rom. 12:13). Husbands and wives must be helpful to one another here, for as it is required of husbands (1 Tim. 3:2), so also of wives to be hospitable while they are married (1 Tim.

5:10), together with their husbands, and when they are widows, of themselves. Abraham and Sarah were a help to one another when the three angels in shapes of men came to their house (Gen. 18). So were the Shunammite and her husband when Elisha the prophet came to their house (2 Kings 4:8).

For hospitality, that it is a commendable duty belonging to those who are house keepers and able to serve guests, is evident by the precepts and examples before specified, as also by the blessing which God has brought to the houses of them that were so given, which the apostle implies in these words, "thereby some have entertained angels unawares" (Heb. 13:2). Now therefore husbands and wives being (as we have heard) joint governors, as in other things, so in this they ought to lend a helping hand to each other for these reasons:

1. Because in showing hospitality there are various things to be done, some of which are proper to the husband's position, and some to the wife's. To order the provision of things out of doors is more fitting for the husband; Abraham did it. To order the smaller things within doors is more fit for the wife; that was left to Sarah (Gen. 18:6–7).

2. Because it is fitting that guests should know they are welcomed both by the husband and by the wife, so that they may be more cheerful.

3. Because a mutual consent and cheerful help here will be a special means, as to show their mutual affection, so to hold the hearts of husband and wife firm and close together, and make them better like and love one another, especially if the husband shall show himself as ready and willing to welcome his wife's friends and family as his own, and the wife her husband's (as they should). For as they themselves are made one flesh, so ought each of them to esteem of the other's friends as of their own.

4. Because thus they show a mutual desire of bringing God's blessing on each other, and upon their whole family.

Vices Contrary to Mutual Help in Hospitality

Against this duty is for the most part covetousness in the husband, and laziness in the wife. The man, because the responsibility of the family lies on him, distrustfully fears lest he should lack enough for his own. I do not deny that a provident care for our own, and namely for them of the family, is needed and commendable: he that provides not for them is worse than an infidel (1 Tim. 5:8). A man may go overboard in serving guests, if he goes beyond his means, impoverishes his estate, and makes himself unable to provide for his own, as many do. Yet when a man has enough and more, when there is no just cause but merely upon an undue fear and anxiety, and distrustfully to be distressed and resent to show hospitality to any, is improper for a Christian, even also to be worse than an infidel, not worthy to have a house or anything fit for hospitality, not even worthy of common society.

The woman on the other side resents the labor she must do and trouble she must undergo about serving guests, and hates the thought that any at any time should come to their house. Concerning a wife, I do not deny that a husband may over burden her by being too jovial, as they speak, and bringing guests too often into the house, especially if they are guests of bad reputation, and by that means make her weary of her life. Yet for a wife to refuse all labor of that kind, and to be discontent when her husband invites any friends, or when any come (as the three angels did to Abraham) unexpectedly, shows that there is no loving affection, nor wife-like submission to her husband in her.

These faults are so much the greater when the husband or wife are free and eager to welcome their own family and friends, but are reluctant and resent showing hospitality to each other's friends and family. From this commonly arises much heart-burning of one against the other, even much discord and fighting between them. From dislike of the practice of one another in this kind often follows a dislike of one another's person, so that as the fault is bad in itself, it proves to be much worse in the trouble that follows upon it.

Husbands' and Wives' Mutual Help in Relieving the Poor

The last shared duty in which husband and wife ought to be helpful to each other, concerns those that are outside the house, namely the *poor*, and those who stand in need of their help, who are to be relieved and assisted. Because husband and wife usually eat together, and are joint partakers of God's good creations, they must remind one another of that precept of love which was given to the Jews when they were at their meals, sending portions to them for whom none is provided (Neh. 8:10). The good wife which is set forth by the Holy Spirit for a pattern and example to others to follow, and her husband, are noted to be helpful to one another in this duty. She is said to stretch out her hand to the poor, and to the needy, and he is said to praise her, encouraging her to keep on doing those good things which she did (Prov. 31:20, 28). What liberty the wife has, or how far forth she may be restrained in case her husband utterly refuses to give consent, we shall later declare in the particular duties of wives. The point here noted is, that the husband himself according to his ability must be both generous to the poor, and allow his wife, even provoke her so to be, and in addition allow her to be generous. Addionally, the wife also must stir up her husband to generosity in this respect, and herself open her hand to the poor in the things which lawfully she may give.

There is nothing whereby a man or wife can bring more profit to the house than by giving to the poor. That which is given to the poor is lent to the Lord, and He will repay it with great increase (Prov. 19:17). It is as seed, which, being abundantly sown, will bring forth a plentiful harvest (2 Cor. 9:6). It is a means to make us friends, to speak a good word for us at the bar of Christ's judgment seat (Luke 16:9); and it brings not only the blessing of men (Job 29:13; 31:20), but of God also (Matt. 5:7), even the greatest blessing of all, the blessing of eternal life (Matt. 25:34–35), for it is a sacrifice with which God is well pleased (Heb. 13:16). The apostle notes this to be one of Christ's sayings, which by word of mouth He left to His disciples, "It is more blessed to give than to receive" (Acts 20:35).

Besides, husbands and wives in distributing help to the poor, may receive good direction from one another, the husband by telling the wife who are fit to be relieved (for commonly husbands better know those which are outside of the family), and the wife by telling the husband what things are best to be given away, for wives commonly know of what things there is greatest supply, and what may be spared in the house.

Husbands' and Wives' Mercilessness to the Poor

Against this is the mercilessness of many husbands, who are not only hard-hearted themselves, never giving anything unless they are forced by the law of the land, and then they part with that which is given so resentfully, as it is not at all acceptable to God (for God loves a cheerful giver, 2 Cor. 9:7), but also tie their wives' hands, and allow them to give nothing. They bring both the cry of the poor, and also the groans and grief of a merciful wife who is thus restrained, upon their own necks, and aggravate their sin in a high degree.

On the other side, the mercilessness of many wives is also contrary to this duty, for there are many, who, though they have liberty to give of the common goods and also allowance of their own out of which they may give, covetously hoard up all they can get, give not a penny's worth, but rather allow food and other things to perish in the house, and when they are spoiled to throw them away, than that anything should be given out of the house while it is good. Shall not the creations which are spoiled in a house, and the poor that have lacked, make a loud cry in the ears of the Lord against them? Furthermore, many wives are grieved at their husband's generosity, and move him to shut his hand, and give no more. Are they not plain devils in this, opposing that which is good?

8

A Wife's Respect for Her Husband

Ephesians 5:22–24 says, "Wives, submit yourselves unto your own husbands, as unto the Lord. For the husband is the head of the wife, even as Christ is the head of the church: and he is the saviour of the body. Therefore as the church is subject unto Christ, so let the wives be to their own husbands in every thing."

In the particular declaration of wives' duties, the apostle notes two points, the duty required and the reason to enforce it. In setting forth the duty, he declares both the matter in which it consists and the manner how it is to be performed. In the matter we may note, the thing required, submission, and the person whom it respects, their own husbands. The manner respects both the quality of the submission and the extent of that submission.

To declare the quality of wives' submission to their husbands, two rules are set down. First, that it be such a submission, as should be performed to Christ (as unto the Lord). Secondly, that it be such a submission such as the church performs to Christ (as the church is subject unto Christ). The extent of wives' submission stretches itself very far, even to all things ("in every thing").

The reason to enforce all these points is taken from that place of honor and authority, where the husband is set above his wife, which is presented under the metaphor of a head (for the husband is the head of the wife), and amplified by that resemblance which he has there to Christ.

Of this resemblance two points are noted. First, that the husband, by virtue of his place, carries the very image of Christ (even as Christ is the head of the church). Secondly, that the husband by virtue of his office is a protector of his wife (as Christ is Savior of the body).[1]

A Wife's Submission in General

The first point to be handled in the treatment of wives' particular duties is the general matter of "submission" under which all other particulars are included, for it has as large an extent as that honor which is required in the first commandment, being applied to wives. When the Lord first declared to the woman her duty, He set it down under this phrase, "Thy desire shall be subject to thy husband" (Gen. 3:16).[2]

Objection: Was that a punishment inflicted on her for her transgression?

Answer: And a law too, for testing of her obedience, which if it is not observed, her nature will be more corrupted, and her guilt increased.

Besides, we cannot but think that the woman was made before the fall, that the man might rule over her. Upon this ground the prophets and apostles have often urged the same. Sarah is commended for this, that she was subject to her husband (1 Peter 3:6). By this the Holy Spirit would teach wives that submission ought to be as salt to season every duty which they perform to their husband. Their very thought,

---

1. For Gouge's exposition of Eph. 5:22–24, see *Building a Godly Home*, 1:28–49.

2. Gouge here quotes the Geneva Bible. The KJV says, "thy desire shall be to the husband," but the idea of submission is also present in the KJV of Gen. 3:16, where the Lord said, "he shall rule over thee."

feeling, speech, action, and all that concerns the husband, must taste of submission.

Against this is the disposition of many wives, whom ambition has tainted and corrupted within and without. They cannot endure to hear of submission. They imagine that they are made slaves by it. But I hope partly by that which has been before delivered concerning those common duties which husband and wife mutually owe to each other, and partly by the particulars which under this general subject are included, but most especially by the duties which the husband in particular owes to his wife, it will evidently appear that this submission is no slavery. But were it more than it is, seeing God requires submission of a wife to her husband, the wife is bound to yield it. And there is good reason she who first drew man into sin, should now submit to him, lest by similar feminine weakness she fall again.

A Husband's Authority Over a Wife Should Be Acknowledged by Her

The submission which is required of a wife to her husband implies two things. First, that she acknowledge her husband to be her authority. Secondly, that she respect him as her authority.

That acknowledgment of the husband's higher rank is twofold, first, generally of any husband, and also particularly of her own husband.

The general is the ground of the particular, for till a wife is informed that a husband, by virtue of his position, is his wife's authority, she will not be persuaded that her own husband is above her, or has any authority over her.

First therefore concerning the general, I will lay down some evident and undeniable proofs, to show that a husband has authority over his wife. The proofs are as follows:

1. God who ordained all powers that be (Rom. 13:1) has power to place His image in whom He will, and to whom God gives higher rank and authority, ought to be acknowledged as due to them. But God said of the man to the woman, "he shall rule over thee" (Gen. 3:16).

2. Nature has honored the male over the female, so that where they are linked together in one yoke, it is given by nature that he should govern, and she obey. This the pagans observed by light of nature.[3]

3. The titles and names by which a husband is set forth in the Bible imply a higher rank and authority in him, as "lord" (1 Peter 3:6), "master" (Est. 1:17),[4] "guide" (Prov. 2:17), "head" (1 Cor. 11:3), and "image and glory of God" (1 Cor. 11:7).

4. The persons whom the husband by virtue of his place, and whom the wife by virtue of her place, represent, most clearly prove as much, for a husband represents Christ, and a wife the church (Eph. 5:23).

5. The circumstances noted by the Holy Spirit at the woman's creation imply no less, because she was created after man, for man's good, and out of man's side (Gen. 2:18–24).

6. The very attire which nature and custom of all times and places have taught women to put on, confirms the same, as long hair, veils, and other coverings over the head. This and the former argument the apostle himself uses to this very purpose (1 Cor. 11:2–16).

The point then being so clear, wives ought in conscience to acknowledge that a husband has higher rank and authority over a wife. The acknowledgment of this is a main and principal duty, and a ground of all other duties. Until a wife is fully instructed there and truly persuaded of it, no duty

---

3. Gouge cites the Greek philosopher Aristotle (384–322 B.C.) from his treatise *Politics*, book 1.

4. Gouge notes the Hebrew term *baal* in Esther 1:17, which may be translated, "husband, master."

can be performed by her as it ought, for submission has relation to higher rank and authority. The very definition of the word implies as much. How then can submission be yielded, if husbands are not acknowledged as having a higher rank? It may be forced, as one king conquered in battle by another may be compelled to bow to the conqueror, but yet because he still thinks in himself that he is not a bit subordinate, he will hardly be brought willingly to yield a subject's duty to him, but rather expect a time when he may free himself and take revenge on the conqueror.

The Foolish Idea that Husband and Wife Are Equal in Rank

Against this submission is the opinion of many wives, who think themselves as good as their husbands in every way, and in no way subordinate to them.

The reason of this seems to be that small difference which is between the husband and the wife in dignity. Of all degrees in which there is any difference between people, there is the least disparity between husband and wife. Though the man be as the head, yet the woman is as the heart, which is the most excellent part of the body beside the head, far more excellent than any other member under the head, and almost equal to the head in many respects, and as necessary as the head. As an evidence that a wife is to the man as the heart to the head, she was at her first creation taken out of the side of man where his heart lies (Gen. 2:21); and though the woman was at first from the man, being created out of his side, yet the man is also by the woman (1 Cor. 11:12). Ever since the first creation man has been born and brought forth out of the woman's womb, so that neither the man is without the woman, nor the woman without the man. Yes, the husband does not have power over his own body, but the wife does (1 Cor. 7:4). They are also heirs together of the grace of life (1 Peter 3:7). Besides, wives are mothers of the same children of which their husbands are fathers, for God said to both, multiply and increase (Gen. 1:28), and mistresses of the same servants of which they are masters, for Sarah is called mistress (Gen. 16:4), and in many other respects there are rights shared between husbands and wives. From this many wives gather that in all things there ought to be a mutual equality.

But to infer a generality from some particulars is a very weak argument.

1. Does it follow that because in many things there is a common equity between Judges of Assize, justices of peace, and constables of towns,[5] that therefore there is in all things equality between them?

2. In many things they do not share the same rights, for the husband may command his wife, but not she him.

3. Even in those things where they share rights, there is not an equality, for the husband has a higher rank in all things. If there be any difference even in these instances, the husband must have the final decision, as in giving the name of Rachel's youngest child, where the wife would have one name, the husband another, that name which the husband gave, stood (Gen. 35:18).

Though there seems to be ever so little difference, yet God having so plainly appointed submission, it ought to be acknowledged. Though husband and wife may mutually serve one another through love, yet the apostle does not allow a woman to rule over a man.

---

5. *Judges of Assize, justices of peace, and constables*: officials in high courts, lower courts, and local law enforcement.

A Wife's Acknowledgment of Her Own Husband's Higher Rank

The truth and life of that general acknowledgment of a husbands' honor, consists in the particular application of it to their own proper husbands.

The next duty therefore is that wives acknowledge their own husbands, even those to whom they are joined in marriage by God's providence, to be worthy of a husband's honor, and to be their authority. This much the apostle intends by that little word "own" (Eph. 5:22, 24) which he uses very often. Likewise does Peter, exhorting wives to submit to their *own* husbands (1 Peter 3:1–5), and here limiting the commendation of the good wives of ancient times for their submission to their own husbands.

Objection: What if a man of low status be married to a woman of high status, or a servant be married to his mistress, or an old woman to a youth, must such a wife acknowledge such a husband to be her authority?

Answer: Yes, truly, for in giving herself to be his wife, and taking him to be her husband, she advances him above herself, and submits herself to him. It means nothing what either of them were before marriage. By virtue of that matrimonial bond the husband is made the head of his wife, though the husband were before marriage a beggar, and from a family with little status in society, and the wife very wealthy and of a noble family, or though he were her apprentice, or bondslave, which also holds in the case between an aged woman and a youth, for the Scripture has made no exception in any of those cases.

Objection: But what if a man of wicked and beastly character, as a drunkard, a glutton, a profane boaster, an ungodly swearer and blasphemer, be married to a wife, a sober, religious mother; must she count him her authority, and worthy of a husband's honor?

Answer: Surely she must. For the evil quality and disposition of his heart and life, does not deprive a man of that position of honor which God has given to him. Though a husband in regard of evil qualities may carry the image of the devil, yet in regard of his position and office[6] he bears the image of God. So do magistrates in the nation, ministers in the church, parents and masters in the same family. Note for our present purpose, the exhortation of Peter to Christian wives which had unbelieving husbands, to be in submission to them; let her conduct be in respect (1 Peter 3:1–2). If unbelievers do not carry the devil's image, and are not, so long as they are unbelievers, vessels of Satan, who are? Yet wives must be subject to them, and respect them.

Wives Denying Honor to Their Own Husbands

Against this is a very perverse disposition in some wives who think they could better submit themselves to any husband, than their own. Though in general they acknowledge that a husband is his wife's authority, yet when the application comes to themselves they fail and cannot be brought to yield that they are their husbands' subordinates. This is a vice worse than the former. To acknowledge no husband to be authority over his wife, but to think a husband and wife are in all things equal, may proceed from ignorance of mind, and error of judgment. But for a wife who knows and acknowledges the general principle that a husband is above his wife, to imagine that she herself is not subordinate to her husband, arises from horrible self-conceit, and intolerable arrogance, as if she herself were above her own sex, and more than a woman.

Contrary also is the practice of such women who purposely marry a man so far lower than themselves for the

---

6. *Office*: a God-given responsibility or calling.

very end that they may rule over their own husbands, and of others who are aged, who for that end marry youths, if not boys. That is a very inappropriate mindset and practice, and completely thwarting God's ordinance. But let them think of ruling what they like, the trust is that they make themselves subjects both by God's law and man's, of which such wives often feel the heaviest burden. Solomon notes this to be one of the things for which the earth is disturbed, when a servant reigns (Prov. 30:22). Now when can a servant more domineer than when he has married his mistress? As for aged women who marry youths, I may say (as in another case it was said), "Woe to thee, O wife, whose husband is a child" (cf. Eccl. 10:16). It is inappropriate that an old man should be married to a young maid, but much more inappropriate for an old woman to be married to a youth.

A Wife's Inward Respect for Her Husband

Our discussion to this point has been of a wife's acknowledgment of her husband's higher rank. It follows for us to speak of that fitting respect which she ought to have toward him. A wife-like respect of her husband consists in two points, reverence and obedience.

The reverence which she owes to him is both inward and outward. Inward reverence is respect filled with awe which a wife has in her heart for her husband, esteeming him worthy of all honor for his place and office's sake, because he is her husband. Doubtless Sarah had in her heart a reverent respect and honorable esteem of her husband, when being alone, and thinking of him in her very thought she gave him the title "lord" (Gen. 18:12). This inward reverence the Scripture includes under this word "reverence," as where our apostle says, "Let the wife see that she reverence her husband" (Eph. 5:33) and where Peter exhorts wives to have their conversation in "fear" (1 Peter. 3:2). It is no slavish fear of her husband which ought to possess the heart of a wife, dreading blows, frowns, bitter words, or similar mistreatment; but such respect and awe of him that makes her (to use the apostle's word) care how she may please him (1 Cor. 7:34). This wife-like respect is manifested by two effects: one is joy, when she gives contentment to her husband, and observes him to be pleased with what she does. The other is grief, when he is justly offended and grieved, especially with anything that she herself has done.

Unless this inward reverence and due respect of a husband be first placed in the heart of a wife, either no outward reverence and obedience will be performed at all, or if it is performed, it will be very poorly grounded, being only a show, hypocritical and deceitful. For according to one's inward affection and disposition will the outward action and conversation be shaped. Michal first despised David in her heart, and from this it followed that she uttered most irreverent and vile speeches of him, even to his face (2 Sam. 6:16). Therefore, after the judgment of a wife is rightly informed of a husband's higher rank, and her will persuaded to account her own husband her *head* and *guide*, it is necessary that her heart and affection be accordingly seasoned with the salt of good respect, and high esteem, which breeds reverence. In order that her heart may be seasoned, she should often and seriously meditate of his position and office, and of that honor which the Lord by virtue of it has planted in him. And if he has gifts worthy of his position, such as knowledge, wisdom, piety, self-control, love, and similar graces, she ought to take notice of it, and to think him worthy of double honor.

A Wife's Low Esteem of Her Husband

Contrary to this inward reverence of the heart is a low and vile esteem which many have of their husbands, thinking no better of them than of other men; no, worse than of others;

despising their husbands in their heart, like Michal. This, as it is in itself a vile vice, and a cause of many other vices, like presumption, rebellion, and even adultery itself many times, and it is also a main hindrance of all duties.

It commonly arises from three causes: (1) Self-conceit by which wives esteem their own gifts too highly, thinking them so excellent as they need no guide or head, but are rather fit to guide and rule both their husbands and all the household, of which proud and presumptuous spirit Jezebel seems to have been, who with an audacious and impudent face said to Ahab her husband, "Dost thou now govern the king-dom of Israel? Up, I will give thee the vineyard of Naboth" (1 Kings 21:7). Likewise were all those wives which are noted to draw away their husband's hearts from the Lord, as the wives of Solomon (1 Kings 11:4), Jehoram (2 Kings 8:18), and others. This they learned of their great grandmother, Eve (Gen. 3:6).

(2) Some weakness of mind, body, or life, which they see in their husbands, from which it comes to pass that many husbands who are highly honored and greatly accounted of by others, are much despised by their wives, because their wives always conversing with them know the secret weak-nesses that are concealed from others.

(3) Worst of all, from unjust assumptions and suspicions, suspecting many evil things of their husbands of which they are no way guilty, and misinterpreting and perverting things well done.

For curing this enormous vice, wives ought first to purge out their heart's pride and self-conceit, thinking humbly and lowly of themselves, even regarding the weakness of their sex, and if the Lord has endowed them with any gift above the ordinary sort of women, to note well their own infirmi-ties, and to lay them by their eminent gifts. Thus by looking on their black feet, their proud peacock feathers may be cast down.[7] When they behold any weaknesses in their husbands, they ought also to reflect their eyes on their own weaknesses, which may be as many and as grievous, if not more in number, and more heinous in their nature and kind—at least let them consider that they are subject to the same, if God leave them to the influence of their own corruption.

Secondly, wives ought in regard to their husbands to assume no evil if they have not sure proof and evidence, but rather interpret everything in the best light, and follow the rule of love, "which beareth all things, believeth all things, hopeth all things, endureth all things" (1 Cor. 13:7). If they note any defects of nature, and deformity of body, or any enormous and notorious vices in their husband, then ought they to turn their eyes and thoughts from his person to his position, and from his vicious qualities to his honorable office (which is to be a husband) and this will lessen that vile esteem which otherwise might be occasioned from these means.

A Wife-Like Sobriety

A wife's outward reverence towards her husband is a manifestation of her inward due respect of him. Now then, because the intent of the heart and inward disposition cannot be discerned by man, in order that the husband may know his wife's good affection towards him, it is necessary that she manifest the same by her outward reverence.

A wife's outward reverence consists of her respectful *gesture* and *speech*.

For the first, that respectful gesture and conduct is appropriate for a wife, was implied in ancient times by the veil which the woman used to put on, when she was brought to her husband, as is noted in the example of Rebekah

---

7. According to popular folklore, the peacock is proud of its feathers but deeply ashamed of its feet.

(Gen. 24:65). The apostle alludes to it in these words, "the woman ought to have power on her head" (1 Cor. 11:10). That cover on the woman's head generally implied submission, and particularly this kind of submission, that is, respectful conduct and gesture. But most plainly is this duty set down by Peter who exhorts wives to order their conduct before their husbands, so as it be pure, with submission (1 Peter 3:1).

This respectful conduct consists in a wife-like *sobriety, gentleness, courtesy, and modesty*.

By sobriety I mean such an attractive, serious, and gracious conduct, as gives evidence to the husband that his wife respects his position and the authority which God has given him. Sobriety in general is required of all women by reason of their sex, and surely it well becomes them all, but it much more becomes wives most of all in their husbands' presence. The apostle in particular requires it of deacons' wives, yet not so as restricted to them, but in a further respect pertaining to them not only as wives, but as the wives of deacons (1 Tim. 3:11).

Against this sobriety is silly and immodest behavior. These vices in a wife, especially before her husband, imply little respect, if not a plain contempt, of him.

Objection: By this all playfulness and intimacy between husband and wife shall be taken away.

Answer: Though sobriety is opposed to silly and immodest behavior, yet not to matrimonial intimacy, which is so far permitted to husband and wife, as if any other man and woman should so behave themselves one towards another as a husband and wife lawfully may, it might justly be counted silliness and sin. Consider the example of Isaac and Rebekah, who played together in such a way that Abimelech, knowing them to be those who feared God, gathered by their love-play that they were husband and wife, for he thought that otherwise they would not have been so intimate together (Gen. 26:8).

This intimacy implies both liking and love, and shows that husband and wife delight in one another's persons. But the silliness condemned here in a wife is not so much a mutual closeness with her husband by his good liking, as an immodest flirting with others to his grief and disgrace.

A Wife-Like Gentleness

Gentleness in a wife respects also to the ordering of her facial expression, gesture, and whole conduct before her husband, by which she shows cheerfulness to him, and a contentedness and willingness to be under him and ruled by him. This is set forth excellently in the spouse of Christ whose eyes are said to be as "dove's eyes," her lips to "drop as the honeycomb," and she herself every way "pleasant" (Song 4:1, 11, 13; 7:6). Upon this it is noted that she appeared to her husband as the bright morning (Song 6:10), and that his heart was wounded with her (Song 4:9).[8] Assuredly the clear sky is not more pleasant in time of harvest than a gentle and friendly face and conduct of a wife in her husband's presence. And though her husband should be of a harsh and cruel disposition, yet by this means he may be made meek and gentle. The keepers of lions are said to bring them to some tameness by handling them gently and speaking to them fairly.

Contrary to this gentleness is a frowning brow, a lowering eye, a sullen look, a pouting lip, an angry face, an insulting mouth, a scornful motion of the arms and hands, a disdainful turning of this side and that side of the body, and a fretful rushing out of her husband's presence. All these and other similar contemptuous gestures are as thick clouds overspreading the heavens in a summer's day, which make

8. The Geneva Bible reads in Song 4:9, "My sister, my spouse, thou hast wounded mine heart."

life very uncomfortable. They often stir up much passion in the man, and bring much trouble upon the wife herself.[9]

Wife-Like Modesty in Clothing

Modesty pertaining to a wife is largely displayed in her clothing. Paul requires this modesty in general of all sorts of women (1 Tim. 2:9), but Peter presses it in particular upon wives (1 Peter 3:3). For as it is very fitting to all women, so wives in a particular way in dressing themselves, to choose their clothes first as fits their husband's position and status, then their own birth and position of their own families, but only last their own preferences and desires. A wife's modesty therefore requires that her clothing be neither costly above what her husband can afford, nor unusual in a way inappropriate for his calling. As a poor man's wife must not put on a show of costly clothing, so neither ministers, important officials, wise magistrates, no, nor conscientious Christians' wives hunt after new fashions, or dress themselves in clothing that is immodest or draws attention to themselves. It is a sign of great reverence in a wife towards her husband to have an eye to his position and status in her clothing.[10]

On the contrary, such proud ladies who must have their own will in their clothing, and think it does not belong to their husbands to order them there, who care not what their husband's ability or his position and calling be, show little respect and reverence to their husbands. Such are they who are not moved one bit with their husband's example. Though the man's clothing is plain and grave, yet the wife's shall be

---

9. We omit here Gouge's treatment of "obeisance," or bowing as a gesture of respect for someone of higher rank.

10. Everyone in England had a position in a social hierarchy, and each person was expected to dress and live according to his station. This is far from some modern cultures where social distinctions, courtesy, tradition, and formality are scorned. Readers should consider how a wife's clothing may reflect well or poorly on her husband given his vocation.

costly and showy. There are many that stand in some more awe of their husband's sight, but show little more respect to him, who have their silken gowns, beaver hats, and other similar clothing not fitting for their place and state, lie in the country, in a friend's house where their husbands shall not know it, and when their husbands are not with them, wear them, and paint their faces, lay out their hair, and in everything follow the latest fashion. What can they which behold this think, but that such a wife's care is more to please other foolish persons than her serious, wise husband, or that her husband cannot at all prevail with her. As this stains her own reputation, so it leaves a blot of dishonor even upon him. If the care of a wife were to give evidence of the reverence which she bears to her husband, his desire and example would in this respect more prevail with her, than the desires of her own heart.

Wife-Like Respectful Speech to Her Husband

As by gesture, so by speech also must a wife's reverence be manifested; *this* must be fitting to *that*. By words as well as by deeds, the affection of the heart is manifested, "Out of the abundance of the heart the mouth speaketh" (Matt. 12:34). A wife's respect is shown by her speech, both in her husband's presence, and also in his absence. For this end in his presence her words must be few and meek. First few, for the apostle commands silence to wives in their husband's presence, and enforces that duty with a strong reason in these words, "I permit not the woman to usurp authority over the man, but to be in silence" (1 Tim. 2:12). The inference of the latter clause upon the former shows that he speaks not only of a woman's silence in the church, but also of a wife's silence before her husband, which is further cleared by another similar place where the same apostle enjoins wives to learn of their husbands at home (1 Cor. 14:35). The reason before mentioned for silence, on the one side implies a respectful submission, as on the other side too much speech implies a seizing of authority.

Objection: Then perhaps a wife must always be silent before her husband.

Answer: No such matter, for silence in that place is not opposed to speech, as if she should not speak at all, but to too much talking, to talkativeness. Her husband's presence must somewhat restrain her tongue, and so will her very silence testify a reverent respect. Otherwise silence, as it is opposed to speech, would imply defiant pride and stubbornness of heart, which is an extreme contrary to talking too much. But the middle ground between both is for a wife to be sparing in speech, to wait for a fit time and just occasion of speech, to be willing to listen to the word of knowledge coming out of her husband's mouth. This implies reverence. Elihu manifested the reverent respect which as a younger person he owed to his elders, by refraining to speak while they had anything to say (Job 32:6). How much more ought wives in regard both of their sex and of their place?

Contrary is their practice who must and will have all the babble. If their husbands have begun to speak, their slippery tongues cannot wait till they have finished. If (as very quick and bold they are to speak) they do not get ahead of their husbands, they will surely take his story out of his mouth before he has finished. Thus they disgrace themselves and dishonor their husbands.[11]

Wives' Meekness in Their Speech

Meekness in a wife's manner of framing her speech to her husband also commends her reverent respect of him. This

---

11. We omit here Gouge's section on a wife addressing her husband with respectful titles such as "husband" or "Mr. Smith," a formality quite foreign to our modern culture.

is a special effect of that meek and quiet spirit which Peter requires of wives, which duly he strongly enforces by this weighty argument, "which is in the sight of God of great price" (1 Peter 3:4). Is a wife's meekness much prized by God, and shall not wives hold it both a binding duty, and beautiful ornament, and grace to them? Her meekness shows itself in the form of words which a wife uses in asking or answering questions, or any other kind of discourse which she holds with her husband, and also her moderation in persisting, arguing, and pressing matters, and the gentle expression of her face in speaking.

If she desires to obtain anything of him, she must ask for it pleasantly, as the Shunammite (2 Kings 4:10). If she would move him to perform a binding duty, she must persuade him gently. If she would restrain and keep him from doing that which is evil, she must do even that also with some meekness, as Pilate's wife (Matt. 27:19). If she has reason to tell him of a fault, she ought to manifest humility and respect, by finding a good time, and doing it after a gentle manner as Abigail (1 Sam. 25:36–37), who, as she wisely behaved herself in this respect with her husband, so also with David by intimating his fault to him, rather than plainly reproving him, when she said, "this shall be no grief unto thee, nor offence of heart unto my lord, either that thou hast shed blood causeless" (1 Sam. 25:31). This meekness requires also silence and patience, even when she is reproved.

Contrary is the irritable and argumentative disposition of many wives to their husbands, who care not how quickly and foolishly they speak to them, like Rachel (Gen. 30:1); nor how angrily and sharply, like Jezebel (1 Kings 21:7); nor how contemptuously and bitterly, like Zipporah (Ex. 4:25–26); nor how mockingly, like Michal (2 Sam. 6:20); nor how reproachfully and disgracefully, like Job's wife (Job 2:9). If they are rebuked by their husbands, their husbands shall be rebuked by them; and they are ready to answer again, not only word for word, but ten for one. Many wives by their complaints and criticisms show no more respect to their husbands than to their servants, if so much. The least occasion moves them not only inwardly to be angry and fret against them, but also outwardly to manifest the same by sharp and angry words. The very object upon which many wives usually spit out their venomous words is their husband; when their hearts are full of bitterness, they must vent them on their husbands; thus their guilt is doubled.

Let wives therefore learn first to moderate their passion, and then to keep in their tongues with bit and bridle, but most of all to be careful that their husbands do not taste the bitterness of it, even if they should be provoked by some oversight of their husband's. It is to be noted how Solomon calls the discord between husband and wife, "the contentions of a wife" (Prov. 19:13), whereby he intimates that she commonly is the cause of it, either by provoking her husband, or not bearing with him.

A Wife's Talking about Her Husband in His Absence

The respect which a wife shows to her husband must be further manifested by her speeches about him in his absence. So Sarah showed her respect (Gen. 18:12), and so must all those who desire to be accounted the daughters of Sarah. The church speaking of her Spouse, does it with as great respect as if she were speaking to Him (Song 5:10). It was for the sake of honor and respect, that Mary called Joseph the father of Jesus (Luke 2:48), when she spoke of him.

This shows that a wife's respectful speeches in presence of her husband and to his face, are not in flattery to please him and win his favor, but in sincerity to please God and perform her duty.

Against their duty are those who in presence can afford the most beautiful and meekest speeches that may be to their husband's face, but behind their backs speak most contemptuously of them.

9

A Wife's Not Going Against Her Husband's Will (I)

Having discussed a wife's respect, it follows to speak of her *obedience*. The first law that was ever given to woman since her fall laid upon her this duty of obedience to her husband, in these words, "Thy desire shall be to thy husband, and he shall rule over thee" (Gen. 3:16). How can a husband rule over a wife, if she does not obey him? The principal part of that submission which in this text (Eph. 5:22) and in many other places, is required of a wife, consists in obedience. Therefore it is plainly commended to wives in the example of Sarah who obeyed Abraham (1 Peter 3:6). Thus by obedience the church shows her submission to Christ.

The position in which God has set a husband to be a head (Eph. 5:23) and the authority which He has given to him, to be a lord (1 Peter 3:6) require obedience of a wife. Is not obedience to be yielded to a head, lord, and master? You will take away all authority from a husband, if you exempt a wife from obedience.

Contrary is the stubborn pride of such wives who must have their own will, and do what they like, or else all shall be disrupted. *Their* will must be done, *they* must rule and over-rule all, *they* must command not only children and servants, but husbands also, if at least the husband will be at peace. Look into families, observe the state and condition of many of them, and then tell me if these things be not so. If a husband be a man of courage, and seeks to stand upon his right and maintain his authority by requiring obedience of his wife, it is strange to behold what a hurly burly[1] she will make in the house, but if he is a milk-sop,[2] and dishonorably yields to his wife, and allows her to rule, then it may be, there shall be some outward quiet. The ground of this is an ambitious and proud spirit in women, who must rule or else they think themselves slaves. But let them think as they like. Surely here they oppose God's ordinance, pervert the order of nature, deface the image of Christ, overthrow the ground of all duty, hinder the good of the family, become a bad example to children and servants, lay themselves open to Satan, and bring much other trouble which cannot but follow upon the violating of this main duty of *obedience*, which if it be not performed, how can other duties be expected?

When a Wife Has Authority to Order the House without Her Husband's Consent

A wife's obedience requires *submission* in yielding to her husband's mind and will, and *contentment* in resting satisfied and content with his state and ability.

That submission consists in two things; first, in abstaining from doing things against her husband's will, and secondly, in doing what her husband requires. The former of these requires that a wife have her husband's consent for the things which she does. To better understand this, we are to consider,

1. What kind of husbands they must be whose consent is required.

2. How many ways his consent may be given.

3. What are the things about which his consent is to be sought.

---

1. *Hurly burly*: much noise and commotion.
2. *Milk-sop*: a man with no courage or backbone, like a piece of bread soaked in milk.

For the first, as on the one side it often happens that a wise, diligent, purposeful, and religious man is married to a foolish woman, a true idiot, that has no understanding, of whom there can be no question, but that such a wife is to do nothing by herself, and of her own head, but altogether to be ordered by her husband. On the other side, it often happens that a virtuous wife and gracious woman is married to a husband destitute of understanding, or to one as stupid as a rock, unfit to manage his affairs through some problem of mind or body. In such a case the whole responsibility to lead lies upon the wife, so as her husband's consent is not to be expected.

Question: What if the husband is a wicked and profane man, and so blinded and stupefied in his soul? Does not this spiritual blindness and stupidity give a religious wife as great liberty as natural stupidity?

Answer: Certainly not, for Peter exhorts faithful wives that were married to unbelieving husbands to be subject to them in fear (1 Peter 3:1–2).

The reason is clear, for spiritual blindness does not take away the ability to govern earthly matters. Indeed nothing that such a man does is acceptable to God or helpful to his own salvation; but yet it may be profitable to his family. A wicked man may provide enough for wife, children, and his whole family in outward temporal things.

Again, it often happens, that a husband is absent a long time from the house, sometimes by reason of his calling, as an ambassador, soldier, or sailor, sometimes also carelessly or willfully neglecting house, goods, wife, children and all, and in his absence has left no directions for the ordering of things at home. In this case also there is no question but that the wife has power to manage matters without her husband's consent, provided that she follow those rules of God's Word concerning justice, equity, truth, and mercy, which a husband in his management of them ought to follow.

The first of these cases declares an *inability* in the husband, the other an *impossibility* for him to order matters. Therefore, the wife being next to the husband, the power of ordering things falls on her, and she is not bound to have his consent.

Different Kinds of Consent

Consent may be *general* or *particular*. A general consent is given when, without distinct respect to this or that particular, liberty is granted to a wife by her husband to do all things that seem good in her eyes. That excellent wife, and famous housewife that is set forth by the wise man, had such a consent (Prov. 31:10–31). For first, it is said, "The heart of her husband trusteth in her" (v. 11); and then it is inferred that she orders all the things of the house, many particulars of which are specified. I gather that her husband, observing her to be a godly, wise, faithful, and diligent woman, gave her authority and liberty to do in the household affairs what she thought good, he being a public magistrate, for he was known in the gates, sitting among the elders of the land (v. 23), and accordingly, she used her liberty.

A particular consent is that which is given to one or more particular things, as that consent which Abraham gave to Sarah (Gen. 16:6) about Hagar, and that which Elkanah gave to Hannah about staying at home till her child was weaned (1 Sam. 1:23).

This particular consent may be expressed or implied. An expressed consent is when the husband communicates his good liking by word, writing, message, or sign, whether his consent be asked (as was noted in the example of Elkanah) or freely offered.

Consent is implicit when, by your best guess, it may be gathered that the husband's will is not against such a thing, though he have not manifested his mind concerning that very particular. This implicit consent may be gathered by his silence when he is present to see a thing done, or otherwise has knowledge of it, or else where he is absent, by his former conduct or disposition in other similar cases. The Scripture counts a husband's silence to be consent, when he knows a thing and may, but does not forbid it, as in the case of a wife's vow (Num. 30:8). For all we know (2 Kings 4:10) the Shunammite had no other consent to prepare a room for the prophet, and to go to him, than her husband's silence and not forbidding it when he knew it.

As for the other kind of implicit consent, it may be set forth in this following instance. Suppose a good wife has a husband whom she knows by his former conduct and disposition to be a man of pity and love, taking all opportunities to show mercy, and in his absence there happens a fit and needed opportunity of showing mercy. If she takes that opportunity to show mercy she has an implicit consent, for she may well think that if her husband knew it he would approve of what she does. It is to be supposed that Hannah upon some such ground vowed her children to God (1 Sam. 1:11). It is not likely that she who would not stay at home to wean her child without her husband's consent, would much less vow him to the Lord (which was a far greater matter) without some persuasion of her husband's good liking of it. Now that a wife may show she deals uprightly in this case upon a true persuasion of her heart concerning her husband's mind, she ought (when conveniently she can) to make known to her husband what she has done, as Hannah did without question, and as much may be gathered out of these words which Elkanah uttered to Hannah, "the LORD establish his word" (1 Sam. 1:23).

The Things about which a Wife Must Have Her Husband's Consent

The things about which a husband's consent is to be sought are those which he by virtue of his position and authority has power to order, as for example, ordering and disposing the goods, livestock, servants, and children of the family, welcoming strangers as guests, even ordering his wife's going abroad and making of vows. To lay down a wife's duty in this first branch of obedience distinctly, it is that *a wife must do nothing which belongs to her husband's authority simply without, or directly against his consent.* Do not the words of Genesis 3:16 imply as much? I do not deny that there may be various things proper and particular to a wife in which I will not restrain her liberty, and therefore I use this phrase "which belongs to her husband's authority." And I grant general and implicit consent to be true consent, so as there need not be an express particular consent for everything, and therefore I have added these clauses "simply without, or directly against his consent."

That is done *simply without consent* which is done without any authorization from the husband so covertly that she is afraid it should come to his notice, imagining he would by no means like it, as Rachel's taking her father's idols without any consent from Jacob (Gen. 31:32).

That is done *directly against consent* which is plainly forbidden by the husband.

But to get down to the details mentioned before, first I must speak about the possessions of the family. It is a controversial question whether the wife has power to dispose them without or against the husband's consent. Before I determine the question, I think it necessary to declare what goods and what occasion of giving the question is about.

The Things which a Wife May Manage without Her Husband's Consent

For the possessions, some are the particular property of the wife, and others are shared. Possessions that are the property of the wife are those which before marriage she or her friends except from the husband to her sole and proper use and disposing, to which he also yields, or those which after marriage he gives to her to dispose as she pleases. Suppose it be some rent, annuity, fees, veils, or something similar.

These kinds of goods are exempted out of the question in hand; the wife has liberty to manage them as she pleases without any further consent than she had by virtue of her husband's former grant.

To these I may refer other possessions, but of another nature, namely those which some friend of hers, suppose father, mother, brother, or any other, observing her husband to be a very hard man, not allowing enough for herself, much less to distribute for charitable uses, shall give to her to dispose as she pleases, commanding her not to let her husband know of it. Now because it is in the power of a free donor to order his gift as he pleases, and because he so orders this gift as he will not have her husband to know of it, I doubt not but she may of herself according to the donor's mind without her husband's consent, dispose such goods. She is acting here but as a trustee.

Again of common goods some are set forth by the husband to be spent about the family, others he reserves for a stock, or to lay forth as he shall see occasion. Concerning those which are set forth to be spent, I doubt not but that the wife has power to dispose them; neither is she bound to ask any further consent of her husband. It is the wife's place and duty to guide or govern the house by virtue of these, providing sufficiently for the family; she may, as she sees good occasion, of such goods as are set apart to be spent, distribute to the poor, or otherwise. This I have noted for such tender consciences who think they cannot give a bit of bread or scrap of meat to a poor person, or make a pot of soup or medicine for a sick person, except they first ask their husband's consent. This is assuming that her husband does not expressly forbid this liberty, and she does not use it except as necessity requires. But our question is concerning such goods as the husband has not set apart, but reserves to his own disposing.

A Wife's Liberty in Extraordinary Matters

When it comes to managing property, the situation may be ordinary or extraordinary—extraordinary being for the good of the husband himself, and others in the family, or those who are out of the family. If an extraordinary occasion happens where the wife, by managing the property without or against the consent of her husband may bring a great good to the family, or prevent and keep a great evil from it, she is not to wait for his consent. Consider the example of Abigail (1 Sam. 25:18). Thus a faithful, wise wife observing her husband to run loose, and to spend all he can get in gambling and drinking, may without his consent lay up what goods she can for her husband's, her own, her children's, and the whole household's good. This is no part of disobedience, but a point in which she may show herself a great help to her husband, for which she was first made (Gen. 2:18).

Concerning those who are out of the family, if they are in great need and require present relief, though the wife knows her husband to be so hard-hearted that he will not suffer her to relieve such, without his consent she may relieve him. The ground of this and other similar cases is that rule laid down by the prophets and by Christ Himself, "I will have mercy and not sacrifice" (Matt. 9:13). If God dispenses with a duty due to Himself in cases of mercy, will He not much more dispense with a duty due to a husband?

A Wife's Limitation in Managing Property, and the Reason Why

From all these principles I deduce the true state of the question in controversy concerning the power of wives in managing the goods of the family to be this, *whether a wife may privately and simply without, or openly and directly against her husband's consent distribute such common property of the family as her husband reserves to his own management, if there is no extraordinary necessity.* The most ancient and common answer to this question has been negative, namely, that a wife has not the authority to do so. For my part, I agree to this.

The basis of this answer is taken from that primary law of the wife's submission, "Thy desire shall be subject to thine husband" (Gen. 3:16).[3] How is her desire subject to her husband, if in the case proposed she does not base her government of the home upon his consent? It is further confirmed by both proofs already given, and also by all other proofs that might be produced out of the Scripture concerning the submission of wives to their husbands. If in ordering the possessions of the family she does not yield submission, in what shall she yield it?[4]

Objection: Again it is objected that that old law is to be expounded of weighty matters.

Answer: The apostle, who was guided by the Spirit of the law-maker, extends that law to everything (Eph. 5:24). But is not this matter of disposing goods a weighty matter? The

---

3. Gouge here quotes the Geneva Bible. The KJV says, "thy desire shall be to thy husband," but the idea of submission is also present in the KJV of Gen. 3:16, where the Lord said, "he shall rule over thee."
4. We omit Gouge's brief digression to discuss Gen. 4:7 and the rights of firstborn over the goods of the family.

consequences which I shall later note to follow will show it
to be a matter of importance.

The Example of the Shunammite in Asking
Her Husband's Consent

As another reason why the wife must not use the family property without her husband's consent may be presented from
the example of the Shunammite who asked her husband's
consent before she prepared the things that were thought fitting to show hospitality to the prophet, and before she used
the things which were for her journey (2 Kings 4:9, 22).

Objection: It is indeed commendable for wives to seek
their husband's consent as she did, but where such consent
cannot be had, it is not necessary.

Answer: This example being grounded upon a law (as we
showed before) it does not only declare what may be done but
also what ought to be done. If a wife is bound to have her
husband's consent for doing a thing, by consequence it follows
that she is prohibited from doing it without her husband's consent. Furthermore, they that take exception against this reason
taken from example, use the same reason in other points, as
the examples of Abigail, Joanna, and Susanna for the contrary.

Objection: In the Shunammite's example there was more
than a merciful relief of the prophet, namely bringing him
into the house to eat and to lodge, in which the husband
must have the final decision.

Answer: The Word of God does not make that difference between relieving the poor and showing hospitality. It
extends a wife's submission to *everything*; therefore the husband has the final say as well in the one as in the other.

The Law of a Wife's Vow

A third reason why the wife must obtain her husband's consent to use their property is taken from the law of a wife's

vow (Num. 30). It generally implies that a wife might not make a vow without her husband's consent. From this it follows as an argument taken from the greater to the less, that she may not use property without his consent. Yes, the law (v. 13) further plainly says that though she has vowed, her husband has power to nullify her vow. Note here how the Lord will rather depart from His own right (as I may so speak) than have the order which He has appointed between man and woman broken. The Lord's right was to have what was vowed to Him performed. The order which He appointed was to have the wife submit to her husband. Rather than the wife should do that which the husband would not have done, the Lord released a wife's vow in case her husband would not consent to have it performed. Now then, I demand, is the management of property a greater matter than the performing of a vow? Or has a wife in these days more liberty than in former days? If she has, by what law? Was there ever under the law a more demanding command laid upon wives than this, "Let wives be subject to their husbands in everything"?

Objection: That point of a woman's submission in performing her vow is a particular case, but not this of managing property.

Answer: The Scripture by particular laws and examples teaches directions for other cases like them. Arguments drawn by just and necessary consequence are counted as plain testimonies. Whereas it is said that this particular in question is not plainly decided, I take the reason of it to be this, that in former times they so well marked the extent of the general law of a wife's submission, that they made no question of doing this or other similar things without their husband's consent. Neither did good wives take that liberty, neither had they any supporters of such liberty.

Objection: The case of a wife's managing property is unlike to that of vows, because vows are voluntary, but managing property as a work of mercy is necessary.

Answer: Though it is a voluntary thing to make or not to make a vow, yet a vow being made, it was not in the power of the party that made it not to perform it. It is a necessary duty to perform a vow, even plainly commanded (Num. 30:3; Deut. 23:21; Eccl. 5:4). As for the argument from a work of mercy, I will later show that a wife is not necessarily tied to it.[5]

The Problems of a Wife Managing Property without Her Husband's Consent

Another good reason may be taken from the trouble which would fall out if this liberty were given to women, which are these that follow:

1. The estate of the family might be wasted before any solution could be thought of, for if the wife may use their property without her husband's consent, it must also be granted without his knowledge. It is to be supposed that if he knew of that which he did not like, he would hinder it. If without his knowledge, then may that which he thinks to be remaining as family savings, be spent by the wife, and nothing be left. Whereas if he knew of the spending of that savings, it might be he would be more thrifty and sparing in other expenses.

Objection: This liberty is not granted to wives beyond their husband's ability.

Answer: Wives cannot always know their husband's ability, for their husbands may have much debt, and yet to maintain his credit, by which he hopes to raise his estate, may allow ample support for his household. If his wife concludes that he is very rich, and is accordingly very generous in her

---

5. We omit Gouge's next reason, which pertains to the laws of England at that time.

gifts, she may soon go beyond his ability and so increase his debt that he shall never be able to recover himself.

2. Persons of contrary religions and dispositions being out of the family might be supported by the property of the same family. If the husband were of one religion, and the wife of another, he without her knowledge might support those of his religion, and she without his knowledge might support them of her religion.

Objection: This liberty of managing property given to the wife is limited within the bounds of the household of faith.

Answer: If theologians grant them this liberty, they will themselves judge and determine who is of the household of faith. Popish wives will say (whatever we say to the contrary) that Jesuits, priests, and friars[6] are of the household of faith, even leading members of it.

3. Many quarrels and fights would arise from this between husband and wife, for if a wife shall persist to do that which her husband will not consent to, surely one of a thousand will not put up with it, but will rather seek all the ways he can to frustrate her, thinking himself despised, if she has her way regardless of what he wants.

Objection: Wives must use this liberty with all due respect to their husband's authority.

Answer: If the husband decisively stands upon his authority, and by all the fair means that can be used, will not yield

---

6. *Jesuits*: members of the Society of Jesus, formed in 1540 by Ignatius of Loyola and Francis Xavier to counter the Reformation and spread papal authority. *Friars*: members of Roman Catholic religious orders such as the Dominicans, Franciscans, Carmelites, and Augustinians, formed in the eleventh and twelfth centuries. English Reformed writers viewed the Roman church with grave suspicion since the Church of England had broken with the Pope in 1534. In 1605, less than twenty years before Gouge published this book, some Roman Catholics were implicated in the Gunpowder Plot, a failed attempt to assassinate the King of England by blowing up the House of Lords. Anti-catholic feelings were running high in England at this time.

this liberty, I know not what better respect she can show to this authority than to refrain and abstain from doing that which otherwise she would most gladly do. But if when it comes to the uttermost point, and she shall say it is her right, and if she cannot have his consent, she will do it without his consent, she shows no great respect.

Many other problems might be brought up, but I will no longer insist on them, only from these let it be well considered whether it is not better for a family that the husband should be barred from managing the property without consent of his wife (so that there might be according to the proverb, only one hand in the purse) than both husband and wife to have liberty to use them without each other's consent.[7]

7. We omit here some sections dealing with property rights and family law in England at that time.

10

A Wife's Not Going Against Her Husband's Will (II)

I have already considered many questions about how a wife should obey her husband through seeking his will about how to manage their household. In this chapter I will consider more cases and questions regarding her submission.

The Submission of Wives in Using Property for Charity

Some that grant that a wife is subjected to her husband in household and personal matters, that she may not use any part of their property at her pleasure, deny that this submission extends to giving to help the poor, and similar charitable uses.

Let it be said first that in case a wife is forbidden or restrained by her husband, she ought to use all the good means she can by herself and her friends to move her husband to grant her some liberty, that she may have some way to show her mercy and charitable disposition. If she cannot prevail then she ought to make known to her husband such persons' cases as she thinks fitting to be helped, and use all the motives she can to persuade him to grant them some assistance.

But consider the case of a wise, religious, merciful wife, married to a greedy lover of this world, who, though he has intelligence and understanding enough to manage earthly affairs and to provide for the outward temporal state of the household, has no heart to help the poor, and is not only unwilling himself to do good in that kind, but will not allow his wife to do it. Would he allow her privately to take of such goods as he has reserved to his own control, and simply without any kind of consent give them away to charitable uses, or though he plainly forbid her, yet directly against his consent use them?

With reverent respect to better judgments, I think she may not. For it being before proved in general that she had no such liberty in disposing goods, I cannot see how this particular purpose of giving to the poor can suspend her general obligation to submission "in everything," unless there is some particular authorization for it in God's Word.

How Far General Exhortations to Works of Mercy Bind Wives

Objection: The many general exhortations to works of mercy, which without limitation to any particular persons, are indefinitely directed to all, do give sufficient authorization to wives: such as, "Give alms" (Luke 11:41), "Let us do good" (Gal. 6:10), and "But to do good and to communicate forget not" (Heb. 13:16).

Answer: All these are strong motives for wives to be merciful and charitable in such things as they may, by any means with their husband's consent, or in such things as by their husbands are given to them. They are also strong motives to provoke husbands to allow them liberty to give to the poor. But in the case proposed they give no liberty to wives. It is a rule laid down by Christ Himself that works of charity must be done, and alms must be given of such things "as ye have" (Luke 11:41), or which are in our power to give. Now if the husband will not give her that power, she has not power to give, and so is excused. In this case her true will and her faithful and earnest desire shall be accepted for the deed, according to that which the apostle says, "if there be first a willing mind, it is accepted according to that a man hath, and not according to that he hath not" (2 Cor. 8:12). Many cases may be given in which subordinates are restrained from works of mercy. Suppose a son or servant be desirous to visit one sick or in prison, but his parent or master (though permission is asked) will not allow him, but commands him not to go out of doors or to go with him another way; shall this son or servant, disregarding that command, do that work of mercy?

Obedience to a Husband in Such Things that He Sinfully Forbids

Objection: This restraint is not "in the Lord" (Col. 3:18) but rather against Him and His Word; therefore a wife is not bound to it.

Answer: Though the husband sin in restraining his wife, she in that restraint may obey "in the Lord" because the Lord who has commanded her to be subject "in everything" has nowhere warranted her not to be subject in this (Eph. 5:24). It is plainly said in the law concerning a wife's vows, that "if he shall any ways make them void after that he hath heard them; then he shall bear her iniquity" (Num. 30:15). Did not he sin in restraining her, and was she not guiltless though she yielded to his restraint? The condition between husbands and wives in this case, is not unlike the case between others in authority, and their subordinates in submission. But other subordinates may lawfully abstain from such things as their governors do sinfully command them to abstain from. For suppose that a son who has grown to be a man lives in his father's house at his father's finding, and has no set portion of his own, and his father will not give him permission to give anything for charitable uses. Is he now bound to give to the poor? Shall the curse be executed on him if he does not give? A cross indeed I acknowledge it to be, both to such a son, and also to a wife so restrained, but not a curse or sin. The sin and curse lie on their heads who restrain them by virtue of their authority, in which they abuse their authority. Other governors may do and often do this, and yet neither is liberty granted thereby to subjects, nor is authority taken from governors. In this resemblance between a son and a wife I desire not to be mistaken; for I mention it not to make the state of a wife and a son entirely the same, but to show that those general precepts of giving to the poor may have their exceptions, as they which in particular handle that point, give other examples. There must therefore be a further ground than the general commandment of giving to the poor to prove the liberty of wives which we are discussing.[1]

A Wife's Submission to Her Husband about Children

A wife may not simply without, or directly against her husband's consent, order and manage the children in giving them names, clothing their bodies, choosing their vocations, where they live, marriages, or inheritances.

Giving names to children is throughout the Scripture for the most part the responsibility given to the husband, as to Abraham (Gen. 17:19), to Zacharias (Luke 1:13), and to others, and that accordingly husbands have ordinarily done, as for example, Adam (Gen. 5:3), Lamech (Gen. 5:29), Abraham (Gen. 21:3), and others. It is to be noted that when there was a difference between the man and his wife in giving a child's name, he giving one name, she another, the name which he gave, stood. Though Rachel (Gen. 35:18) named her youngest son Benoni, Benjamin (which name Jacob gave) was the child's name. Also when Elizabeth (Luke 1:62) told her friends that her child's name must be John, they would

---

1. We omit Gouge's answers to objections based on the actions of Zipporah (Ex. 4:25) and Joanna (Luke 8:2–3) because in neither case is it clear that these women acted without their husband's consent.

not rest there till Zacharias had ratified that name. Though Joseph were but the supposed father of Jesus, because he was the husband of Mary the mother of Jesus (Matt. 1:21), he had the honor given him to give the name to her child. Although in Scripture it is sometimes said that the mothers named their children, as Leah (Gen. 29:32), Rachel (Gen. 30:24), and others, it is supposed that they had their husband's consent.

For making decisions about residence and marriage it is noted that Rebekah (Gen. 27:43) asked the consent of her husband; though she told her son Jacob that he should go to Haran to his uncle Laban to be kept in safety from the fury of Esau, yet she would not send him till Isaac had given his consent for his residence there, and taking a wife from there (Gen. 28:1–2).

For directing a child to a vocation, it is noted of Hannah, that though before the child was born she had by solemn vow dedicated him to the Lord (1 Sam. 1:11), yet when the child was born she asked her husband's consent about it (1 Sam. 1:22).

That which is noted of Hannah's carrying a little coat to her son year by year when she went up with her husband (1 Sam. 2:19), shows that she did it with her husband's consent. Women are for the most part prone to promote their children above their husband's position and vocation, and therefore there is good reason that they should be governed by their husbands.

Objection: What if husbands are more ambitious to have their children dressed in an inappropriate way than wives?

Answer: A wife must do what she can to hinder it. If she cannot prevail with him, she is much more excused by reason of her submission than he could be, if he would allow his wife to have her will.

The law that lays the responsibility upon husbands to give such and such inheritances to his children and the answerable practice of husbands from time to time (Deut.

21:15–16), show that the wife of herself does not have the power to order them.

A Wife's Submission to Her Husband about Ordering Servants and Livestock

If wives must have their husband's consent in ordering and disposing of their children which come out of their womb, much more of their servants.

They may not hire or fire servants against their husband's will. In this point, as in many others, Sarah showed her wife-like obedience, in that she would not deal roughly with her servant even though she was provoked (Gen. 16:5), much less throw her out of the house till she had made the matter known to her husband (Gen. 21:10). Though she failed in the manner in which she did it, in the thing itself she is a good example. It is further noted and approved in the Shunammite that she asked her husband's consent about sending a servant with her (2 Kings 4:22).

My meaning is not that such wives who have servants given them to wait upon them should ask their husband's consent whenever they need their services; for their husbands by allowing them men for their attendance made their will and consent clear that they may use them as they see need for it. But they should not use and employ their servants in such things as they know their husbands would dislike, unless they can gain their husband's consent.

Objection: Wives are parents of their children as well as husbands, and mistresses of servants as well as their masters, and therefore have altogether as great power over them as their husbands.

Answer: Indeed if the authority of the husband comes not between, that may be granted in relation between her and them, but her power being subordinate to her husband's she has not so great a power; the power of a wife that we speak now of is directly related to her husband.

The same may be said of their animals and cattle, a particular point noted also in the example of the Shunammite, who having occasion to use a beast went to her husband, and said, "Send me, I pray thee, one of the young men, and one of the asses" (2 Kings 4:22).

A Wife's Submission in Welcoming Travelers and Making Vows

If wives may not at their pleasure use the things pertaining to the house, much less may they bring strangers into the house and entertain them without or against their husband's consent. The good Shunammite first asked her husband's consent before she lodged a prophet of the Lord (2 Kings 4:10).

The same pattern is also commended to wives to move them not to journey abroad without their husband's consent. Though that good wife had a very weighty and just reason to go to the prophet, she would not before she knew her husband's mind (2 Kings 4:22).

As for a wife's power to make vows, in that the law gives a husband power to nullify her vow when he knows it (Num. 30:8), it implies that she ought to have his consent in making it, if at least she desires to have it established, which she ought to desire, or else she mocks God.

I have thought it good to mention these particular points for illustration of a wife's submission, because all of them are grounded on God's Word; many others might be added to them, but these are sufficient.

A Wife's Insubordination in Doing Things without or against Her Husband's Consent

Now we consider the usual vices and errors contrary to those duties. The general sum of all is for a wife to take on herself to do what she likes, whether her husband wills it or not, either not willing that he should know what she does, or not caring though it is against his will. Of this sort are:

1. Those who privately take money out of their husbands' closets, desks, or other similar places where he puts it, never telling him of it, nor willing that he should know it. Likewise are those who take merchandise out of the shop, grain out of the bin, sheep out of the flock, or any other possessions to sell and make money or to give away, or otherwise to use so as their husbands shall never know, if they can hinder it. Such wives sin heinously in many respects.

First they disobey the ordinance of God in a main branch of their particular calling, which is *submission*. Secondly, they poorly repay the care and labors which their husbands perform for their good. Many such wives pay back evil for good, which is a devilish quality. Thirdly, they are often a means to reduce and impoverish their husband's estate. Fourthly, they show themselves no better than petty thieves. All that can be justly and truly said for their right in the family property cannot defend them from the guilt of theft; they are the more dangerous by how much the more they are trusted, and less suspected, and their act is so much the more heinous by how much the more dear their husbands ought to be to them. Fifthly, they are a very bad example to other subordinates in the house, for seldom has a man a deceitful wife but some of the children or servants are made accomplices, being made her instruments to take the property, and hide them as she orders, and are made unfaithful. Sixth, they make themselves slaves to their own children and servants, whom they dare not displease, lest they should tell what was done. Seventh, they teach their children and servants to be thieves, for besides being used by their mistresses to steal, they will also steal for themselves when their mistresses shall not know it. So as what with the wives stealing one way, and the children or servants another way, a man's estate may be wasted as dew before the sun, and he not know which way.

2. Those who will have what allowance they think best for themselves and family, and scornfully say, they will not be at their husband's finding: they know best what allowance is fittest for the family, and that it shall have. Many will make their husband's ear tingle again, and even make the whole house (if not the street also) ring of it, if they think their allowance be not as big as the full extent of their husband's estate. This impatience and insolence crosses God's ordinance, and so it makes both their lives uncomfortable.

3. Those who pamper, clothe, or in any way bring up their children otherwise than their husbands would, even to the grief and dishonor of their husbands, keeping them at home when their husbands would have them abroad for better education. As these sin in hindering the good of their children, so also in not yielding to their husbands.

4. Those who will have their own will about servants, hiring and firing whom they please, and when they please, using some servants whom they find on their side against their husbands and carrying themselves so sharply and harshly to others that are on their husband's side, as a good, trusty, faithful servant cannot long stay in the house.

5. Those who secretly lend out their husband's horses, or other livestock, more respecting the pleasure of a foolish friend than to please a good husband. This fault is so much the greater, when it is done to the damage and hurt of the husband.

6. Those who are then most playful and happy, when their husbands are furthest off and cannot know it. Solomon sets it down as a mark of an adulteress to dress up her house and to seek for guests, when her husband is gone a journey far off (Prov. 7:19). Then ought she to be

most solitary by abstaining from parties to show that nothing throws a wet blanket on her happiness more than the absence of her husband.

7. Those who think their houses a prison to them, that cannot stay long at home. They think they have power to go wherever they will, and to stay out as long as they like, whatever their husbands think. The apostle lays this down as a mark of a sinful wife, and a lazy housewife, "idle, wandering about from house to house" (1 Tim. 5:13). Therefore, in another place he exhorts them to be keepers of the home (Titus 2:5). The wise man goes further, and notes another mark of an adulteress, that "her feet abide not in her house" (Prov. 7:11), which we may see verified in the Levite's adulterous wife, whose fearful end was a stamp of God's judgment on such loose immorality (Judg. 19:2).

8. Those who do not care how or what they commit themselves to without their husband's consent or knowledge. Especially offending are those who, being seduced by Jesuits, priests, or friars,[2] take the sacrament and bind themselves by solemn vow and oath never to read an English Bible, nor any Protestant books, no, nor to go to any of their churches, or to hear any of their sermons, and most of all those who enter into some popish nunnery and vow never to return to their husbands again.

Objection: Hannah vowed her child to God without her husband's consent (1 Sam. 1:15); why may they not much more vow themselves to God?

Answer: Surely she was persuaded that her husband would not be against it, and so had an implicit consent, which may well be deduced, because afterwards she made it known to him, as both the name given to the child, and that speech of Hannah, "I will bring him that he may appear

---

2. *Jesuits...friars:* members of Roman Catholic orders operating in England to undermine the Reformation.

before the LORD, and there abide for ever," and the answer of her husband, "The LORD establish his word" (1 Sam. 1:22–23), and his going up with her when he was dedicated to the Lord (1 Sam. 2:19), do all show.

Thus far we have discussed the first branch of a wife's submission in abstaining from doing things without her husband's consent. The second branch now follows in doing the things which he requires.

–11–

A Wife's Active Obedience
to Her Husband

It is a good proof and test of a wife's obedience, to abstain from doing such things as otherwise she would do, if her husband's contrary will did not restrain her. Yet that is not sufficient; there must be an active as well as a passive obedience yielded. That old law earlier mentioned, "thy desire shall be subject to thine husband, and he shall rule over thee" (Gen. 3:16), implies as much also. If she refuses to do what he would have her to do, her desire is not subject to him, but to herself; neither does he rule over her.[1]

This active part of her obedience covers both his *commandments*, to willingly do what he lawfully commands, and his *reproofs*, carefully to correct what he justly tells her is wrong.

For the first, so far ought a wife to be from thinking it contemptible to be commanded by her husband, that the very knowledge which by any means she has of her husband's mind and will, ought to have the force of a straight commandment with her. This readiness to obey is commended in the wives of Jacob, to whom when Jacob had declared what motives he had to depart from their father's house, implying by it that he meant to depart, and would have them to go with him, yet before he particularly expressed his will,

___
1. As noted earlier, Gouge quotes the Geneva Bible here, The KJV does not contain the word "subject" in the first part of this verse, but the second part still clearly affirms the husband's authority.

they readily answered, "whatsoever God hath said to thee, do" (Gen. 31:16). By this they led him to understand that they were ready to yield to whatever he would have done.

A Wife's Willingness to Dwell Where Her Husband Chooses

To make this part of a wife's obedience somewhat more clear, I will exemplify it by two or three particular instances, recorded and approved in God's Word.

The first is, that *a wife ought to be willing to dwell where her husband will have her dwell.* The wives of Abraham, Isaac, and Jacob manifested their wife-like obedience here. Though their husbands brought them from their own country and from their father's house, they did not refuse to go with them, but dwelt in a foreign country, even in tents.

Note in particular what Jacob's wives say to their husband in this case, "Is there yet any portion or inheritance for us in our father's house?" (Gen. 31:14), implying that seeing it was their husband's pleasure to leave, they would not any longer stay in their father's house, to look for any more portion or inheritance there.

These examples further show that if a husband has good reason to move from one country to another, or from place to place, his wife ought to yield to go with him. Note what the apostle says, "have we not power to lead about a…wife?" (1 Cor. 9:5). That question implies a strong affirmation. Wives then ought to submit to that power of husbands to lead about a wife from place to place. This clause, "as well as other apostles, and as the brethren of the Lord and Cephas," shows this was not only a power which might be used, but one which was used by husbands and yielded to by wives.

Objection: These examples are extraordinary, and from extraordinary occasions.

Answer: Yet they may be patterns for ordinary occasions which are lawful and justifiable. Was it not extraordinary of Elijah to pray first that there might be no rain, and then again that there might be rain? Yet this is proposed as a general pattern to move us to pray for lawful things.

Now in laying down this duty I added the clause and caveat of *good reason*, to meet both with those who upon discontent or superstition leave the land where the true gospel is maintained and preached, and go into idolatrous places, and also with such wandering unstable minds as only to satisfy their own desires, and to see fashions, as we speak. Such can never rest in a place, but are continually moving from country to country, and from place to place. I think, to use the words of the apostle, "a wife is not under bondage in such cases" (1 Cor. 7:15).

But if a man be sent as an ambassador by his prince or country, or if a preacher or professor be called into another country, as Martin Bucer[2] and Peter Martyr[3] were into England in King Edward's days, or if a man be sentenced to long imprisonment, and requires his wife to be with him, she ought in duty to yield to his demand.

Against this is the mind and practice of many wives, who being affected and addicted to one place more than another, such as the place where they were brought up, where most of their best friends dwell, refuse to go and dwell where their husband's calling lies, though he requires and desires them never so much. Thus many husbands are forced to their great damage for the sake of peace to yield to their wives, either to relinquish their calling or to have two houses; from which it follows, that sometimes they must neglect their servants

---

2. Martin *Bucer* or Butzer (1491–1551): reformer of Strasbourg who spent his latter years in England.

3. *Peter Martyr* Vermigli (1500–1562): reformer from Italy, who served with Bucer in Strasbourg, taught in England, was imprisoned by Queen Mary, and then returned to Europe.

and calling, and sometimes be absent from their wives, if not from their children also. Some wives pretend that they cannot endure the smoke of the city, others that they cannot endure the air of the country. Indeed their own wills and conceit stuffs them more than either city smoke or country air. I cannot call these the daughters of Sarah in this. They are not like those holy women that trusted in God, and were subject to their husbands (1 Peter 3:5–6), but rather similar to that unfaithful housewife of the Levite, who would not dwell in her husband's house at Mount Ephraim, but at her father's house in Bethlehem Judah (Judg. 19:2). Such wives as I speak of, in matrimonial chastity may be more honest, but in wife-like submission are little more faithful. Let this be taken for a fault, and it will be more quickly corrected.

A Wife's Readiness to Come to Her Husband When He Requires

Another particular instance of a wife's readiness to yield to her husband's commandments is *to come to her husband when her husband requires it*, either by calling her or sending for her. The wives of Jacob being sent for to their husband in the field where he was, made no excuse, but came immediately (Gen. 31:4). So far ought wives to subject their wills to their husband's here, that though it may seem to them some dishonor to come, if their husbands will have it so they must yield, otherwise they seem even to despise their husbands (Est. 1:17).

Against this is Vashti-like pride, when wives think and say that it is a servant's part to come when they are called or sent for, and they will never yield to be their husband's servant and come at his command. By this reason all duties of submission may be rejected. But for this particular case, let such proud ladies note the result of Vashti's stubbornness (Est. 1:16). As many excuses might be made for her as I think for anyone else. First, she was royally descended, being the daughter of a king. Secondly, she was then among the honorable women of the kingdom. Thirdly, the king was drinking when he sent for her. Fourthly, he sent for her to show her beauty before multitudes of men, which was not fitting. But all these were not sufficient to excuse her fault and free her from blame. First, though she was of a royal family, yet she was a wife, and her husband sent for her. Secondly, being among the noble women of the kingdom, she should instead have shown herself as a pattern of submission. Thirdly, though he was drinking, he remained a husband, and the thing which he commanded did not require her to sin. Fourthly, if she thought the thing inappropriate, she should first have used all the fair means she could to have been spared, but if she could not have prevailed, then she should have yielded.

Objection: Her fault was not in that as a *wife* she came not to her *husband*, but in that as a *subject* she came not to her *sovereign*.

Answer: Her fault was in both, and in the judgment passed against her, that by her example all women might learn to "despise their husbands" (Est. 1:17).

Objection: Her act is rebuked like this by pagan men that had no understanding of God's Word.

Answer: First, the Holy Scripture by the circumstance so distinctly noted implies that her rebellious act was a serious sin. Accordingly, both wise commentators and also preachers do accuse her of sinful disobedience to her husband. Secondly, though they were pagan, they showed what submission is required of wives to their husbands by the very light of nature, by which this sin is made inexcusable. Thirdly, Abimelech was but a pagan man, yet his sentence concerning a woman's submission in these words, "he is to thee a covering of the eyes" (Gen. 20:16), is taken to be wise, and approved by the Holy Spirit to be a good proof. As for the specifics about Vashti, why is it so distinctly recorded in the Scripture but for instruction and admonition to wives?

A Wife's Readiness to Do What Her Husband Requires

A third particular application of a wife's readiness to yield to her husband's commandment is *to perform what business he requires of her.* When three men came to Abraham suddenly and he desired to welcome them, he asked his wife to "make ready quickly three measures of fine meal" (Gen. 18:6) and she did it accordingly. Jeroboam, having a serious reason to send a message to Ahijah the prophet, thought it fitting to send it by his wife; she accordingly (though a queen) went (1 Kings 14:2). She did as her husband would have her.

Opposed to this is the spirit of many wives who will not do anything upon command. If such a wife's husband suddenly desires to have a friend over for dinner and uses Abraham's phrase, "Make supper ready quickly," she will say, "Let him come and do it himself; if he will have it so quickly done, I will not be his slave." Or, if having a matter of importance and secrecy, he asks his wife herself to do it, she will reply, "I am not one of your servants; cannot you give it to one of them, or do it yourself?" Yet such wives will be ready to command their husbands to do every little thing, and if he does not, they can reply, "Is this such a big matter? May not a wife speak to her husband?" Were the point of obedience well learned, it would cast such wives into another mold.

These few particulars may serve for direction in many hundreds. I proceed to the other part of a wife's active obedience, which covers the reproofs of her husband.

A Wife's Meekly Taking Reproof

The husband, having authority over his wife, has power, even duty, as necessary, to rebuke her. By just consequence therefore it follows, that it is her duty to yield obedience. This ought rather be done because the chief test of sound obedience lies in this. For nothing goes so much against one's pride as reproof. She that yields when she is rebuked will much more when she is asked gently. This point of obedience is manifested two ways, both by meekness in taking reproof, and by working to fix what is justly reproved. The very point of obedience especially consists in this latter. The former is a good preparation without which it will hardly be done, at least not well done.

Meekness in this case is one of the most principal fruits of that meek and quiet spirit which Peter commends to wives (1 Peter 3:4). However, Rachel justly deserved blame for coming in a rush of rage with a dictatorial command to her husband (Gen. 30:1), yet in that she meekly took his sharp reproof her example is commendable, for she did not reply against it, but meekly gave a direction to better accomplish her desire (Gen. 30:2). It is commendable I say, not in the content of her direction, but in her patient bearing of reproof.

Much wisdom may be learned by this, for when any meekly receives reproof, by this they suppress their anger, and keep it from rising as a cloud before their understanding and darkening it, and so may better judge of the matter reproved, whether it be just or not, and whether it need fixing or not. They who are angered by reproof and fret and rage against it, cannot so well judge. Mary made good use of Christ's reproving her (John 2:4–5), and learned and taught a good point of wisdom, to refer our affairs to Christ as we expect His pleasure, and not dictate to Him what time, means, manner, or any other circumstances.

Question: What if the husband's reproof is bitter?

Answer: He there forgets his place, yet even in this she must not forget her duty. If Jacob's reproof be well noted, we shall find it very sharp, for it is expressly said that "his anger was kindled against Rachel" (Gen. 30:2), so that he spoke in anger. The manner and form of his words being with a question, and the matter also, "Am I in God's stead?"[4] and so on, declare sharpness. Yet (as was declared before) she showed meekness.

Question: What if his reproof is unjust?

Answer: Meekness may still not be forgotten. In such a case a wife may make a just defense to clear her own innocence and show her husband's error, but if he refuses to hear her or will not believe her, then (as Peter speaks in another case) she must "endure grief for conscience toward God" (1 Peter 2:19–20).

The two reasons which Peter there gives in that other case may be rightly applied to this.

1. In general this is *worthy of thanks*. It is a grace, a glory to her, a matter that deserves praise and commendation.

2. In particular it is *acceptable to God*. However their husbands may deal roughly and untowardly with them, God will graciously look on them if they shall patiently in obedience to His ordinance bear their husband's unjust reproofs.

3. I may add this reason also, that thus they shall show themselves good Christians indeed, in that they are not "overcome of evil" (Rom. 12:21).

Contrary is the mind of those who by no means will bear a rebuke at their husband's hands. It matters not whether it is just or unjust; if their husbands reprove them, they shall be sure to have the reproof rebounded back again upon their faces with greater violence than it ever came from them. Some seem to be very good wives till they are tried by the touch-stone of reproof, but then, though the reproof be for a very right concern, delivered very gently, and in private between their husbands and themselves, they grow so impatient, or rather crazy, that they do not refrain from giving

---

4. *God's stead*: God's place. Only God can give children, which Rachel demanded of Jacob.

their husbands the most defiant speeches that they can invent, using with them bitter swearing and cursing, and threaten to hurt themselves if their wills be crossed. Furthermore, if wise husbands shall patiently bear with them in their tantrum, and after it is cooled down tell them how inappropriately they acted for their position, they will seek to justify themselves and lay all the blame on their husbands for crossing their will. Or, if they cannot but see their fault, yet they will only say, "It is my weakness," but still continue in that weakness. Though they make a show of fearing God, they do not labor to purge this corrupt attitude out of their hearts. This is how most fights arise between husband and wife. If wives would learn in this point to be submissive, many quarrels, which from time to time arise between them, would be calmed if not prevented. Michal, the wife of David (2 Sam. 6:20), and Job's wife (Job 2:10) shall rise up in judgment against these wives, because they were silent after they were reproved. Solomon often titles those who cannot bear rebuke "scorners" (Prov. 9:7–8), so by it wives show that they are very scornful.

A Wife's Readiness to Make Right What Her Husband Justly Reproves in Her

A further degree of obedience in bearing reproof is that *a wife willingly makes right what is justly reproved by her husband.* I say justly, because where no fault is, no change is needed. Patience may be needed, but no repentance of that which is not wrong. But where anything is wrong, she must make it right. Rachel did wrong in bringing idols into her husband's house (Gen. 31:19), her husband in asking her among others to put away their foreign gods, reproved them all. In response, she with all the rest gave to him all their foreign gods (Gen. 35:2–4). This was a good way to make things right.

A reproof may be justly given either for a good duty omitted, or for an evil thing committed; and accordingly must the rectifying or change be. A duty formerly omitted must after the reproof be more carefully observed and performed if it is a continual duty and may be performed again. Otherwise the way to make it right is a testimony of true sorrow for that wrong. When an evil is committed, if any means can be used to make up the hurt, and make right the trouble that followed from it, it must be done; if not, sorrow as before must be testified, and care taken that the same not be committed again.

Because a good conscience requires as much of all Christians by whomever they be reproved, so the respect which a wife owes to a husband requires it in a special way. Otherwise her fault is doubled both by persistence in her sin, and by disobedience to her husband.

Against this is their spirit who become worse after reproof, being like those scorners (of whom Solomon speaks) that hate those that reprove them (Prov. 9:8). Some wives say that if their husbands would let them alone they would do better, but upon rebuke they will never change. The more their husbands find fault, the more will they go on in doing what they do. What other judgment can be given of them than that which the wise man gives, "there is more hope of a fool than of him" (Prov. 26:12).

A Wife's Contentment with Her Husband's Present Estate

Contentment is also a part of obedience. It covers a man's outward estate and ability, in and with which a wife must rest satisfied and contented, whether it be high or low, great or ordinary, wealthy or needy, and above, equal, or under that estate in which she was before marriage. Though a man have been sometimes great in estate, if he loses wealth and is brought to a low estate, she ought to rest content. Thus much Job implies in his reply to his wife, saying, "Shall we receive good at the hand of God, and shall we not receive evil?" (Job 2:10). The evil he speaks of was the loss of his goods, servants, and children, together with other miseries that Satan inflicted upon him through God's permission. The receiving of evil which he speaks of was a resting content with it, and a patient bearing of it. Evil may be laid on any, and so they be forced to bear it, but they only receive it who are content with it. Now in that he uses the plural "we" and speaking to his wife he shows that he and his wife ought to rest content in that poor and miserable estate, for

1. Husband and wife being one flesh, both his promotion and also his demotion is hers. As she rises with him, so she falls with him. Therefore as she is willing to be promoted with him, so she must be content to be demoted with him.

2. If at the time of marriage her husband was of lower estate than she, she voluntarily put herself into that low estate, for a wife takes her husband (as he her) "for better or for worse, for richer or for poorer." And shall she not be content with her own act? If after marriage his estate decays and becomes lower than it was, she is to be persuaded that it was so ordered by God, and that God aimed at *her* humiliation as well as *his*. As a result of this she ought to be patient and content in her dutiful submission to God's over-ruling providence. This Job implies under this phrase, "The Lord takes away."

3. A wife's contentment is a great comfort to her husband lying under a cross, and it makes the burden seem much lighter than otherwise it would, if at least he is a kind husband, and affected with his wife's feelings, as he ought to be. For a loving husband in every distress is more perplexed for his wife than for himself.

A Wife's Unhappiness at Her Husband's Estate

Against this contentment is the impatience and unhappiness of wives at the lowness and (as they think) embarrassment of their husband's estate, which is manifested many ways.

1. Some when they are married, finding their husband's estate weaker than they imagined, regret their marriage, and refrain not to tell their husbands that if they had before known them to be no better men than they find them to be, they would not have married them. They betray their foolish indiscretion by saying, when it is too late, "If I had thought this," and they additionally manifest their own rashness and failure to make an informed decision, in that they gave their hands and plighted their troth[5] to those whom they did not know. If they say they were deceived by their friends whom they trusted, I answer that marriage is too weighty a matter to be wholly deferred to the trust of friends. Everyone that yields to be married ought to know well the party to whom they yield, and above all, they ought to seek direction, help, and blessing from God. If despite all the means which they could possibly use, they are deceived, they are to look to God, and to behold His providence there, and duly to weigh whether the Lord has crossed their desire for their humiliation, or for testing of their patience, wisdom, and other similar graces, or else to wean them from some empty and worldly delights, to which they were too addicted.

2. Others observing their husband's estate to be reduced and destroyed, never search after the cause, but lay all the blame upon their husbands, and with their discontented looks, angry words, and impatient conduct, so torment their hearts, that they make the cross much heavier than otherwise it could be. Though the estate should be overthrown by

---

5. *Plighted their troth*: promised their faithfulness, from the traditional wedding vow in the Book of Common Prayer, "till death us do part, according to God's holy ordinance; and thereto I plight thee my troth."

the financial mistakes of a husband, a wife ought to look to God's providence there, as was noted before.

3. Others are too proud to stoop and to come down to their husband's present condition, and through their pride and empty conceit are a great means to make his estate much the worse. They, as long as they can get it by any means, will not reduce anything of their fancy clothes, elegant pleasures, expensive furniture, and other things which are causes of great expense to their husbands. By this it also often comes to pass that husbands are thought to be wealthier than indeed they are, and so greater taxes and fees than they can bear are laid upon them for king, country, church, the poor, and similar causes.

4. Others, unhappily lie long sluggish in their beds, or sit still and do nothing when they are up, and will not take a bit of trouble to get up and increase their husband's estate, by which God is provoked more and more to weaken their estates, that He may more punish such pride and laziness in wives.

A Wife's Submission to Christ First

So much of the distinct branches of a wife's submission, the *limitation* and *manner* of performing it follows next. To know the limitation of a wife's obedience, and the manner how she ought to yield submission to her husband, two things must be considered, both the position of a husband and the position of a wife.

The husband's position is noted in this phrase, "as unto the Lord" (Eph. 5:22), which shows that the husband even by virtue of his position is to his wife in Christ's place, which is further more plainly laid down in these words that follow: "the husband is the head of the wife, even as Christ is the head of the church" (v. 23).

The wife's position is implied in these words, "as the church is subject unto Christ, so let wives be to their own husbands" (v. 24), which makes clear that the obedience which a wife performs to her husband must be such obedience as the church performs to Christ.

From the position of a husband, I deduce this general principle concerning a wife's submission, that submission *must be yielded to the husband as to Christ*. Two conclusions will follow, one *negative*, which is *the wife must yield no other submission to her husband than what may stand with her submission to Christ*.

The former is a necessary condition required of all subordinates in their submission, and obedience much more in a wife's submission to her husband, because of all persons of different rank there is the least difference between husbands and wives.

Hence for our present purpose, I deduce these two other more particular conclusions, the first of which is this, *if God plainly commands the wife any duty, and her husband will not by any means give consent, but forbids her, she may and ought to do it without, or against his consent.*

Cases Where a Wife Ought to Forbear What Her Husband Requires

The other particular conclusion is this, that *if a husband require his wife to do that which God has forbidden she should not do it.*

Two cautions are to be observed about this point. First, that she be sure (being truly informed by God's Word) that that which she refuses to do at her husband's command is forbidden by God. Secondly, that she first labors with all meekness and by all good means that she can to persuade her husband to stop urging and pressing that upon her which with a good conscience she cannot do.

A similar proof may be brought for this as was for the former, for we know that a wife is not bound to greater submission to her husband than a son is to a father. But, a son may in the case proposed refrain from doing that which his father requires and commands him to do. Consider the approved example of Jonathan who refused to bring David to Saul to be slain, though his father commanded him so to do (1 Sam. 20:31). I might also give the example of the same in Saul's subjects and servants, who refused to slay the priests of the Lord at his command (1 Sam. 22:17). Though a husband is not reckoned in particular among those to whom we are forbidden to hear if they entice us to idolatry, by the rule of relation he is implied, and by just consequence deduced from this clause, "thy friend which is as thine own soul" (Deut. 13:6), for who is so dear as a husband?

To give some particular examples as I did in the former case, if a husband shall command his wife to go to mass, to a stage play, to play at dice, to prostitute her body in immorality, to dress in a showy way like a whore, to sell by dishonest weights and measures, or similar sins, she should not do so.

Wives' Faults in Showing More Respect to Their Husbands than to God

Against this limitation is on the one side a cringing, flattering disposition of such wives that seek to please their husbands, so that they do not care about displeasing God. Jezebel was such a one; to please her husband most wickedly she planned Naboth's death (1 Kings 21:7). On the other side is a weak, timid heart which makes them fear their husbands more than they fear God. Good Sarah, that worthy precedent of good wives in other things, failed to some degree in this (Gen. 12:13). If wives rightly considered and always remembered that they have a Husband (namely Christ) in heaven, as well as on earth, and that there is greater difference between *that* and *this* husband than between heaven and earth, and that both in giving reward and taking revenge, there is no comparison between them, their care of pleasing or their fear of offending their Husband in heaven would be much more than of pleasing or offending their husband on earth. If anything were commanded or forbidden them by their husbands on earth against Christ, they would say, "If I do this, or refrain from that, I would be lying to myself; for nothing can be hidden from my Husband in heaven. I would even be obeying Satan rather than God."

The Manner of a Wife's Submission to Her Husband

The second general conclusion concerning the manner of a wife's submission, which was deduced from the position of a husband, was this, that *the wife must subject herself to her husband in that manner, that she would or should subject herself to Christ.* The word "as" in the clause, "as to the Lord," suggests as much.

This very conclusion is also inferred out of the position of a wife: in the same position that the church is to Christ, a wife is to a husband. Therefore such submission as the church yields to Christ, must a wife yield to her husband (Eph. 5:24), which the very words of the apostle plainly affirm. Now we know that every Christian wife in particular ought to yield that obedience to Christ which the church in general does; therefore also she must yield such submission to her husband as she should to Christ.

Question: What if a husband be an enemy of Christ? Must such submission be yielded to an enemy of Christ as to Christ Himself?

Answer: Yes, because in his office he is in Christ's place, though in his heart an enemy. In this case will the wisdom, patience, and obedience of a wife be best tested. It is noted of the church, that she is a lily among thorns (Song 2:2). She remains lily-like, white, soft, pleasant, amiable, though she be joined with thorns, which are scraggy, prickly, sharp. So a wife must be gentle, meek, gentle, obedient, though she be matched with a crooked, perverse, profane, wicked husband. Thus shall her virtue and grace shine forth the more clearly, even as the stars shine forth most brightly in the darkest night. Among wives Abigail deserves great praise, who forgot not her duty, though she was married to a rude, greedy, drunken dolt, a very Nabal in name and deed. As for those who take occasion from the wickedness of their husbands to neglect their duty, they add to their cross a curse, for a cross it is to have a bad husband, but to be a bad wife is a sin, which pulls down a curse. Let wives therefore move their eyes from the disposition of their husband's person to the condition of his position, and seeing he bears Christ's image, be subject to him as to Christ.

This general conclusion might be applied to the matter of submission as well as to the manner, for the church acknowledges Christ her authority, fears Him inwardly, reverences Him outwardly, obeys Him also both by refraining to do what He forbids and also by doing what He commands. Therefore, now to insist in the manner only, there are four virtues which are especially needed for this, by which the church seasons her submission to Christ, and wives also may and must season their submission to their husbands.

These are the four: humility, sincerity, cheerfulness, and perseverance.

Wives' Humility in Every Duty

Humility is that grace that keeps one from thinking highly of himself above that which is proper, and regarding that low view which he has of himself makes him think reverently and highly of others. If humility is placed in a wife's heart, it will make her think better of her husband than of herself, and so make her the more willing to yield all submission to him. The apostle requires it of all Christians as a general flavor to season all other duties (Phil. 2:3; Eph. 4:2), but it is needed especially for subordinates, most of all for wives, because there are many privileges belonging to their position, which may soon make them think they ought not to be subject, unless they be humble in mind. That the church does here season her submission, is clear by the book of Song of Songs, where often she acknowledges her own lowness, and the excellence of her Spouse. *Therefore as the church is humbly subject to Christ, so let wives be to their husbands.*

Wives' Pride

Contrary to humility is pride, which puffs up wives and makes them think there is no reason they should be subject to husbands; they can rule themselves well enough, yes, and rule their husbands too, as well as their husbands rule them. There is no more dangerous vice for a subordinate than this. It is the cause of all rebellion, disobedience, and disloyalty: "only by pride, cometh contention" (Prov. 13:10).

Wives' Sincerity in Every Duty

Sincerity is that grace that makes one to be *within* even in *truth*, what *without* he appears to be *in show*. This is that singleness of heart which is expressly required of servants, and may be applied to wives, for indeed it pertains to all sorts (Eph. 6:5). Because it is only discerned by the Lord, who is the searcher of all hearts (Acts 1:24), it will move a wife to have an eye to Him in all she does, and to work for His approval above all. Therefore, uprightness and walking before God are often joined together. He that is upright will surely walk before God, that is, work for God's approval, as Noah did (Gen. 6:9), and as God commanded Abraham to do (Gen. 17:1).

If there were no other motive in the world to move her to submission, for conscience's sake to Christ she should yield it. Peter testifies of holy women, that they trusted in God and were subject to their husbands (1 Peter 3:5), implying by it that their conscience to God made them be subject to their husbands. Was not Sarah's submission seasoned with sincerity, when within herself, in her heart she called her husband lord (Gen. 18:12)?

There is great reason that wives should submit themselves in sincerity, for:

1. In their submission even to their husbands they have to do with Christ, in whose place their husbands stand, so that, though their husbands who are but men see only

the face and outward behavior, Christ sees their heart and inward disposition. Though their husbands see only the things which they do before their faces, and can hear only of such things as are done before others, Christ sees and knows the things that are done in the most secret places that can be, when no creature beside themselves knows such secrets. Now let it be granted that in their outward conduct they give a lot of happiness to their husbands, and please them every way. Yet if they have been lacking sincerity, with what face can they appear before Christ? He will take another manner of account of them; before Christ all their outward compliments will not help them at all.

2. In this lies a main difference between true, Christian, religious wives, and mere natural women; *these* may be submissive for personal ends, as namely, that their husbands may love them more, or live more quietly and peaceably with them, or that they may the more easily obtain what they desire at their husband's hands, or for fear of their husband's displeasure and wrath, knowing him to be an angry, furious man, so as otherwise it might be worse with them. They might lack many necessary things, or suffer many painful blows if they were not subject. But the *others* respect Christ's ordinance, by which their husbands are made their head, and yield to His Word and will, by which they are commanded to submit.

3. The benefit of this virtue being planted in a wife's heart is very great, and that both to her husband, and also to herself.

To her husband, in that it will make her show her respect of him before others, behind his back, as well as before himself in his presence, and also will make her faithful to him, and careful to do his will wherever he is, whether with her, or from her.

To herself, in that it will minister inward sweet comfort to her, though her husband should take no notice of her submission, or misinterpret it, or require it for evil purposes; for she might say as Hezekiah did, "Remember now, O LORD, I beseech thee, how I have walked before thee in truth and with a perfect heart, and have done that which is good in thy sight" (Isa. 38:3).

That the church does season all her submission with sincerity is clear, in that she is said to be "all glorious within" (Ps. 45:13). *Therefore as the church is sincerely subject to Christ, so let wives be to their husbands.*

Wives' Submission in Mere Compliments

Contrary to sincerity is hypocrisy, and mere outward submission in words, when a wife even despises her husband in her heart, as Michal did David (2 Sam. 6:16), and yet carries a fair face before him, as "an adulterous woman; she eateth, and wipeth her mouth, and saith, I have done no wickedness" (Prov. 30:20). Solomon makes it a mark of a wicked wife to "flatter with her words" (Prov. 2:16). Though such a wife should perform all the duties named before, all those would be nothing to God if they were done with a double heart, and not in singleness of heart. For as many outward imperfections are pardoned by God, where sincerity is, so no outward actions are accepted of Him though they seem never so fair, where there is no sincerity.

Wives' Cheerfulness in Every Duty

Cheerfulness is more apparent than sincerity, and makes submission the more pleasing not only to God, but also to man, who by the effects of it may easily discern it.

For God, as He does all things willingly and cheerfully, so He expects that His children should follow Him, and thereby show themselves His children. "God loveth a cheerful giver" (2 Cor. 9:7), not only a cheerful giver of money to the poor, but of all duty to God and man.

For men, it makes them also accept much better any duty when they observe it to be done cheerfully. This ravished David with joy, to see his people offer their gifts willingly to the Lord (1 Chron. 29:9); similarly when a husband sees his wife willingly and cheerfully perform her duty, it cannot but raise up love in him. This cheerfulness is manifested by a ready, quick, and speedy performance of her duty.

That thus the church submits herself to Christ is evident by that which David says, "Thy people shall be willing in the day of thy power" (Ps. 110:3). *Therefore as the church is cheerfully subject to Christ, so let wives be to their husbands.*

Wives' Sullen and Forced Obedience

Against this cheerfulness is the sullen disposition of some wives, who will indeed be subject to their husbands, and obey, but with such a drooping and sour face, with such pouting and muttering, as they grieve their husbands more in the manner than they can be pleased with the thing itself that they do. They show themselves like to a cursed cow, which having given a fair amount of milk, kicks over the bucket with her hoof, and so the proverb is true, "As good never a bit as never the better." Such submission is in truth no submission. It can neither be acceptable to God, nor profitable to their husbands, nor comfortable to their own souls.

Wives' Perseverance in Doing Their Duty

Perseverance is a virtue which makes all the rest perfect, and sets the crown upon them; without which they are all nothing. This is in those who after they have begun well, continue to do well to the end, and thereby reap the fruit of all. It has respect both to *continuance* without inconsistency, and also to *endurance* without deserting and giving completely over. So as it is not enough to be subject by starts and fits, one while yielding all good obedience, another while proud and rebellious. Neither is it sufficient in former times to have been a good wife, and later prove to be bad, but there must be daily proceeding and holding on from time to time, so long as husband and wife live together.

This grace was in her of whom it is said, "She will do him good, and not evil all the days of her life" (Prov. 31:12). Such were all the holy wives commended in Scripture; among other particulars, mention is made of the wife of Phinehas who on her death-bed showed the reverent and good respect she bore to her husband, though he was a wicked and immoral man (1 Sam. 4:21). This grace does the church add to all her other virtues, she in all parts of her submission remains persevering, and faithful to the death. It comes to pass, that at length she receives the reward of her holy obedience, which is full and perfect communion and fellowship with her spouse Christ Jesus in heaven. Regarding her unshakable perseverance, it is said that the "gates of hell shall never prevail against her" (Matt. 16:18). *Therefore as the church is perseveringly subject to Christ, so let wives be to their husbands.*

Wives Turning Back from Their Former Goodness

Against this perseverance is first *inconsistency of duty*, a returning to it, and a leaving it off by turns, like one that is sick with an intermittent fever, sometimes well, sometimes ill, one while hot, another while cold. That sometimes ceasing takes away all the virtue, grace, and glory from sometimes doing. Besides, it is twenty-to-one that through the corruption of nature, that diversity and alternating fits after a while will cease, and end in the worse. It is very likely that Michal was such a one, for once she showed herself so full of respect to David, that for his sake she provoked the king, her father's displeasure (1 Sam. 19:11), but later in her heart she despised him, and with her tongue taunted him (2 Sam. 6:16–20).

Also contrary to the forenamed constancy is *apostasy*, that is, a total relinquishing of the former good course, as if a wife repented her of her former good beginning. Such a one is she who "forsaketh the guide of her youth, and forgetteth the covenant of her God" (Prov. 2:17). For anything we read to the contrary, Job's wife was such a one. And such are many who in their younger years, while their religious parents lived (as Joash while old good Jehoiada lived, 2 Chron. 24:2) have behaved themselves very well like good dutiful wives, but being grown to elder years, have grown also so proud and rebellious, as if they completely turned back from their former good beginning. This revolt arises sometimes from the evil counsel of wicked gossips, and sometimes from their own proud spirit. I may say of these wives' submission, as the prophet says of the righteousness of those who later rebel: their submission shall not be remembered, but in their rebellion they shall die (Ezek. 18:24). *Therefore as the church is subject to Christ, let wives be to their husbands.*

The Extent of a Wife's Obedience

The extent of a wife's submission (which remains now to be handled) is set down under these general terms (*in everything*) which are not so generally to be taken as if they admitted no restraint or limitation, for then would they contradict such cautions as these, "in the fear of the Lord," "as to the Lord," "in the Lord" (Eph. 5:21–24; Col. 3:18). For man is so corrupt by nature, and of so perverse a disposition, that often he wills and commands that which is contrary to God's will and commandment, which when he does, that Christian principle laid down as a settled decision by the apostle must take place, "We ought to obey God rather than men" (Acts 5:29).

Question: Why then is this extent laid down in such general terms?

Answer: First, to teach wives that it is not sufficient for them to obey their husbands in some things, as they themselves think fitting, but in all things whatever they be in which the husband by virtue of his higher rank and authority has power to command his wife. Thus this general extent excludes not God's will, but the wife's will. She may do nothing against God's will, but many things must she do against her own will if her husband requires her. Secondly, to show that the husband's authority and power is very large: it has no restraint but God's contrary command, of which if a wife is not assured, she must yield to her husband's will.

A Wife's Laboring to Align Her Judgment with Her Husband's

From that extent I gather these two conclusions:

1. *A wife must labor to bring her judgment and will to her husband's.*

2. *Though in her judgment she does not think that most fitting which her husband requires, she must yield to it in practice.*

In the former of these, I do not say simply that a wife is bound to align her judgment to her husband's, for he may be deceived in his judgment, and she may see his error, and then unless her understanding would be blinded, she cannot conceive that to be true which he judges so. Rather, I speak of effort (when she does not have sure and undeniable grounds to the contrary) to suspect her judgment when it's contrary to her husband's, and to think she may be in an error, and not be too absolute and resolved in contradicting her husband's opinion. This submission even of her judgment concerns not only things necessary for which her husband has a plain and decisive basis in the Scripture, but also things doubtful and indifferent, for even so far does this clause ("in everything") extend. The submission of a wife concerns not only her practice, but her judgment and opinion also, which if she can bring to the lawfulness and appropriateness of that which her husband requires, she will much more cheerfully perform it. To this purpose (as I take it) may be applied that exhortation of the apostle, that women "learn in silence with all subjection" (1 Tim. 2:11). Though it is primarily meant of learning in the church, it does not exclude her learning at home from her husband; for in the next words he adds, "I suffer not a woman to usurp authority over the man, but to be in silence."

Wives' Too High Opinion of Their Own Wisdom

The presumption of such wives that think themselves wiser than their husbands and able better to judge matters than they can is against this principle. I do not deny that a wife may have more understanding than her husband, for some men are very ignorant and stupid; and on the other side, some women are well instructed, who by this have attained to a great measure of knowledge and discretion; but many, though they have husbands of sufficient and good understanding, wise and discrete men, yet think that what they have once conceived to be a truth must be so. Such is their dogmatism that they will not be brought to think that they may make a mistake, but say they will never be brought to think otherwise than they do, though all the husbands in the world should be of another opinion, not much unlike to the wise-man's fool, who thinks himself wiser than "seven men that can render a reason" (Prov. 26:16).

A Wife's Yielding to Her Husband in Such Things that She Does Not Think to Be Fitting

The latter conclusion concerning a wife's yielding in practice to that which her husband requires, though she cannot bring her judgment to think as he does about the fitness of it, covers indifferent things, namely, such as are neither in their particulars commanded, nor forbidden by God, as the outward affairs of the house, ordering it, managing property, showing hospitality to guests, etc.

Question: May she not reason with her husband about such matters as she thinks inappropriate, and labor to persuade her husband not to persist in the pressing of it, working to bring her husband to see the lack of wisdom (as she thinks) of that which she sees?

Answer: With modesty, humility, and reverence, she may do so, and he ought to hear her, as the husband of the Shunammite did (2 Kings 4:23–24), but, if despite all that she can say, he persists in his resolution, she must yield.

First, her submission is most manifested in such cases. Here she clearly shows that what she does, she does in respect of her husband's place and power. Were it not for that, she would not do it. Other things are not as evident proofs of her submission to her husband, for if he commands her to do that which God has plainly commanded, as she ought to, whether her husband command it or not, it may be thought she does it on God's command, and not on her husband's. If her husband commands her to do that which God has plainly forbidden, then by no means ought she to yield to it. If she does, it may be termed a joint conspiracy of husband and wife together against God's will, as Peter said to Sapphira the wife of Ananias, "How is it that ye have agreed together to tempt the Spirit of the Lord?" (Acts 5:9), rather than submission to the image of God in her husband.

Secondly, her yielding in indifferent things contributes much to the peace of the family, as subjects yielding to their magistrates in such cases makes much to the peace of the nation. For in differences and dissensions one side must yield, or else great trouble is likely to follow. Now of the two, who should yield but the subordinate?

Care in Choosing Such Husbands That Wives May Be Subject to without Grief

Objection: If the case be such between husband and wife, it is not good to marry.

Answer: This is not a good deduction; for all the seeming hardness of a wife's case is in the wickedness of a husband, who abuses his position and power, and not in that submission which is required by God. For if a husband carries himself to his wife as God requires, she will find her yoke to be easy, and her submission a great benefit even to herself.

Therefore I would exhort parties that are unmarried, whether young women or widows, to be very careful in their choice of husbands, and in their choice to respect above all, their good qualities and conditions, their bearing the image of Christ, as well as in their office, and authority, so that their wives may with joy and comfort, not with grief and anguish, be subject to them. Then will submission prove an irritation, when the husband is an ignorant, profane, idolatrous, worldly, wicked man. Wives of such husbands are often brought into many hardships. You widows and young women who are free, do not be too free and eager in giving your consent to whom you know not. Among other motives, often think of this point of submission, to which all wives are bound. After you are married it is in vain to think of freedom from submission. By taking husbands, and giving yourselves to be wives, you bind yourselves to the law of the man, as long as he lives. Then as you desire to be accepted by God, and to find mercy and comfort from him, you must bear this yoke, how heavy and grievous it seem to be.

The Reasons to Motivate Wives to Do Their Duties

Enough of wives' duties; the reasons noted by the apostle to enforce those duties now follow. They are laid down in these words: "Wives, submit yourselves unto your own husbands, as unto the Lord. For the husband is the head of the wife, even as Christ is the head of the church: and he is the saviour of the body. Therefore as the church is subject unto Christ, so let the wives be to their own husbands in every thing" (Eph. 5:22–24).

The main ground of all the reasons which the apostle here implies, is taken from the *position* in which God has set a husband, which is first by consequence implied in these words, "as unto the Lord," and then more plainly and directly expressed in these, "the husband is the head of the wife." The word set before these words, "for" being a causal conjunction, shows that they are set down as a reason, which is first proposed under a metaphor, "head," and then explained by that similarity which a husband has to Christ ("even as Christ") which is further commended by the virtue and benefit that proceeds from the headship of Christ properly, and of a husband also by consequence, in these words, "and is the Savior of the body." Upon a husband's similarity to Christ, he deduces that a wife should resemble the church, and so concludes, "Therefore as the church is in subjection to Christ, so let wives be to their husbands."

From the ground of a wife's submission, and the many explanations of it, and the deduction made upon it, five distinct reasons may be drawn out to enforce a wife's submission to her husband. The first is taken from a husband's *position*: he is in the Lord's place to his wife. The second from his *office*: he is a head to his wife. The third from the *image* he bears, or from the *similarity* between him and Christ. The fourth is from the *benefit* that his wife receives from him. The fifth is from the *example* and pattern of the church.

A Husband's Position

The *place* in which God has set a husband not only serves to direct a wife in the manner of her submission, but it also serves to move a wife to yield such submission as is required, which will appear evident by these two conclusions.

1. *A wife by subjecting herself to her husband, there is subject to Christ.*

2. *A wife by refusing to be subject to her husband, there refuses to be subject to Christ.*

That these two conclusions are rightly and justly deduced from the forenamed ground I prove by similar conclusions which the Holy Spirit deduces from the same ground. It is evident that Christ Jesus, even incarnate and made flesh, was in the place of His Father, for which reason Christ said to Philip, who desired to see the Father, "he that has seen me has seen the Father" (John 14:9). Now notice what Christ deduces both on the one side: "he that receiveth me receiveth him that sent me" (Matt. 10:40); and on the other side: "he that honoureth not the Son, honoureth not the Father which hath sent him" (John 5:23). It is also evident that ministers of the gospel stand in the place of Christ, for thus says the apostle of himself and other ministers, "Now then we are ambassadors for Christ, as though God did beseech you by us: we pray you in Christ's stead, be ye reconciled to God" (2 Cor. 5:20). Now notice again the conclusions deduced by Christ, on the one side, "he that heareth you, heareth me," and on the other, "he that despiseth you, despiseth me" (Luke 10:16). On this ground God said to Samuel concerning the people that rejected his government, "they have not rejected thee, but they have rejected me" (1 Sam. 8:7).

To apply this reason, I hope such wives who live under the gospel have so much religion and piety in them as to acknowledge it well suits them to be subject to the Lord Christ Jesus. Here then learn one special and principal part of submission to Christ, which is to be subject to your husbands. Thus shall you show yourselves to be the wives of the

Lord Christ, as the apostle says of obedient servants, they are "the servants of God" (1 Peter 2:16).

Again I hope none are so empty of all religion and piety as to refuse to be subject to Christ. Take notice that if you willfully refuse to be subject to your husbands, you willfully refuse to be subject to Christ. I may apply that to wives, which the apostle speaks of subjects, "whosoever resisteth the power and authority of a husband, resisteth the ordinance of God: and they that resist shall receive to themselves judgment" (cf. Rom. 13:2).

This first motive is a strong motive. If it were duly considered by wives, they would more willingly and cheerfully be subject than many are; they would not think so little of their husband's position, nor so contemptuously speak against God's ministers who plainly declare their duty to them, as many do.

A Husband's Office

The second reason is similar to this, taken from a husband's office,[1] that he is the wife's "head" (1 Cor. 11:3), which is also urged to this very purpose in other places.

This metaphor shows that to his wife he is as the head of a natural body, both higher in place, and also more excellent in dignity, by virtue of both which he is a ruler and governor of his wife. Nature teaches us that this is true of the head of a natural body, and the apostle by entitling a husband "a head" teaches us that it is as true of a husband, from which it follows, that it stands with common equity, and with the light of nature, that the wife should be subject to her husband This argument the apostle in plain terms urges elsewhere, saying, "doth not even nature teach you" (1 Cor. 11:14).

---

1. *Office*: a God-given responsibility or calling.

Go therefore, O wives, to the school of nature, look upon the outward parts and members of your bodies. Do they desire to be above the head? Do they hate to be subject to the head? Let your soul then learn from your body. Is it not unnatural for the *side* to be advanced above the *head*? If the body should not be subject to the head, would not destruction follow upon head, body, and all the parts of it? As unnatural, and much more unnatural is it for a wife to be above her husband: and as great, yes and greater disturbance and ruin would fall on that family. The order which God has set there would be completely overthrown by it. They that overthrow it would show themselves opposers of God's wisdom in establishing order. This reason drawn from nature is of force to move even pagans and savages to yield submission, how much more Christian wives, it being also agreeable to God's Word, and ratified by it?

The Similarity between Christ and a Husband

The third reason taken from a husband's *similarity* to Christ here, adds an edge to that former reason: in being a head, he is like Christ. So there is a kind of fellowship and co-partnership between Christ and a husband. They are brothers in office, as two kings of different places.

Objection: There is no equality between Christ the Lord from heaven, and an earthly husband; the difference between them is infinite.

Answer: Yet there may be likeness, similarity, and fellowship; inequality is no hindrance to these. Two kings may be more different in estate than a subject and a king; yet those two kings are brothers and fellows in office. There may be similarity where there is no parity, and likeness where there is no equality. The glorious and bright sun in the sky, and a dim candle in a house, have a kind of fellowship, and the same office, which is to give light, yet there is no equality between them. So then a husband resembles not only the head of a natural body, but also the glorious image of Christ, and is that to his wife which Christ is to His church. To apply this point, notice how two positions (worthy to be noted) arise from it.

1. *Submission is due to a husband as well as to Christ.* I say not "as great," because of the difference in glory, but "as well," because of the likeness in office. A constable (though a poor average man) must be obeyed as well as a high sheriff.[2] A beggar's child must obey his father, as well as a king's child. Such wives therefore who are not subject wrong their husbands as well as those who are not subject to Christ wrong Christ.

2. *They who by their submission maintain the honor of their husband's position, maintain by it the honor of Christ's place;* and again by the rule of contraries, they who by refusing to be subject challenge the honor and authority of their husband's position, by it challenge the honor and authority of Christ's position.

The obedience of a poor man's child or servant justifies that obedience which king's children and servants owe their father and sovereign, and so on the contrary, disobedience in small ones, dishonors the place of great ones.

The argument of Memucan[3] drawn from the greater to the lesser in these words, "Vashti the queen has not done wrong to the king only, but also to all the princes, and to all the people" (Est. 1:16) may be applied from the lesser to the greater. Disobedient wives do wrong not only to their own particular husbands, but also to all heads, even to Christ the head of the church.

---

2. *Constable*: local law enforcement officer. *High sheriff*: officer appointed by the king to oversee the justice system in a shire or county.

3. *Memucan*: a prince of Persia and Media (Est. 1:14).

From the last principles I discussed (namely, that the obedience of a good wife maintains the honor of Christ's position, and on the contrary side that the disobedience of a bad wife impairs the honor of it), I may rightly deduce two other conclusions.

1. That *Christ will assuredly reward the good submission of good wives*, for He has said (and what He has said He can and will perform), "them that honour me will I honour."

2. That *He will sorely revenge the rebellion of evil wives*: for again He has said, "they that despise me, shall be lightly esteemed" (1 Sam. 2:30).

We know that those who share a similar office are ready to stand for the honor of one another's position, and to maintain the honor of it, and not without good reason, for by it they maintain their own honor.

Therefore as good wives may well expect a reward at Christ's hands, however their husbands respect their obedience, whether well or badly (a great encouragement for wives to perform their duties, though their husbands be never so bad), so evil wives have just cause to fear revenge from Christ's hand, however their husbands bear with them.

They who duly weigh this reason taken from that similarity between Christ and the church, cannot but hold it to be a motive of great importance.

The Benefit which a Wife Has by a Husband

The fourth reason, taken from the *benefit* which a wife receives from her husband, further presses the point in hand. Though Christ be properly the Savior of the body, yet even here a husband carries a similarity of Christ, and is after a manner a "Savior," for by virtue of his position and office he is her *protector*, to defend her from hurt and preserve her from danger, and a *provider* of all needed and necessary things for her. In this respect she is taken from her parents and friends, and wholly committed to him, as Jacob's wives said, "Have we any more portion or inheritance in our father's house?" (Gen. 31:14)—yes, she herself, and all she has is given to him. He again shares whatever he has to her good and for her use. David compares a wife to a vine in relation to her husband (Ps. 128:3), suggesting that she is raised by him to that height of honor she has, as a vine by the tree, or frame near to which it is planted. By his honor she is dignified, by his wealth is she enriched.

He is, under God, all in all to her; in the family he is a *king* to govern and aid her, a *priest* to pray with her and for her, a *prophet* to teach and instruct her. As the head is placed in the highest place over the body, and understanding placed in it, to govern, direct, protect, and every way seek the good of the body, and as Christ is united to the church as a spouse, and made her head, that she might be saved, maintained, and provided for by Him; so for this end was a husband placed in his place of higher rank; and his authority was committed to him, to be a *savior* of his wife. Therefore if none of the former motives prevail with wives to move them to be subject to their husbands, yet this should.

From this reason flow these two conclusions:

1. The submission required of a wife is for her own good.

2. In refusing to obey she shows herself both ungrateful to her husband, and also harmful to herself.

That her submission is for her own good is evident by this end for which a husband is made a head, to be a savior, not to puff him up, to make him insult and act like a tyrant over his wife. So as if she is subject to him, she may reap much good from him. As the church is wisely governed, and safely protected by subjecting herself to her head, Christ Jesus; and as the body partakes of much good and is preserved from much evil by subjecting itself to the head, so if a wife is subject to her husband, she will fare much the better thereby. All the ease, profit, and benefit of it will be hers. If therefore she would do herself good, this is a way and means ordained of God for this end; let her seek it here.

If despite this she refuses to be subject to her husband, does she not (as we say) stand in her own light? Being the weaker sex, and more unable to help herself, if she shall reject this good help which God has provided for her, is she not most harmful to her own self? And considering the care and labors her husband undergoes for her sake, is it not very unnatural ingratitude, inwardly to despise, or outwardly to scorn such a head? No better testimony of a grateful heart can be given by a wife to her husband than cheerful and ready submission. No greater ingratitude can be shown than rebellion and disdain. Now among vices ingratitude is one of the most offensive to God and man, so as both to avoid the black spot of ingratitude, and to carry away the name of gratefulness, wives should be subject.

The Example of the Church Set before Wives

The last reason taken from the *example* of the church is also of good force to persuade wives to submission. Example prevails more with many than precept. If any example may be of force, then this most of all: for it is not the example of one only, but of many; not of many ignorant and wicked persons, but of understanding, wise, holy, and righteous persons, even all the saints that ever were, are, or shall be. For the church includes all under it, even that whole society of saints, which are chosen of God in His eternal counsel, redeemed of Christ by His precious blood, and effectually called by the gospel of salvation, God's Spirit working inwardly and powerfully upon them, those very souls of just and perfect men now triumphing in heaven, also included. Notice how this church is described in the 26th and 27th verses. Let this example therefore be often thought of; no one will regret following it, for it is the only right path to eternal glory, to which they shall surely come that follow it.

But to show the force of this reason a little more distinctly, note these two conclusions following from it:

1. *Wives are as much bound to be subject to their husbands, as the church to Christ.* Why else would this example be thus set before them, and pressed upon them? Why are husbands set in Christ's place, and compared to Him?

2. *A wife's submission to her husband, corresponding to the church's submission to Christ, is evidence that she is of the church,* guided by the same Spirit that the church is. For it cannot be performed by the power of nature, it is a supernatural work, and so an evidence of the Spirit.

Therefore, O Christian wives, as your husbands resemble Christ by their position, so you resemble the church by your practice. Of the two this is the more commendable, for that is a dignity, this a virtue, but true virtue is much more glorious than any dignity can be.

These reasons being well poised, and the force of them all joined together, they cannot but work on the proudest heart that exists. Therefore if this point of submission seems to be too bitter a pill to be well digested, let it be sweetened with the syrup of these reasons, and it will much more easily be swallowed, and do its good work.

–13–

A Husband's Affectionate Authority over His Wife

Ephesians 5:25 says, "Husbands, love your wives, even as Christ also loved the church, and gave himself for it."

As the wife is to know *her* duty, so the husband much more *his*, because he is to be a guide, and good example to his wife, he is to dwell with her "according to knowledge" (1 Peter 3:7). The higher his position is, the more knowledge he ought to have how to walk worthy of it. Neglect of duty in him is more dishonorable to God, because by virtue of his position he is "the image and glory of God" (1 Cor. 11:7), and more destructive not only to his wife, but also to the whole family, because of that power and authority he has, which he may abuse to support his wickedness, having in the house no higher authority to restrain his fury. Whereas the wife, though never so wicked, may by the power of her husband be kept under, and restrained from outrage.

Therefore to go on in order, in laying down the husband's duties (as we have the wife's), we are to consider both the *duties* themselves and the *reasons* to enforce them.

In setting down the duties we must note the *matter* in which they consist and the *manner* how they are to be performed. The apostle includes the whole matter of them all under *love*, which is the sum and head of all. We will handle this first, and then proceed to other particulars.

That Love which Husbands Owe Their Wife

This head of all the rest, *love*, is plainly set down, and alone mentioned in this and in many other places of Scripture, whereby it is evident that all other duties are included under it.

To omit other places where this duty is urged, in this place *love* is expressed by name four times, beside that it is implied under many other terms and phrases (Eph. 5:25, 28, 33).

Whoever therefore takes a wife, must, in this respect that she is his wife, love her; as it is noted of Isaac (the best pattern of husbands noted in the Scripture), he "took Rebekah, and she became his wife; and he loved her" (Gen. 24:67).

Many good reasons for this may be given.

1. Because no duty on the husband's part can be rightly performed except it be seasoned with love. The apostle exhorts all Christians to do all things in love (1 Cor. 16:14), much more ought husbands. Though in position they are above their wives, love may not be forgotten.

2. Because of all persons on earth a wife is the most proper object of love. Neither friend, nor child, nor parent ought so to be loved as a wife. She is termed, "the wife of thy bosom" (Deut. 13:6), to show that she ought to be as his heart in his bosom.

3. Because his high position, and power of authority may soon puff him up, and make him abuse his wife and trample her under his feet, if an entire *love* of her is not planted in his heart. To keep him from abusing his authority, love is so much pressed upon him.

4. Because wives through the weakness of their sex (for they are the weaker vessels) are much prone to provoke their husbands. So as if love is not ruling in the husband, there is likely to be but little peace between husband and wife. Love covers a multitude of imperfections.

5. Because as Christ by showing first His love stirs up the church to love Him, so a husband by loving his wife should

stir up her to love him in return. Showing himself like the sun which is the fountain of light, and from which the moon receives what light she has, so he should be the fountain of love to his wife.

Objection: Love was before laid down as a common duty pertaining both to husband and wife; how is it then here required as a particular duty of a husband?

Answer: In regard of the general extent of love it is indeed a common duty belonging to the one as well as to the other, yes, belonging to all Christians, to all men, for it is the very nature of love, and a special property of it, to seek not her own things (1 Cor. 13:5), but the good of others, which all are bound to do by virtue of the bond of nature. More than others, Christians are to love others by virtue of the bond of the spirit; among Christians, especially wives and husbands by virtue of the matrimonial bond; of married couples, most of all husbands by virtue of their position and responsibility. Their position is a position of *authority*, which without love will soon turn into *tyranny*. Their responsibility is especially and above all, to seek the good of their wives. Because wives are the most important and greatest responsibility of husbands, so their most vigorous and greatest care must be for them. The parents and friends of wives as they give over all their authority to their husbands, so they cast all care upon them; therefore that husbands may take more care of their wives, and better seek their good, they should in a special way love them. Husbands are most of all bound to love, and bound to love their wives most of all.

Thus this affection of *love* is a distinct duty in itself, especially belonging to a husband, and also a common condition which must be joined to every other duty of a husband, to season and sweeten them. His look, his speech, his conduct, and all his actions, in which he has to do with his wife, must be seasoned with love. Love must show itself in his commandments, in his reproofs, in his instructions, in his admonitions, in his authority, in his familiarity, when they are alone together, when they are in company before others, in civil affairs, in religious matters, at all times, in all things. As salt must be first and last upon the table, and eaten with every bit of meat, so must love be first in a husband's heart, and last out of it, and mixed with everything in which he has to do with his wife.

A Husband's Hatred and Lack of Love

Hatred of heart is against love. This vice as it is very offensive and detestable in itself, so much more when the wife is made the object of it. As love provokes a husband to do his wife what good he can, so hatred to do her what harm he can. Moses notes a man's hatred of his wife to be a cause of much harm (Deut. 22:13). The nearer and dearer any persons be, the more violent will that hatred be which is fastened on them.

Hence was it that divorce was allowed to be made between a man and his wife, in case he hated her (Deut. 24:3). Without question, this law was made for relief of the wife, lest the hatred which her husband conceived against her should cause her some harm, if he were forced to keep her as his wife. Christ seems to imply that in these words, "Moses, because of the hardness of your hearts, suffered you to put away your wives" (Matt. 19:8). This therefore being so deadly a poison, let husbands watch out not to allow it to soak into them.

Neither is it sufficient for a husband not to hate his wife, for even the lack of love, though it be only the absence of good, is a great vice and contrary also to the duty of love. Where this lack of love is, no duty can be performed well, even as when the great wheel of a clock, the first mover of all the rest, is out of frame, no other wheel can be in good order.[1] They that think of love as having little importance show that there is little or no love of God in them at all. For if the apostle's deduction is good, taken from a man's neighbor or brother whom he has seen, it will much more be good having relation to a wife; for how can he who does not love his wife (whom God has given to him as a token of His favor, and as a help meet for him, to be in his bosom and ever in his sight, even to be no longer two, but one flesh), love God whom he has not seen (1 John 4:20)? If any man says he loves God and hates his wife, he is a liar. Let husbands therefore by loving their wives give evidence that they love God.

A Husband's Wise Maintaining of His Authority

All the branches which grow out of this root of *love*, as they cover husbands' duties, may be drawn to two heads:

1. A wise maintaining of his authority.
2. A right managing of the same.

That these two are branches of a husband's *love*, is evident by the place in which God has set him, which is a place of authority; for the best good that any can do, and so the best fruits of love which he can show forth to any, are those which are done in his own proper position, and by virtue of it. If then a husband relinquishes his authority, he takes away his ability to do that good, and show those fruits of love which otherwise he might. If he abuses his authority, he turns the edge and point of his sword in the wrong direction. Instead of holding it over his wife for her protection, he stabs her body to her destruction, and so shows by it more hatred than love.

Now then to handle these two separately, and distinctly:

1. That a husband ought wisely to maintain his authority, is implied under this apostolic precept, "Husbands, dwell

---

1. Before the invention of electronics, clocks consisted of wheels or gears driven by suspended weights.

with [your wives] according to knowledge" (1 Peter 3:7), that is, as those who are well able to maintain the honor of that position in which God has set you, not as dolts and fools without understanding. The same is also implied under the titles of honor which the Scripture attributes to husbands, as lord, master, head, guide, image and glory of God, etc.

The honor and authority of God, and of His Son Christ Jesus, is maintained in and by the honor and authority of a husband, as the king's authority is maintained by the authority of his Privy Council[2] and other magistrates under him; yea, as a husband's authority is in the family maintained by the authority of his wife: for "he is the image and glory of God: but the woman is the glory of the man" (1 Cor. 11:7).

The good of the wife herself is thus also much promoted, even as the good of the body is helped forward by the head's abiding in his position. Should the head be put under any of the parts of the body, the body and all the parts of it would certainly receive much damage by it: even so the wife and whole family would feel the damage of the husband's loss of his authority.

1. *Question*: Is it in the power of the husband to maintain his own authority?

Answer: Yes, in his more than in any others: for notice the counsel of the apostle to Timothy, though in another case, yet very pertinent to this purpose, "Let no man despise thy youth" (1 Tim. 4:12). It was therefore in Timothy's power to maintain his honor, and not to allow it to be despised; and so is it in a husband's power.

2. *Question*: How may a husband best maintain his authority?

Answer: That direction which the apostle gives to Timothy to maintain his authority, may first be applied for this

---

2. *Privy Council*: powerful political leaders appointed to advise and assist the king (or queen) of England.

purpose to a husband: "Be thou an example of the believers, in word, in conversation, in charity, in spirit, in faith, in purity" (1 Tim. 4:12). It is as if he had said, If you walk before them in a manner worthy of your place and calling, and worthy of that honor and respect which is owed to it, showing forth the fruits of love, faith, and other similar graces, surely they will respect you; but if otherwise thou conduct thyself shamefully, and not fitting for a minister, you give them good reason to despise you. Even thus may husbands best maintain their authority by being an example in love, seriousness, piety, honesty, etc. The fruits of these and other similar graces showed forth by husbands before their wives and family must work a reverent and dutiful respect in their wives and whole house towards them, for by this means they shall more clearly discern the image of God shine forth in their faces.

Objection: True goodness and grace itself is hated by wicked and ungodly wives: it was an act of piety that made Michal despise David.

Answer: 1. I may grant it to be so, yet this may be a good direction for such husbands as have not such wicked wives.

2. This does not always so happen, no, nor yet for the most part in those that are wicked; true virtue and integrity does often cause admiration in those who love it not.

3. Though some are of so crooked and perverse a disposition as to take occasion of contempt, where none is given, yet shall that husband justify himself before God and man, that conducted himself worthy of his position.

Husbands Losing Their Authority

Contrary is their practice who by their irreverence, partying, drunkenness, immorality, failure to take life seriously, wasting money, and other similar dishonorable conduct, make themselves contemptible, and so lose their authority. Though a wife should not take these occasions to despise her husband, yet is it a just judgment on him to be despised, seeing he makes himself contemptible.

Contrary also to the directions I just gave is the stern, rough, and cruel conduct of husbands, who by violence and tyranny go about to maintain their authority. Force may indeed cause fear, but the fear of slaves, such a fear as produces more hatred than love, causes more inward contempt than outward respect.

And contrary is their groveling disposition, who against their own judgment yield to their wife's inclination in such things as are unlawful; they will lose their authority rather than make their wife unhappy. This is a fault plainly forbidden by the law (Deut. 13:6–7), and yet a fault in which not only wicked Ahab (1 Kings 21:7, 9), but also wise Solomon fell (1 Kings 11:4). How heinous a fault, and how grievous a fall this was in Solomon, the fearful result of it shows! Similar to him not in wisdom, but in its point of enormous folly, are those who upon their wife's instigation, allow priests and Jesuits,[3] to lurk and celebrate masses in their houses, and yield to be present at them themselves.

Similar to Ahab are such magistrates as suffer their wives to oversway them in course of justice, which it comes to pass that more petitions and suits are made to the wives of magistrates in the cases of justice than to the magistrates themselves and the favor of their wives is more esteemed than their own, so as the power of governing, and the final decision in determining matters, is from their wives. They are but the mouths and instruments of their wives, in so much as among the common people the title of their places and offices is given to their wives.

Some husbands allow this by reason of their fearful and foolish disposition, lacking courage and wisdom to maintain

---

3. *Jesuits*: members of the Roman Catholic order, the Society of Jesus.

the honor of their positions against the pride of their wives. Others upon a subtle, covetous, wicked mind, that by the means of their wives there may be more freedom for receiving bribes. Among these I may reckon those who against their own mind, to satisfy their wife's mind, allow both their wife and children to follow the latest fashion, to dress themselves in a way inappropriate to their positions, to frequently be with foolish friends, and so on; and also those who upon their wife's insistent nagging are moved (as Samson was) to reveal such secrets as should not be known. Husbands may listen to their wives' suggesting good things, but they may not obey them in evil things; if they do, their fault is double: 1. in doing evil; 2. in losing their authority.

Let husbands therefore be very watchful against their wives' evil instigations. Satan labored to overthrow Job by his wife, and by this does he corrupt many in these days.

Husbands' High Esteem of Their Wife

As authority must be well maintained, so must it be well managed, for which purpose two things are necessary: a husband must tenderly respect his wife and he must give provident care for her.

A husband's tender respect of his wife is both inward and outward. *Inward* in regard of his opinion of her and affection to her, *outward* in regard of his conduct towards her.

For a husband's *opinion* of his wife, two things are to be weighed: her position and her person.

1. Her *position* is indeed a place of subordination and submission, yet the nearest to equal rank that may be, a place of shared rights in many respects, in which husband and wife are after a sort even associates and partners. From this then it follows that the husband must count his wife a coworker and companion (1 Peter 3:7). This is one point of giving honor to the wife; and it is implied under that phrase by which the

end of making a wife is noted (Gen. 2:18), which in our English Bible is translated, "meet for him," word for word "as before him," that is, like himself, one in whom he might see himself, or even (to use our apostle's word) "himself" (Eph. 5:28). These phrases imply a kind of fellowship, as also the many privileges that are common to both.

As a wife's acknowledgement of her husband's higher rank is the foundation of all her duties, so a husband's acknowledgement of that fellowship which is between him and his wife will make him conduct himself much more friendly, intimately, lovingly, and every way that suits a good husband towards her.

Fellowship between Husband and Wife Despite a Wife's Subordination

Objection: Fellowship between husband and wife cannot stand with a wife's *subordination* and *submission*.

Answer: They are of very small minds that cannot see how these may stand together. Is there not a fellowship between higher and lower magistrates in relation to their subjects? Scripture mentions a fellowship between Christ the head and other saints in relation to the glory of which all are made partakers for it calls us "joint heirs with Christ" (Rom. 8:17), and in relation to God's people a fellowship between God and His ministers, for it calls them "labourers together with God" (1 Cor. 3:9), yet none can deny the saints and ministers to be subordinate and in submission to Christ and God. But to answer the objection directly:

1. There may be not only a fellowship, but also an equality in some things between those that in other things are one of them subordinates and subject, as between husband and wife in the power of one another's bodies, for in that the wife (as well as the husband) is both a servant and a master, a servant to yield her body, a master to have the power over his.

2. There may be fellowship in the very same things in which is subordination, for fellowship covers the thing itself, subordination to the measure and manner. In giving light the sun and moon have a fellowship, but in the measure and manner the moon is subordinate. The moon has less light than the sun, and that which it has it has from the sun. In governing, the king and other magistrates have a fellowship, but in the measure and manner of government they are subordinate to him. So is it between husband and wife. In many things in which there is a fellowship, the wife is nevertheless subordinate, so subordination may stand with fellowship.

3. There are no persons of different rank between which there is so near an equality as between husband and wife. If therefore there may be a fellowship between any that are authority and subordinate to one another, then much more between husband and wife.

As the soul therefore rules over the body, by a mutual and loving consent and agreement, so must a man over his wife.

Husbands' Too Low Esteem of Their Wife

Working against this is the idea of many who think there is no difference between a wife and servant except in intimacy, and that wives were made to be servants to their husbands because submission, fear, and obedience are required of them. From this it comes to pass that wives are often used little better than servants, an idea and practice that smells too much like paganism and drunken arrogance. Did God at first take the wife out of man's side, that man should tread her under his feet rather than set her at his side next to him above all children, servants, or any other in the family, however near or dear to him? None can be nearer than a wife, and none ought to be dearer.

Husbands' Good Esteem of Their Wife

For the *person* of a wife, *a husband ought to esteem that particular person to whom by God's providence he is joined in marriage, to be the fittest and best for him.* This is implied under that word, "own," noted by the apostle where he says "husbands love your *own* wives" (Eph. 5:25), and again presses it under a comparison of the body, "as your *own* bodies" (Eph. 5:28).[4] Everyone thinks his own body best and fittest for him. A man might sometimes wish some defects or problems in his own body to be changed, and desire that his were like others, more slender, strong, and handsome than his own, yet would he not have his head to be upon that other man's body. A man that would love his wife ought to have the same opinion of her.

There is good reason for him to do so. The proverb is true, if it is rightly taken, "marriages are first made in heaven," that is, God has a ruling hand in ordering them. Solomon implies this by that opposition which he makes between wealth and a wife (Prov. 19:14): *that* is from our fathers, *she* from the Lord. In this respect he says, "Whoso findeth a wife findeth a good thing, and obtaineth favour of the LORD" (Prov. 18:22). If therefore you are loved by God, and love Him, He will make your wife prove a good thing to you.

Objection: A wife may be a very immoral and wicked woman; how then can she be accounted the best wife?

Answer: First, it may be she was good enough when first she was brought to you, but you by your evil example or negligent leadership or harshness have made her as bad as she is. If it be so, then is she to be considered not as you have marred her, but as you did marry her. Secondly, though compared to other wives she is not in the best of condition, yet compared to you she may be the best in event, if not for your

---

4. Though it is not reflected in English translations, the same Greek word for "your own" is used in Eph. 5:25, 28.

peace and quiet, yet for testing your wisdom and patience, and she may be as a school of virtue to you. As a skillful pilot's competency is tested and known by stormy seas, so a man's wisdom by a troublesome wife. Yes, she may be given to you as a punishment of some former sins, as seeking after a beautiful, honorable, rich, proper wife, rather than a religious and honest one, or seeking her without any direction or help first sought from God, or otherwise than you have authorization from God, as by stealth, and without parents' consent; or some other sin in another kind, to bring you to repentance, or as a means to restrain and wean you from some future sins to which you are subject, and so prove a blessed cross to keep you from a fearful curse.

Husbands' Preposterous Opinion of Their Wife

A corrupt and perverse opinion which many have of their own wives, thinking of them as the worst and least fit, is contrary to this, even though they are those who every way, both in gifts and qualities of mind, and also in grace and attractiveness of body, deserve all good respect and esteem. Whereas others (which look with a single eye) commend their good qualities, they misinterpret and are prejudiced in every way. If their wives are religious, they think them *hypocrites*; if serious, sober, and modest, *depressed*; if they go out for good reasons, *restless and running around*. This bad opinion of their wives is a cause that their hearts are completely removed from their own wives, and set upon strange flesh, by which the devil gains what he desires, that is, to separate those whom God has joined together, and to join those whom God has separated.

Husbands' Wholehearted Affection to Their Wife

A husband's *affection* to his wife must be answerable to his opinion of her. He ought therefore to delight in his wife wholeheartedly, that is, so to delight in her as wholly and only delighting in her. In this respect the prophet's wife is called the desire, or delight, or pleasure of his eyes (Ezek. 24:16), that in which he most of all delighted.

Such delight did Isaac take in his wife as it drove out a contrary strong feeling, namely the grief which he had for the death of his mother: for it is noted that "he loved her, and Isaac was comforted after his mother's death" (Gen. 24:67).

This kind of affection the wise man elegantly sets forth in these words, "Rejoice with the wife of thy youth. Let her be as the loving hind and pleasant roe[5]…and be thou ravished always with her love" (Prov. 5:18–19). Here notice both the metaphors and the hyperbole which are used to set forth a husband's delight in his wife. In the metaphors again note both the creatures to which a wife is compared, and the attributes given to them. The creatures are two, a hind and a roe, which are the females of a hart and a roe-buck.[6] Now it is noted of the hart and roe-buck, that of all other beasts they are most enamored (as I may speak) with their mates, and even crazy in their heat and desire after them.

These metaphors Solomon has used to set forth that sincere and eager, wholehearted and burning affection which a husband ought to have for his wife. Being taken in a good sense, and rightly applied, so as they exceed not the bounds of Christian modesty and decency, are very fit, and pertinent to the purpose. If we stretch them beyond modesty, we wrong the writer of them, or rather the Holy Spirit that directed him, and propose a harmful pattern to husbands.

The attributes given to the creatures much amplify the point; the former is termed "a loving hind," the latter "a pleasant" roe, word for word a hind of loves, a roe of favor, that is, exceedingly loved and favored, for to set forth the

---

5. *Hind…roe*: female red deer and female roe deer.
6. *Hart and roe-buck*: male red deer and male roe deer.

extent of God's love to His Son, Christ is called "the son of his love" (Col. 1:13, Greek).

These comparisons applied to a wife vividly set forth that delight which a husband ought to take in her, and it is yet much further amplified by the hyperbole used in this phrase, "be thou ravished always with her love," word for word, "err thou in her love," by which no sinful error or stupidity is meant, but a lawful, eager affection. It implies two things especially.

First, to make a man overlook some such blemishes in his wife, as others would soon see and dislike, or else to count them no blemishes, delighting in her not a bit the less for them. For example, if a man has a wife, not very beautiful or proper, but having some deformity in her body, some imperfection in her speech, sight, gesture, or any part of her body, yet so to treat her, and delight in her, as if she were the most beautiful and in every way most perfect woman in the world.

Secondly, it implies to esteem her so highly, to feel such fervent affections, to regard her so tenderly, that others may think him even to dote[7] on her. A husband's affection to his wife cannot be too great if it is kept within the bounds of honesty, sobriety, and propriety. The wife's affection ought to be as great to her husband, yet because of the husband's place of authority, he must especially take all occasions to show his inward affection. Read the Song of Songs, and in it you shall observe such affection manifested by Christ to His spouse, as would make one think He did (with reverence in a holy manner to use the phrase) even err in His love and dote on her. This is a good pattern and example for husbands, for nothing is more lovely than a good wife.

---

7. *Dote*: to act delirious or head-over-heels in love.

The Stoic Disposition of Husbands to Their Wife

Against this is the disposition of such husbands who have no warmth or heart of affection in them, but, like Stoics,[8] delight no more in their own wives than in any other women, nor count them any dearer than others, a disposition in no way authorized by the Word. The faithful saints of God before mentioned, as also many others similar to them, were not Stoics, without all affection. Nor did they think it a matter inappropriate for them to delight especially in their wives (witness Isaac's playing with his wife in Genesis 26:8) for this is a privilege which belongs to the state of marriage.

But so that I not be misunderstood here, let it be noted that the affection of which I speak is not a carnal, sensual, beastly affection, but such as is consistent with Christian seriousness and sobriety, relating to the soul of a man's wife as well as to her body, grounded both on the intimate relationship of marriage, and also on the inward qualities of his wife.

I have written enough of a husband's inward respect of his wife; it follows to speak of his outward conduct towards her.

---

8. *Stoics*: followers of a fatalistic ancient philosophy who sought to live by logic and put down strong emotions.

14

A Husband's Humble Gentleness to His Wife

Peter gives a general rule for a husband's outward conduct to his wife, which is that he dwell with her "according to knowledge" (1 Peter 3:7), that is, as a man able to order his conduct wisely to his own honor and his wife's good, that so she may have good reason to bless God that ever she was joined to such a husband.

Out of this general principle these two branches sprout forth. First, that a husband give no just offence to his wife. Secondly, that he respond wisely to that offence which is given by her.

To avoid giving of offence he must have respect to that which she does as duty to him and to that which he does as duty to her.

Regarding the former, two things are required: both that he kindly accept what she is willing and able to do and that he wisely praise and reward what she does well.

Thus having presented this outline, I will distinctly handle the various points.

The first particular in which a husband shows himself to be a man of knowledge in walking before his wife, is by *a kind and thoughtful acceptance of every good duty which his wife performs.* Abraham, to testify of his good acceptance of Sarah's work in nursing her child, made a great feast when the child was weaned (Gen. 21:8), and Elkanah in a similar respect gave liberty to his wife to do what seemed her best (1 Sam. 1:23).

A great encouragement this must be to wives to be subject to their husbands in all things, when they observe no part of their submission to be carelessly neglected, but rather graciously accepted. It quickens the spirit of a wife to think that her concern and labors in pleasing her husband shall not be in vain.

Husbands' Despising and Rejecting Their Wife's Goodness

Against this is the practice of those, who thinking all which a wife does to be just her duty, take little or no notice of it, or if they cannot help taking notice of it, regard it as of little importance and pass it over with scarcely a thought. This often makes a wife even regret the good she has done, as David regretted the service which he had done for Nabal (1 Sam. 25:21). The truth is that wives ought to look to God for His acceptance rather than to their husbands, and though their husbands will take no notice, or not regard what good thing they do, for conscience sake, and for the Lord's sake, to do their duty. But even considering our weakness and slowness to do every duty, it cannot be denied but that a husband's slight regarding of his wife's goodness is an influence to make her weary of it, and that he does as much as he can to make her regret it.

But what may we say of those who mock and reject their wife's attempts to do her duty, even like them the worse for being conscience of it, and so (contrary to the rule of Christianity) overcome goodness with evil (Rom. 12:21)? Surely they show a very diabolical spirit to be in them, and cannot but cause much grief and offence to their wives, and make that which they do to be very tiresome and tedious. Fathers should not provoke their children, much less husbands their wives (Eph. 6:4).

Husbands' Courteous Accepting Their Wife's Respectful Conduct

To better understand this necessary point I will somewhat more particularly and distinctly apply the same to the duties of a wife, which were drawn to two headings: respect and obedience.

For the first, if a wife shows her due respect of her husband by any reverent behavior, gesture, or speech, he ought to meet her (as we say) halfway, and manifest his gracious acceptance of it by some similar courteous behavior, gesture, and speech, being appropriate, not foolish.

Objection: Thus shall a husband lower himself, and disgrace his position.

Answer: The courtesy which I speak of as it comes from an authority, being a mere voluntary matter and a sign of kindness and favor, is not degrading himself, but honoring his subordinate, a great grace to her, and no disgrace to him. Abram was counted by the Hittites a prince of God, yet in talking with them he bowed to them (Gen. 23:6–7). It is noted as a commendable thing in Esau, that though at that time he was his brother's superior (at least he took himself so to be), yet observing how Jacob respected him, bowing seven times to the ground, he ran to meet him, and embraced him, and fell on his neck (Gen. 33:3–4). Most relevant to the point is the example of King Ahasuerus, who beholding Esther's respectful standing before him, held out his scepter to her, which in a king is a great courtesy (Est. 5:2).

But to put the matter beyond doubt, let the example of Christ noted in Solomon's Song be observed, and we shall find His courtesy in every way corresponding to the reverence of His spouse.

Husbands' Too Great Aloofness

Contrary is the aloof conduct of husbands to their wives, who overlook all respect showed by wives, treating their wives in this case no better than children or servants, or no better than kings do respect the honor shown them by their subjects. Often have I noted that there is a great difference between a wife and all other subordinates, and therefore every way she shows respect to her husband should be acknowledged all the more by him. We know that kings and queens will put out their hands to be kissed by their subjects when they kneel before them, which is a sign of courtesy. How much more ought husbands to show courtesy? They are unworthy to be respected by their wives, who too are so lordly that they do not acknowledge them.

Husbands' Ready Yielding to Their Wife's Humble Suits

Again, it being a sign of respect in a wife humbly to make known her desire to her husband, he ought to show so much courtesy as willingly to grant her desire. This courtesy Ahasuerus afforded to Esther (Est. 5:3), David to Bathsheba (1 Kings 1:28), Isaac to Rebekah (Gen. 28:1), Abraham to Sarah (Gen. 16:6), and many other husbands to their wife. Abraham showed such respect to his wife, that though the thing which she desired grieved him, he yielded to his wife (Gen. 21:10–11).

Objection: God first commanded him so to do.

Answer: This adds the more force to the argument, showing that it is God's plain will, that a husband should show this kind of courtesy to his wife. Much more ought a man to do his wife's request than any other's, whether friend, child, or parent. Much more free, eager, and cheerful should he be to show himself in granting his wife's request than any other's, assuming that her desire be of that which may lawfully be granted. To yield in things unlawful is to lose his authority.

Husbands' Harshness to Their Wife

Against this is the harshness of their disposition who yield to their wives' request as a cow that yields her milk with difficulty, not without much trouble, by which the grace of all their yielding is taken away. There can be no courtesy in yielding, when it is forced from them against their mind and will. Their wife must ask, and beg again and again, even be forced to use the mediation of others to persuade their husband to yield to their request before they will yield, if at all they yield. What is this but to proclaim to all the world that there is no affection in them to their wife? If a wife's breath is strange[1] to her husband, surely his heart is first strange to her, which is the ready way to make him set his heart on strange women.

Husbands Refraining to Demand All That They May

As a wife's respect so also her obedience must be answered with her husband's courtesy. To testify of this, *a husband must be ready to accept that in which his wife shows herself willing to obey him.* He ought to be sparing in demanding too much of her. In this case he ought so to frame his conduct towards her, that the obedience which she performs may rather come from her own voluntary disposition, from a free conscience toward God, even because God has placed her in a position of submission, and from a wife-like love, than from any demands on her husband's part, and as it were by force.

---

1. *Breath is strange*: Gouge alludes to Job 19:17, where Job refers to his wife's alienation from him by saying, "My breath is strange to my wife." Gouge plays on this word to warn that if a man despises his wife's requests ("breath"), that shows that his heart is hostile to her, and he is on the path to adultery ("strange women," see Prov. 5:30).

Husbands ought not to demand of their wife, whatever wives ought to yield to if it be exacted. They must observe what is lawful, necessary, convenient, helpful, and fit for their wife to do, and what they are most willing to do before they are too determined to demand it. For example,

1. Though the wife ought to go with her husband, and dwell where he thinks fitting, he should not (unless by virtue of some urgent calling) move her from place to place, and carry her from that place where she is well settled without her glad consent. Jacob consulted with his wives, and tested their willingness before he carried them from their father's house (Gen. 31:4).

2. Though she should cheerfully show hospitality to whatever guests he brings into the house, he should not be painful and burdensome to her. The greatest care and labors for serving guests lay on the wife; she should therefore be treated tenderly here.

If he sees that she is conscientious and wise, well able to manage and order matters about the house, yet hating to do anything without his consent, he ought to be ready and free in yielding his consent, and satisfying her desire, as Elkanah (1 Sam. 1:23). If she is bashful and backward in asking consent, he ought voluntarily to offer it, and to give her a general consent to order and manage matters as in her wisdom she sees fitting, as Elkanah did, and the husband of that good housewife which Solomon describes (Prov. 31:11).

A general consent is especially required for the ordering of household affairs, for it is a charge laid upon wives to "guide the house" (1 Tim. 5:14), by which it appears that the businesses of the house most properly belong to the wife. Husbands ought to refer matters to their ordering there, and not restrain them in every particular matter from doing anything without a special permission and direction. To present this in some particulars, it belongs particularly to a wife,

1. To order the decorating and organizing of the house (Prov. 31:21–22).

2. To manage the ordinary provision of food for the family (Prov. 31:15).

3. To rule and govern female servants (Gen. 16:6).

4. To bring up children while they are young, and so on (1 Tim. 5:10; Titus 2:4).

These therefore ought he to refer to her discretion with a general consent (2 Kings 4:19), with limitation only of two cautions.

1. That she have in some measure sufficient discretion, intelligence, and wisdom, and not be too ignorant, foolish, simple, lavish, etc.

2. That he have a general oversight over all, and so use his authority that he tolerates nothing that is unlawful or improper to be done by his wife about house, children, servants, or other things, for, the general responsibility of all lies mainly upon him, he shall give an account to God for all things that are wrong in his house, and the blame of all will also before men lie upon him.

But those two cautions provided, he should together with his general consent put trust in his wife (Prov. 31:11), as Potiphar did in Joseph (Gen. 39:6), making here a difference between a wife and all others, whether adult children, friends, or servants whom he employs in his affairs. In every particular he may direct them for matter and manner, and take a strict account of them for expenses laid out, or other things done, because what they do is wholly and only for another. To his wife, who is a joint parent of his children, and governor of his house, to whose good the husband's wealth returns, and thus does for herself that which she does for her husband, greater liberty, and permission must be given.

Husbands' Too Much Strictness towards Their Wife

Against this is the rigor and austerity of many husbands who stand upon the uttermost step of their authority, and yield no more to a wife than to any other subordinate. Such are they:

1. Who are never contented or satisfied with any duty the wife performs, but always demand more and more.

2. Who do not care how painful and burdensome they are to their wife, painful by bringing such guests into the house as they know cannot be welcome to her, burdensome by too frequent and untimely inviting of guests, or imposing other similar extraordinary businesses, over and above the ordinary affairs of the house. Too frequent imposing of such things cannot but cause much fatigue. Demanding things with poor timing, as when the wife is weak by sickness, child-bearing, nursing, or other similar means, and so not able to serve as well as otherwise she would, will certainly greatly disturb and offend her.

3. Who hold their wife under as if they were children or servants, restraining them from doing anything without their knowledge and particular, explicit consent.

4. Who are too busy in prying into every business of the house, and will have their hand in them all. Besides that such husbands give no opportunity to their wife of giving proof of the understanding, intelligence, wisdom, care, and other gifts with which God has blessed her; additionally, they take away that main end for which a wife was given to man, namely, to be a help (Gen. 2:18). Such husbands cannot help but neglect other more weighty matters, which more properly belong to them. For observe it and you shall find, that such husbands as are most busy about the private affairs of the house pertaining to their wife, are most negligent of such affairs as pertain to themselves. They think they walk in integrity, but yet are they neither just nor wise, for "the just man walketh in *his* integrity" (Prov. 20:7), and "the

wisdom of the prudent is to understand *his* way" (Prov. 14:8). That integrity belongs to his own particular position and his own way, but "every fool will be meddling" (Prov. 20:3) with things not his responsibility.

5. Who are too suspicious of their wife, and because of that too strict in taking account of her. Paul calls suspicions evil (1 Tim. 6:4), and not without good reason, for they are evil in their *nature*, and evil in their *effects*, being the cause for much trouble, but in none so evil as in husbands over their wife. If a wife's fidelity (to whose good the welfare of the family, and increase of the family savings returns as well as to the husband's) be suspected without good reason, who shall be trusted? It is the overthrow of many families that servants are trusted and not wives.

This ends our discussion of a husband's kind acceptance of that which his wife is willing and able to do.

Husbands' Encouraging Their Wife in Good Things

The love which a husband owes to his wife further requires that he wisely *praise* and *reward* what she has well done. That which the apostle says of the magistrate's authority, may appropriately be applied to a husband's in relation to his wife, "Do that which is good, and thou shalt have praise of the same" (Rom. 13:3). It is plainly noted in the description of a good husband, that he praises his wife (Prov. 31:28–29), and in that he says, "Give her of the fruit of her hands" (Prov. 31:31), it is implied also that he rewards her.

This is an undeniable evidence of his good acceptance of her duty, and a further encouragement to stir her up to go on and continue in doing well. This is also an evidence of his joy and delight both in her person, and also in her doing well. If there is no delight in one's person, doing well will stir up envy rather than joy, and they that envy a man's doing well, will never praise or reward him for it.

In a husband's praising of his wife this caveat must be put, that he so order his praise as it does not tend to flattery, or excessive or foolish affection, nor yet stirs up coveting or envy in others.

Husbands Discouraging Their Wife by Ingratitude

Contrary is an ungrateful, if not envious disposition of such husbands, as passing by many good things ordinarily and usually every day done by their wife without any approval, praise, or reward. They are ready to criticize the least slip or neglect in them, and in such terms as if they never did anything well, so that their wife may well complain as it is in the proverb,

Often did I well, and that hear I never:
Once did I ill, and that hear I ever.

Yet such will be ready to praise other men's wives, and criticize their own wives with the examples of those others, when their own do far excel them in all kinds of goodness. What does this show but that either they take no notice of their own wife's goodness, or else by reason of the commonness of it, regard it little? If their wives have not the more grace in them, this disposition is enough not only to discourage them from doing any good duty, but also to cause jealousy in them, and to alienate their hearts from them.

A Husband's Gentleness

To this point we have covered that respect which a husband is to have of that duty which his wife performs to him. For avoiding just offence, a husband must further *give good attention to that which as duty he does to his wife*. As *kindly* he must accept duty at his wife's hands, so *gently* he must perform that duty which he owes to her.

This gentleness is a special fruit and evidence of love, and a notable means to take away all offence that otherwise might be taken from many things which he does. Sugar and honey are not more pleasant to the tongue than gentleness to the heart. It causes such things as otherwise are annoying and painful to the soul to be well taken and applied, even as bitter pills dipped in sweet syrup, or rolled up in the soft pulp of an apple, are soon swallowed down and well digested. If a husband desires to be counted a servant of the Lord he must learn this lesson, for "the servant of the Lord must...be gentle unto all men" (2 Tim. 2:24). If any other servant of the Lord, much more husbands; if to "all men," most of all to their wife, and in many respects.

1. Because of the close union between husband and wife.

2. Because of the joint authority she has with him over others, that here he may be an example to her.

3. Because of her weakness; mirrors are tenderly handled, for a small knock quickly breaks them.

Husbands' Bitterness

Against this is *bitterness*, a vice expressly forbidden, particularly to husbands, a vice that cannot be consistent with husband-like love. Upon this the apostle, commanding the one, forbids the other, "Love...and be not bitter" (Col. 3:19). Nothing more turns the edge of his authority, perverts the use of his leadership, provokes the pride of his wife, makes his words and deeds less regarded, than *bitterness*. It is as gall and wormwood[2] mixed with sweet and wholesome foods, which causes that they cannot be well digested, but are spit out again with violence as soon as they are tasted. Men in authority are very prone to this, and therefore, O husbands, be so much more watchful against it. Love your wife and be not bitter to her.

---

2. *Gall and wormwood*: bitter, nauseating flavors.

A Husband's Manner of Instructing His Wife

The *gentleness* of a husband must be manifested in his speech and conduct. For as far as *reverence* extends itself in the duties of wives, *gentleness* must be extended in the duties of husbands. Whether a husband's speech be to his wife before her face, or her behind her back, it must be sweetened with gentleness.

Regarding his speech to her, the instructions which he gives her, the commandments which he lays upon her, the reproofs with which he checks her, must all be mixed with *gentleness*.[3]

To instruction the apostle plainly adds meekness. Instruct, says he, with meekness, "those that oppose themselves" to the truth (2 Tim. 2:25). If ministers must use meekness when they instruct their people, much more husbands when they instruct their wife. If meekness must not be laid aside in cases of opposition, then in no case, at no time may it be ignored.

In this case to show meekness, let these rules be observed:

1. Consider the understanding and capacity of your wife, and suit your instructions to her ability. If she is of low capacity, give precept upon precept, line upon line, here a little and there a little. A little at once often given, namely, every day something, will accumulate in time to a great measure, and so accumulate, that, together with knowledge of the thing taught, love of the person that teaches will increase.

2. Instruct her in private between yourself and her, that so her ignorance may not be put on public display. Private actions passing between husband and wife are signs of much kindness and intimacy.

3. In the family so instruct children and servants when she is present, as she may learn knowledge by it. There can

---

3. We omit Gouge's discussion of appropriate titles for a husband to give his wife, as being specific to his culture.

be no more meek and gentle manner of instructing, than by one to instruct another.

4. Together with your precepts mix sweet and forceful persuasions, which are testimonies of great love.

Against this is a harsh and rough manner of instructing, when husbands go about to thrust into their wives' heads, as it were by violence, deep mysteries which they are not able to understand, and yet if they do not understand, they will be angry with them, and in anger speak with abusive language, and proclaim their ignorance before children, servants, and strangers. This harshness is ordinarily so fruitless, and additionally so exasperates a woman's spirit, as I think he would be better off to completely omit the duty than do it after such a manner.

A Husband's Manner of Commanding His Wife Anything

The commandments which a husband gives to his wife, whether they be affirmative (telling her to do something) or negative (forbidding her to do this or that) must all be seasoned with gentleness. For which end respect must be had to the *matter* and *manner* of his commandments.

Regarding the *matter* of the things which he commands his wife to do, they must be indeed lawful and honest, such as she is persuaded to be so, such as fit her position, and of significance and importance.

And on the contrary, the things which he forbids must be against God's law, which he can evidently prove to her to be against God's law, such as are inappropriate for her position, and will have some evil and harmful effect if they are done.

To command an unlawful thing, or forbid a thing which ought to be done, is to bring his own authority into opposition with God's, in which case he brings his wife into this dilemma, either to reject God's commandment or his.

How then can she think that her husband loves her, when he brings her into such traps and distresses, that she must fall into the gulf of God's displeasure, or smash against the rock of her husband's offence? Gentleness is far from such commandments.

The same may be said of such things which seem to a wife's conscience to be sinful, if they be asked of her; or her binding duty, if they be forbidden, especially if she has any ground for her conscience out of God's Word. The conscience is subject to God alone; if it is forced it would be a fearful horror, and a very hell in that party whose conscience is forced. She that doubts is condemned if she does that about which she has doubts (Rom. 14:23).

Objection: In doubtful matters the commanding power of an authority is enough of a basis to satisfy the conscience of them that are under authority.

Answer: First, in things merely doubtful concerning which the party in submission has no warrant out of God's Word one way or other, it may be so. But when the conscience does not doubt and hang in suspense, but is grounded in God's Word and persuaded that that which is commanded is against God's law, or that which is forbidden is a binding duty, then to do this, or to leave that undone, is to the party so persuaded a sin. This is the doubting (of which the apostle speaks) that condemns a man. In this case to urge a wife to do this, or not to do that, is to urge her to sin, which a gentle spirit and loving heart will not do.

Secondly, though the husband's command be enough of a reason to the wife, and if he absolutely presses her to this or that, she ought to yield, yet the love and gentleness required of a husband should make him so tender towards her as to let go of some of his rights, and when he sees her conscience troubled about his command, to relieve her conscience by refraining to press that which seems so burdensome to her.

A husband may sin in pressing too much upon his wife some command that does not require her to sin.

A Husband's Wise Conduct When His Wife is Wrongly Scrupulous

Objection: What if a husband upon his knowledge observes his wife to be wrongly scrupulous,[4] and to misinterpret and misapply the Word of God which she makes the ground of her scruple?

Answer: He must first labor to resolve her conscience by a plain discovery of her error, which is a true and great sign of love. If despite all that he can do in that way she cannot be brought to yield to that which he would have, then he must carefully observe these two things, whether her refusing to yield is obstinacy or weakness, and whether it be about a small or important matter.

By the reasons which she renders, and her manner of pressing them, he may discern whether weakness or obstinacy makes her stand against him. If the reason from God's Word on which she rests is doubtful, and to one that has not a good sound judgment and a sharp discerning mind, it may appear to make something for her, it is to be presupposed that there is more weakness than stubbornness in her. But if she can give no good reason, but only show any way that seems to incline her, and holds her opinion with determination, and stiffly stands on her own resolution, though the emptiness of her arguments be plainly shown to her, so that she has nothing further to object, or if she render no reason at all but her own thought, opinion, and will, and yet refuses to yield, surely obstinacy possesses her heart. In case of obstinacy it is very helpful that a husband insist upon his power to maintain his authority, and by the best wisdom he

---

4. *Scrupulous*: controlled by false fear or guilt because the conscience is confused about right and wrong.

can (using only such means as are lawful) bring her to yield from her stubbornness to that which he requires, especially if the matter is important. Consider the case of a religious man married to a popish wife, and she will be moved by no reason to refrain going to mass, or yield to go to the preaching of the gospel. But if through weakness she cannot be persuaded of the lawfulness of what her husband requires, and the matter required is of no great consequence, nor the weakness of her conscience cause any great error, a husband ought so far to show his gentleness as to refrain to press her conscience.

A Husband's Forbearing to Press Things Inappropriate to a Wife's Position

Things inappropriate to the position of a wife are dishonorable to her. For a husband to urge his wife by strict command to do them, implies more harshness than gentleness. Had the spirit of that stubborn king Ahasuerus been more gentle towards his wife, he would not have so far pressed his wife to so inappropriate a thing as he did, namely, to come before all his princes and people to show her beauty. It is true indeed that she offended in refusing to yield, he absolutely requiring it, but that offence on her part does not justify his act, and free him from all blame. It is noted, that "he was merry with wine" when he gave that commandment (Est. 1:10), by which it is implied that his practice better fit a drunken than a sober man. Such is their practice who demand of their wives to do such businesses as are more appropriate for servants rather than wives, or immoral rather than honest women, as to go to taverns, ale-houses, play-houses, and such places where worthless companions are.

A Husband's Pressing His Authority in Important Matters

If a man invokes his authority when talking to his wife about important and significant matters, then he helps her to feel how weighty such matters are. Thus a wife will either be brought to yield to that which is commanded, or to be convicted of guilt for not yielding. Thus a wife may see that it is not his own will so much which makes him to use his authority in commanding, as the necessity of the thing itself, which returns good especially to her that does it. The performance of a duty is for the most part most profitable to the party that performs it, so that by this a husband shows love to his wife in pressing that which he requires.

That this sign of love may be more clearly seen, it is important that a husband add to his commandment just and weighty reasons, that by them his wife may the better discern the fitness, lawfulness, helpfulness, and necessity of the things commanded. We know that all the things which God commands are weighty and necessary, His will alone (being the very rule and ground of all goodness) makes things absolutely necessary. Yet to His commandments He adds weighty reasons, showing on the one side the benefit and blessedness that will come to those who obey His commandments, and on the other side, the trouble and misery that will fall on their heads who refuse to obey. By this he shows the great and loving concern which He has for us, and the earnest desire He has of our good. Thus may a husband even in his commandments show much love and kindness.

Husbands' Too Great Pride in Commanding

Against this is the rough pride of husbands, when they will have their own will done and it does not matter whether the thing commanded be lawful or against God's law, whether their wives' consciences can yield to it or not, whether it stands with the honor of their positions or not, and whether it be important or insignificant; it is their will that it should be done, and done it shall be—there is all the reason they will give. Some think it a glory to command what they like, and think that there is no proof of their authority and of their wives' submission, but in such things as they command upon their own will without any further ground or reason. If such husbands meet with confrontations, if though they command much, they find not answerable performance, they may thank themselves that they are on the fast track to have their authority despised and even trodden under foot.

Husbands' Rare and Gentle Using of Their Commanding Power

Husbands must consider the *manner* of using their authority in commanding as well as to the *matter*. Regarding the *manner* his commandments must be rare, not too frequent, and by way of making an appeal, not too absolute.

Authority is like a sword, which with too much use will be blunted, and so fail to do that service which otherwise it might when there is most need. A wise, sober, peaceable man, may always have his sword in readiness, very bright, keen, and sharp, but he will not be very ready to pull it out of his scabbard. He rather keeps it for a time of need, when it would give him the best use. Such husbands therefore who are too frequent in their commands, show themselves not sober, nor wise, nor lovers of peace.

As the use of a husband's authority in commanding must be rare, so when there is occasion to use it, it must be tempered with such gentleness and moderation, as a husband (according to Paul's example) though he has power to command that which is proper, yet for love's sake must rather appeal for it (Philemon 9). Note how gently Abram frames his speech to his wife, "Say, I pray thee," says he, "thou art my sister" (Gen. 12:13). Though the thing he required stinks of too much weakness, yet his manner of requiring it fit a kind husband.

Husbands' Insolence and Absolute Demands

Against this is the insolence of many who cannot speak to their wives but by commands. Their authority is like a swaggerer's sword, which cannot long rest in the sheath, but is drawn forth for every little reason. This frequent use of commands makes their commandments regarded as nothing. The same may be said of those who are too absolute in commanding. There must be no saying of "no" to that which they say. Upon command they will have their will done, and no other way. No persuasion, no appeal shall be used. They will rather have their will done not at all than not upon absolute command. They will not allow others, in case of any refusal, to appeal or persuade, but will try what they can do by authority absolutely. Thus as by trying to bend steel as far it will go, it often breaks, so by putting their authority to the uttermost trial, they often lose all their authority, in which case, "The mends," as we speak, "is in their own hands."[5]

---

5. *The mends...is in their own hands*: it is their fault, so let them fix the problem themselves.

15

A Husband's Patient Correcting of His Wife

The authority and responsibility which God has given to a husband over his wife require that when good and right reason presents itself, he should reprove her. This is a special means to draw her from those sins in which otherwise she might live and lie, yes, and die also; and so live, lie, and die under God's wrath. To free a wife out of this misery and wretchedness is as great a sign of love, as to pull her out of the water when she is in danger of drowning, or out of the fire when she is in danger of burning. Solomon thus calls reproofs, a "reproof of life" (Prov. 15:31), and expressly notes reproofs to be the way of life, a means to create and preserve spiritual life, and to bring one to eternal life, and so to escape death and damnation (Prov. 6:23). In these respects rebukes are called a precious balm or excellent oil which may heal a wound, but make none; "which shall not break my head," as the psalmist speaks (Ps. 141:5). Upon this ground, no doubt, it is noted of many good husbands who were undeniably loving, kind, meek, and gentle husbands, that they reproved their wives, as Jacob (Gen. 30:2), Job (Job 2:10), David (2 Sam. 6:21–22), and others.

Neglecting Reproof

Against this is a groveling and fearful mind of many husbands who hate to offend, and (as they think) to provoke their wives; and for this reason choose to let them continue in sin rather than tell them of it. They both dishonor their position and the image of God, which by virtue of their position they carry, and also in effect and in reality hate their wives. This the law implies, where it says, "Thou shalt not hate thy brother in thine heart: thou shalt in any wise rebuke thy neighbour, and not suffer sin upon him" (Lev. 19:17).

Handling the Matter of Reproof Well

That a husband may clearly show that his reproving his wife is indeed a fruit of his love, he must have a special care to sweeten it, especially with gentleness, for it is the bitterest pill that by a husband can be given to a wife. It is a verbal correction, and in that respect a middle means (as I may so speak) between admonition and correction, partaking somewhat of both. It goes no further than words, and so is an admonition. The words of a reproof are sharp, and so it is a correction. Though it is but a gentle correction, yet it is a sharp admonition, and all the correction which a husband by himself can give his wife, for we shall later show that he may not go on to hitting or striking her.

To sweeten reproof with gentleness, consideration must be given (as before was noted of commanding) both to the matter, and also to the manner of it. The matter of reproof must be *just*, and *important*.

Justice requires that it be a truth, and a known truth, even a thing of which he is sure, for which he reproves his wife. Christ, in giving direction for reproving correctly, lays down this principle, "Moreover if thy brother shall trespass against thee, go and tell him his fault" (Matt. 18:15). A trespass therefore must go before reproof. Where no trespass is, there reproof is unjust.

Again, the apostle advises that an accusation should not be received "but before two, or three witnesses" (1 Tim. 5:19).

By this he implies that a groundless report must not be received, but where blame is laid, there must be two or three witnesses to confirm it, so as he that rebukes may have good and sure ground for that which he does. Indeed, that advice was given in particular about an elder, but from the less to the greater it will follow to be a good advice concerning wives, for no kind of person must be more wary in laying blame and reproof upon another than a husband on his wife.

Fairness further requires that the matter for which a husband reproves his wife be important, namely for some fault that is dangerous to her soul, hurtful to their estate, contagious by reason of bad example to children and others in the family, but most of all a sin against God which provokes His wrath, and pulls down His heavy curse upon him, her, and the whole family.

When that for which a wife is reproved is a truth, a known truth, and an important truth, the husband in performing this duty justifies his deed, shows that there was need of it, and so gives evidence of his love, makes his reproof to pierce the more deeply, and so makes her more ashamed of her fault. From this it will follow, that either she will fix her fault or at least will have her mouth stopped so that she shall have nothing to make excuses. The reproof of the three saints before mentioned, Jacob (Gen. 30:2), Job (Job 2:10), and David (2 Sam. 6:21–22), match these points of justice and wisdom, and the effects of it match those which we have noted in this reason, as the silence of the three wives implies, for none of them replied again.

Undue Reproof

Against justice and equity are naïve gullibility and undue suspicion. Gullibility is when belief is given to every groundless report, and as a result blame is laid upon the wife before any fair proof be made of that for which she is blamed. By this it often comes to pass that she is wrongfully and unjustly blamed. If she is, what good fruit can proceed from such reproofs? What evil fruits are not likely to proceed from this, such as secret unhappiness (if not malice and hatred) and open fights and shouting matches?

The same may be said of causeless suspicion, which is the mother of jealousy, and the very bane of marriage, from which the devil takes great advantage against them both, seeking by it to untie that knot which God has so firmly knit between them. Suspicion to the mind is as colored glasses to the eye, which represents things to the sight not as they are in their own true color, but as the color of the glasses is. Suspicion will make a man pervert everything that his wife does, and blame her many times for praiseworthy things. In this case what can be thought, but that a husband seeks advantage against his wife, rather than any good to her?

If to those two vices (gullibility and suspicion) he adds rashness and haste in reproving, and makes every small and insignificant matter which any way he dislikes, matter of reproof, does he not proclaim to all that shall know it that he loves chiding more than he loves his wife? Yes, is not this the ready way to make all his reproof (if not scorned) regarded as nothing? What then will be the profit of them?

Whether A Husband May Reprove His Wife for Such Things He Is Guilty Of

To the *matter* of reproof some add that a husband should not reprove his wife for a fault of which he himself is guilty, but I doubt this direction. I do not deny that he ought to have a special care that he is not guilty of that crime for which he corrects his wife; otherwise, first he blunts the edge of his reproof, so it cannot pierce into her heart as easily. Secondly, he causes it to rebound back again upon himself with these reproaches, "Physician, heal thyself" (Luke 4:23); "Hypocrite, first cast out the beam out of thine own eye" (Matt. 7:5); "Thou therefore which teachest another, teachest thou not thyself?" (Rom. 2:21). Thirdly, he is a heavy witness against himself; for "wherein thou judgest another, thou condemnest thyself" (Rom. 2:1).

But to deduce by this that because he is guilty of such vices as are in his wife, he should not reprove her though she be worthy to be reproved, is hardly sound and good theology. Thus he makes himself guilty of a double fault, *one* of committing the sin himself, *the other* of allowing his wife to lie there, whereas if he reproved his wife, he might by it reclaim both her and himself. I do not doubt that his reproving of his wife would strike deeper into his own conscience than if a third should reprove them both. How Judah and David were stricken to the heart after they had given sentence against such crimes as they themselves were guilty of (Gen. 38:26; 2 Sam. 12:13)! It is good advice that no man be guilty of that which he reproves in his wife, but it is no good rule to say that no man ought to reprove his wife of that of which he is guilty.

Handling the Manner of Reproof Well

Similar directions to those which were given for the manner of commanding must be observed in the *manner* of reproving. Reproofs therefore must be rare and meek.

When reproofs are seldom used except for urgent and necessary reasons, it first shows that a husband takes no delight in rebuking his wife, but is even forced to. Secondly, it makes his wife regard it much more. Thirdly, it is likely to work a more perfect cure, for seldom and rare reproofs commonly pierce most deeply.

Continual scolding and finding fault with a wife for everything wrong are against this. If not only the wife herself, but a child, or servant, or any else in the house do wrong, the wife shall be blamed for it. This is too common a fault in husbands, by which they much provoke their wives and many times make them regard a reproof no more than any other word. For as birds which always abide in bell towers where there is much ringing are not a bit frightened with their loud sound, so wives are not moved at all who have their ears from time to time filled with their husband's rebuke.

That a reproof must be given in meekness is clear by the apostle's general precept of restoring one "in the spirit of meekness" (Gal. 6:1), for a right manner of reproving is here particularly intended. Now of all with whom we have to do, there is no fitter object for meekness than a wife, who in a more particular manner than any other is your own flesh. Meekness covers both privacy of place, and softness of words.

When a husband is alone with his wife is the fittest season for reproof. Thus will reproof be answerable to Christ's direction, "tell him his fault between thee and him alone" (Matt. 18:15), says Christ of a brother, but no brother must be more tenderly dealt with than a wife. Thus will it also soak better into her soul, when no idea of dishonor and embarrassment shall rise up to hinder the work of it, which will be ready to rise when a reproof is given in public before others. Thus likewise will reasons be taken away from children and servants for despising her, which otherwise they would quickly take, if she should be rebuked before them, gathering from this that she is kept under as much as they. Now because she is a joint governor of them with him, he ought by all means to maintain her reputation before them.

Question: What if she does not regard a rebuke in secret?

Answer: He may follow Christ's direction, take one or two more, namely wise, sober, faithful friends, if it may be, of her family, as her parents (if she have any living) or those who are in course of nature next to parents (if they are not partial on her side) and before them rebuke her (Matt. 18:16), but by no means before any of the household under her government.

Question: What if her sin is public, such as may be a bad example to them of the house, being committed in their sight, or brought some other way to their knowledge?

Answer: Wisely he must so show his dislike of her sin, that he no way harms her honor. He may therefore declare that such a thing was not well done, and warn his household against committing the same, even strongly threaten them that if any of them do the same they shall dearly regret it. If those who are under correction offend there, the more surely and severely correct them, even because they have taken example. Thus shall he testify a great good respect of his wife, and also a thorough dislike and hatred of her sin.

"A soft tongue," as Solomon notes, "breaketh the bone," that is, softens a hard heart, and beats down a stubborn pride (Prov. 25:15). How will it then work upon a soft heart, and gentle disposition? If therefore a husband aims to do good by reproving his wife, his reproof must be so ordered, that it may seem to be rather a gentle admonition than a sharp rebuke. He may and ought plainly to declare her fault to her, but in gentle and meek terms, without insulting, contemptuous, and shameful words.

Question: What if her fault be a heinous, scandalous sin?

Answer: In an extraordinary case some sharpness may be used, as the reproofs of Jacob (Gen. 30:2), Job (Job 2:10), and David (2 Sam. 6:21–22) show, for they were all sharp, but this sharpness must not be made bitter by any evil language. A woman's wickedness may not move a husband to be too quick to speak, and furious, but rather to be the more watchful over himself, that he contain himself within the bounds of discretion and moderation. For this end it is proper that husbands lay it down for a rule never to rebuke their wives when they are in a rage. Strong emotions raise a dark mist before the eyes of reason, which, while it remains, keeps reason from giving any good direction. Rage is as a fire, and it so inflames a man, and makes him feverish, that in his disorder he can keep to no standards.

Though a man be not able to rule himself when rage is stirred up, yet, if beforehand while his eye is single, and his whole body light (Matt. 6:22), while he is in tune (as we speak) and in a good frame of mind, he firmly resolves with himself not to do such or such a thing in his rage, that resolution will be a special means to make him refrain from doing that in passion, which if he should do, he could not in passion well order and moderate. If once he begin to do a thing in rage, the least provocation that can be will be as bellows[1] to blow up that fire into a flame.

Regarding the violence of rage (in which women by reason of the weakness of their judgment are for the most part most violent) it is also the part of a wise man to refrain from this duty of reproving his wife even when she is in a rage. As it is necessary that he should be well composed to give a reproof, so as necessary it is that she should be well composed to take a rebuke. Rage both fills and corrupts one's heart. The heart then, being full of rage, what room is left for good advice? Will a man pour wine into a vessel full of water, or wait till all the water is drained out? The heart also being so corrupted that it is characterized by nothing but rage, what good can then good advice do?

It is therefore a special point of wisdom, and shows a good respect that a man bears to his wife, yes, it shows much meekness and moderation for a husband, well to weigh both his own and his wife's temper when he reproves her, and to refrain doing it while either he or she is in a rage.

---

1. *Bellows*: flexible bag or other device used to pump air into a fire to make it burn hotter.

Indiscreetly Reproving a Wife

Against this is the indiscretion of husbands who regard not place, nor persons, nor time, nor temper of themselves or their wives, nor any other circumstance in reproving, but like Saul, who at a table where a great feast was, in presence of his nobles and captains, when he was enraged with anger, with most poisonous and bitter speeches not only rebuked but also shamed his son, and that with such words as he spared not his own wife; for in his rage he called his son, "son of the perverse rebellious woman" (1 Sam. 20:30). Like this foolish and furious Saul, I say, they take the most open place of the family before children, servants, and whole house, to reprove their wives, and with such bitter and disgraceful terms, as either they provoke their wives to answer again for maintaining (as they think) their own honor and reputation, as Jonathan was provoked to answer his father again (1 Sam. 20:32), or else give them of the household that see her thus trampled underfoot, occasion to set their feet also upon her.

Most husbands are eager enough to reprove, but few do it in meekness and moderation. They cannot do it but in company, nor without bitter words. Many in rebuking their wives, do not restrain themselves from using all the evil terms that they can think of, even such as tend not only to their wife's dishonor, but also to their own and their children's infamy. The reason is because they never rebuke but when they are in rage, and so hardly know what they do, by which also they stir up rage in their wives, and yet for all that refrain not a bit more, but rather grow more violent, as when the heat of two fires meet together, the flame must be the greater. This being the preposterous practice of many husbands, is it any wonder that ordinarily so little good, and so much hurt is done by reproving? No, would it not be a wonder, if any good and no hurt should be done by it? This therefore, though it is a duty, it is a duty to be used rarely and with great moderation.

To this point we discussed a husband's gentleness in his speeches to his wife.

16

A Husband's Kind Conduct toward His Wife

A husband's conduct toward his wife must match his speech, or else all the gentleness of it will seem just an empty compliment.

A man's conduct includes under it his facial expression, gestures, and actions, in all of which must gentleness have its place.

A Husband's Friendly Facial Expression toward His Wife

His facial expression in his wife's presence, and towards his wife, must be composed to a friendly cheerfulness. His authority over her, and rank above her, may not make him forget the intimate relationship and union between them.

Under the facial expression I include head, brow, eyes, lips, and such other parts which are, depending upon how they are framed, signs of friendship or unhappiness. Now among and above other parts of the body, the outward composition of facial expression does soonest and best declare the inward disposition of the heart. By Esau's pleasant facial expression Jacob perceived that he was pacified in his heart towards him, and as a result said, "I have seen thy face as though I had seen the face of God," that is, a friendly, gracious face (Gen. 33:10). On this ground David desired God, "to lift up the light of thy countenance [face] upon us," that by it he might know the grace and love of God towards him (Ps. 4:6). On the other side, by a frowning and lowering face, by hanging down the head, putting out the lips, and so on, anger, malice, grief, with other similar affections of heart, are manifested. Consider how by Cain's casting down of his countenance God discerned anger and envy to be in his heart (Gen. 4:6), or by Laban's countenance Jacob observed that his affection was turned from him (Gen. 31:2). A wife then beholding gentleness and amiableness in her husband's face, beholds it as the face of God, and as in a looking glass beholds the kindness and love of his heart, and so has her heart more firmly knit to him, and is moved to respect him more.

Husbands' Too Great Austerity

These attitudes are contrary to friendliness: an arrogant, proud facial expression, as of an emperor over his servants; a grim, stern facial expression, as of a judge over poor prisoners; a drooping, frowning facial expression, as of an unhappy lender over a desperate debtor; a fierce, fiery facial expression, as of an angry king over a subject that has displeased him.

These and such similar countenances manifest a proud, stubborn, furious, unhappy disposition of heart, so they cannot but give great unhappiness to a wife, and even much frighten her, being but a weaker vessel, and alienate her heart and affection from him.

A Husband's Affectionate Gestures with His Wife

A husband's gesture ought to be so affectionate and friendly towards his wife, that others may discern him to be her husband, and his wife may be stirred up to be affectionate with him.

They who are eager to show themselves kind and gentle husbands, are prone to exceed and so to fall into an extreme on the right hand, for some are never content unless they have their wives in their laps, ever snuggling, kissing, and playing with them, regardless of who is around them. Thus they show more thoughtlessness, foolishness, and overheated affection than true kindness and love, which forgets not a husband-like seriousness, sobriety, modesty, and decency.

Some allege Isaac's "sporting" with Rebekah (Gen. 26:8), to justify their sensuality. But they forget that what Isaac did was when he and his wife were alone; he was seen through a window. Much greater liberty is granted to husband and wife when they are alone than in company. Besides, there are many other ways to show kindness and affection than by foolishness and lack of self-control.

A Husband's Coldness to His Wife

Against affection is coldness, when a husband so carries himself towards his wife as if she were a stranger to him. If he comes in company where his wife is, of all other women he will not turn to her, nor take notice of her. This fault is so much the greater if such a man freely shows friendliness to others, and is accustomed to be glad and affectionate with other women. Though his gladness and affection to them are not unfitting a Christian, yet his conduct being of another temper towards his wife, it may be a means to create jealousy in her. Many think outward, kind gestures towards a wife to be foolishness, but if they knew what a means it is to stir up, increase, and preserve love in a wife's heart to her husband, they would think differently.

A Husband's Giving Gifts to His Wife

Actions are the most real demonstrations of true kindness in which a husband must not fail, as he would have his kind speech, facial expression, and gesture to be received in the best way. Kindness and gentleness in action consists in giving gifts (as we speak) to his wife. This is plainly noted in

Elkanah, who every year gave portions to his wives (1 Sam. 1:4–5). Thus a husband like him testifies his love to his wife, so he will much motivate her to do all duty to him. A small gift, as an action of kindness freely given, not upon any debt, but in testimony of love, does more work on the heart of her to whom it is given than much more given upon contract, or for a work done, by which it may seem to be deserved.

In giving gifts to a wife, a husband ought to be more bountiful and generous than to others, so that she may see by it that he loves her above all; as it is noted that Elkanah gave Hannah "a double portion, because he loved her" (1 Sam. 1:5). And in giving gifts it is best to give them with his own hands, unless he is absent from her.

Husbands Beating Their Wives

Against this are the furious and bitter actions of many unkind husbands (with heads too heady)[1] whose favors are buffets, blows, strokes, and stripes, in which they are worse than the venomous viper. For the viper casts out his poison for his mate's sake,[2] and will not you, O husband, regarding that close union which is between you and your wife, lay aside your fierceness and cruelty? Many wives by reason of their husband's fury are in worse situation than servants, for those who will not hit a servant, care not what load they lay upon their wives. Where servants have only a set time to be under the tyranny of such furious men, poor wives are tied to them all their life long. Wives cannot have so good a remedy by the help of law against cruel husbands, as servants may have against cruel masters. Masters have not such opportunity to

---

1. *Heads too heady*: too rash and violent.
2. Gouge cites Basil (c. 329–379), who in his *Hexaemeron* (7.6) said a viper spit out its venom before mating with a lamprey—a model for husbands. The fable comes from, Claudius Aelianus (c. 175–c. 235), *On the Nature of Animals*.

exercise their cruelty over servants as husbands over wives, who are to be continually at board and bed with their husbands. The nearer wives are, and the dearer they ought to be to their husbands, the more horrible must be striking when it comes by a husband's hand than by a master's. Since a husband has less power and authority to strike his wife than a master to strike a servant, his striking seems all the heavier, and the wife's situation is worse than a servant. Therefore such a man (if he may be thought a man rather than a beast) is rightly said to be like a father-killer and mother-killer.[3]

Question: May not then a husband beat his wife?

Answer: With submission to better judgments, I think he may not. My reasons are these:

1. There is no authorization throughout the whole Scripture by precept or example for it. Though this argument is from silence, for the point in hand it is forceful in two respects. First, because the Scripture has so abundantly and particularly declared the various duties of husbands and wives, and yet has given nothing concerning a husband's striking and beating his wife. Secondly, because it has also abundantly and particularly spoken of all those who are to correct, and of their manner of correcting, and of their bearing correction who are to be corrected, and of the use they are to make of it. Yet it says nothing at all concerning a husband's punishing or a wife's enduring it like this. The Scripture being so silent in this point, we may well deduce that God has not ranked wives among those in the family who are to be corrected with the rod.

2. That small difference of rank which is between husband and wife does not permit so high a power in a husband,

---

3. Gouge cites John Chrysostom (c. 347–407), who argued that since a man must leave his parents for the sake of a wife (Gen. 2:24), striking a wife is worse than striking down our parents (*Homilies on 1 Corinthians*, homily 26).

and so low a slavery in a wife, as for him to beat her. Can it be thought reasonable that she who shares a man's bed all their lives, who has power over his body, is a joint parent of the children, a joint governor of the family, should be beaten by his hands? What if children or servants should know of it? (Surely they must, for how can such a thing be done in the house and they of the household not know?) Can they respect her as a mother or a mistress who is under correction as well as they?

3. The intimate relationship and true union that is between husband and wife does not allow such dealing to pass between them. The wife is as a man's self: "They two are one flesh" (Eph. 5:31). No man but an insane, furious, desperate wretch will beat himself. Two sorts of men are in Scripture noted to cut and lance their own flesh, idolaters as the worshipers of Baal (1 Kings 18:28), and demoniacs, as he that was possessed with a legion of devils (Mark 5:5, 9). Such are they who beat their wives, either blinded in their understanding or possessed with a devil.

Objection: He that is clearest in his mind will suffer his body to be stuck with a needle, cut, lanced, and otherwise hurt, if it is needed and appropriate.

Answer: First, a man's heart will not allow him to do any of these himself. There are surgeons whose office it is to do such things. If the surgeon himself has need of any such remedy for his own body, he will use the help of another surgeon. If the case is such that a wife must be beaten, it is better for a husband to refer the matter to a public magistrate (who is as an approved and licensed surgeon) and not to do it with his own hands.[4] Secondly, though some parts of the

---

4. Corporal punishment such as flogging was part of the British judicial system until the mid-twentieth century. Thus Gouge says that in the case of criminal activity, the husband should rely on the judicial system, not his own punishment.

body may be so dealt with, yet every part may not, such as the heart, which the wife is to the man. Thirdly, the comparison does not hold. For sticking with a needle, lancing, etc., is not punishment for any fault, as the beating of a wife in question is; there is no question but a man that has skill may if necessary open a vein, lance a boil, splint a broken bone or disjointed joint in his wife's body, which may be more painful than correction, and here the comparison holds, but not in the other.

Objection: There is as close a relationship between Christ and His church, as between husband and wife, yet Christ does not refrain to correct and discipline His church.

Answer: There is a double relation between Christ and the church. He is a husband to it, having made it "of his flesh, and of his bones" (Eph. 5:30), and a supreme Lord over it, having all power in heaven and earth committed to Him (Matt. 28:18). In this latter respect He disciplines, not in the former. A husband is not such a supreme lord over his wife; therefore Christ's example is no authorization to him.

4. There is no hope of any good to come from a husband's beating of his wife, for where the party corrected is persuaded that the party which corrects has no authority or right so to do, it will not be brought patiently to take it, but will resist and strive if possible to get the mastery. Let a stranger strike such an older child or a servant as will patiently bear many strikes at a parent's or master's hand, they will turn again at that stranger, and try to give as good as he brings. Now a wife having no ground to be persuaded that her husband has authority to beat her, what hope is there that she will patiently bear it, and be bettered by it? Or rather is it not likely that she will, if she can, rise against him, overcome him (as many do) and never do any duty correctly? A fault in a wife is not taken away but increased by blows.

Objection: Stings and pain may make her dread her husband, stand in awe of him, and do her duty the better.

Answer: Such dread and awe fits neither the position of a husband to demand it, nor the position of a wife to yield it. Though she may be brought to yield some outward submission, yet inward hatred to her husband's person may be joined to it, which is as bad, if not worse than outward disobedience.

Objection: She may be of so furious a disposition as, except by force, she will not be kept in any boundaries.

Answer: First, it has been of old time answered, that "no fault should be so great, as to compel a husband to beat his wife."[5] Furthermore, other forceful means may be used besides beating by her husband's hands. She may be denied some of her privileges that she enjoys, and, if no other means will serve the purpose, be put over to the magistrate's hands, that if she be of so despicable a disposition, as by no other means she will be kept under than by fear and force, by hurt and pain, she may fear the magistrate and feel his hand, rather than her husband's.

Objection: If a wife becomes so bold, or rather insane, as to threaten to strike and beat her husband, may he not in that case beat her to make her cease her fury?

Answer: I do not doubt that that good provision which is made in law to preserve a man's life, may be applied to this purpose. The law simply condemns all murder, yet if a man be so assaulted as there is no way to preserve his own life but by taking away his life that assaults him, it does not condemn him as a murderer because he did it in self-defense. So if a husband is set upon by his wife, it is lawful and helpful that he defend himself, and if he can do it no other way

---

5. Gouge again cites John Chrysostom, homily 26 on 1 Corinthians (see note 3 above).

but by striking her, that is not to be reckoned an unlawful beating of her.

A Husband's Bearing with His Wife's Weaknesses

To this point we have covered the husband's avoiding of offence; now I will speak a word concerning his bearing with offence.

It is a general duty, common to all, to "bear ye one another's burdens" (Gal. 6:2), in which even a wife is to bear her husband's burdens, because he, as everyone else, is subject to slip and fall and so needs to be supported. Yet after a more special and particular manner does this duty belong to a husband, and that in two respects.

1. Of the two, he is more obligated than his wife, because in relation to his wife he is the stronger, for she is the weaker vessel (1 Peter 3:7). But the strong are most obligated to "bear the infirmities of the weak" (Rom. 15:1).

2. He is obligated to bear patiently with his wife more than with any other, because of that close relationship which is between them. He that cannot bear with his wife, *his flesh*, can bear with nobody. The reason given by the apostle to move a man to dwell with his wife according to knowledge, and to give honor to her, implied in this phrase, "as unto the weaker vessel" (1 Peter 3:7), shows that this is a particular duty belonging to a husband, in which he may both show his knowledge and wisdom, and also honor his wife. For why is he reminded of her weakness, but to show he should bear with her patiently?

As that phrase implies the duty, so also it implies a good reason to enforce it. For precious things which we highly value, the weaker they are, the more tenderly and carefully are they handled, as china dishes, and crystal glasses, and of all parts of the body, the eye is most tenderly handled. Now what things, what persons are more dear and precious than a wife? Yet for all that she is a weak vessel; therefore she is much to be borne with patiently.

For a husband's better direction here, difference must be made between weaknesses. Some are natural imperfections, others are actual transgressions. Natural imperfections are inward (as slowness in mind, dullness in understanding, shortness of memory, quickness in strong emotions, etc.) or outward (as lameness, blindness, deafness, or any other defect and deformity of body). These infirmities should cause pity, compassion, sympathy, and even greater tenderness and respect, but no offence. Note Abraham's example in this case; his wife was barren, yet he did not despise her for it, nor did he accuse her with any such thing.

Actual transgressions are violations of God's law, and such are meant here which most directly tend to his own disturbance and disadvantage, as argumentativeness, insisting on her own way, being picky, stubbornness, etc. In bearing these must a husband especially show his wisdom in various ways.

1. By using the best and gentlest means he can to cure them, as meek admonition, seasonable advice, gentle appeal, and compassionate affection. Elkanah, supposing that his wife did wrong in her strong emotions, thus dealt with her and supported her (1 Sam. 1:8).

2. By removing the stone over which she stumbles, by taking away the cause (so far as conveniently he can) which makes her to do wrong. Thus Abraham, by God's advice, put Hagar and her son out of the house because they were an offence to Sarah (Gen. 21:14).

3. By turning his eyes away (if the matter be not great, but may be tolerated) and taking no notice of the offence, but rather passing by it, as if he perceived it not. Solomon says, that it is a man's glory to pass over a transgression (Prov.

19:11), and he exhorts a man not to give his heart to all the words that men speak (Eccl. 7:21).

4. By forgiving and forgetting it if notice is taken of it. Jacob took notice of Rachel's wrath and stubborn demand, for he rebuked her for it, yet since he willingly yielded to that which afterwards she asked him to (Gen. 30), it appears that he forgave the offence, if not forgot it.

The best test of a man's affection to his wife, and of his wisdom in ordering the same, is in this point of bearing with offences. Not to be offended with a wife that gives no offence is not praiseworthy; pagan men may go so far. Notice what Christ says of this case, "For if ye love them which love you, what reward have ye? Do not even the publicans the same?" (Matt. 5:46; cf. Luke 6:32–33). Gently to bear with and wisely to pass over offences when they are given, not to be provoked when there is cause of provocation given, is a true Christian virtue, a virtue fitting husbands better than any other kind of men.

Husbands' Quickness to Anger

Contrary is quickness to anger, and irritability, when husbands are moved with the least provocation, like tinder catching fire at the least spark that falls upon it. Many are like gunpowder, which not only takes fire, but also breaks out into a violent flame upon the least touch of fire. As gunpowder is dangerous to be kept in a house, so are such husbands to be joined so nearly to wives as marriage joins them. If it be said, that as gunpowder does no hurt if fire come not at it, so they are good and kind, if they be not provoked and displeased, I answer, that we have a proverb that says, "The devil is good while he is pleased," yet it is not safe to have the devil too near. It is as impossible (considering man's weakness) that he should live and keep company with any, and not give offence, as for flint stones to beat and dash against one another repeatedly, and no spark of fire come from them. How then may it be thought possible for a wife, who is so continually keeping company with her husband, and the weaker vessel, to live without giving him offence? It is no very kind speech, which husbands use, especially if they be told of their unkindness, "Let my wife deserve favor, and she shall have it." How little favor would such husbands have from Christ their Husband, if he should have that attitude toward them?

Thus far has been handled the first part of a husband's well managing his authority, by a tender respect of his wife. The second is a provident care for her.

17

A Husband's Providing for His Wife

A husband that tenderly respects his wife, but does not providently care for her, shows more affection than discretion. He may have a kind heart, but he lacks a wise head. How then can he be a good head to his wife? Some short-term happiness she may have by him, but small profit and benefit can she reap from him. Those duties therefore which have been delivered must be done, but these that follow must by no means be left undone.

A husband's provident care[1] is noted in that office of Christ, in which a husband resembles him, namely, to be "a saviour of the body" (Eph. 5:23). It consists in providing things needed by his wife and in protecting her from things harmful to her.

A careful *providing of things needed* is a most important part of that honor which husbands are to give to their wives. For where the apostle says that elders are worthy of double honor (1 Peter 3:7; 1 Tim. 5:17), he means financial support as well as respect. The apostle counts him worse than an infidel that provideth not for his own, and especially for those of his own house (1 Tim. 5:8). Who are of a husband's house, if not his wife? In his house, who more properly *his own* than his wife? If then a husband does not provide for his wife, what is he to be counted?

---

1. *Provident care*: meeting immediate needs and preparing for future needs.

There is great reason why he should provide for her, because he has taken her from her parents and friends, and has received that portion which they allotted her, and has authority committed to him over her, and she is put in submission under him. Her friends, having given away her portion, and their power over her, and committed all to him, will no longer take care of her. She, being in submission under him, cannot without him provide for herself. Who then shall provide for her if he does not, whose wholly and only she is?

Contrary is the mind of those who take a wife only for their own happiness, or delight, or gain, and never think of that responsibility which together with a wife they take upon themselves. Having the same attitude are those who, when they have a wife, neglect her in everything but what is necessary to accomplish their own purposes. Much have they to answer for, and so much the more, because a wife is a special pledge of God's favor (Prov. 18:22).

A Husband's Providing Means of Spiritual Edification for His Wife

In this provident care which a husband ought to have of his wife, we will consider the extent and duration of it. It ought to extend both to herself, and to others; regarding herself, to her soul and body.

For her *soul*, means of spiritual edification must be provided, and those both private and public. Private means are holy and religious exercises in the house, as reading the Word, prayer, catechizing, etc. These, being the spiritual food of the soul, are to be provided and used every day, as our bodily food. A husband as a master of a family must provide these for the good of his whole house, but as a husband, especially for the good of his wife. To his wife, as well as to the whole house, he is a king, a priest, and a prophet.

By himself therefore, for his wife's good, he should perform these things, or provide that they may be done by some other. Cornelius himself performed those exercises (Acts 10:2, 30). Micah hired a Levite, and though his idolatry was evil, yet his care to have a Levite in his house was commendable (Judg. 17:10). The Shunammite's husband provided a room for the prophet, especially for his wife's sake, for it was at her request (2 Kings 4:11).

Public means are the holy ordinances of God publicly performed by God's minister. The care of a husband for his wife in this respect is so to order his place of residence, and provide other needed things, that his wife may be made partaker of it. It is expressly noted of Elkanah that he so provided for his wives, that they went with him every year to the house of God (1 Sam. 1:7; 2:19); the same is implied of Joseph, the husband of Mary (Luke 2:41). In those days there was a public place and house of God, to which all God's people (however far they dwelt from it) were to return every year. The places where Elkanah and Joseph dwelt were far from the house of God, yet they so provided, that not only they themselves, but also their wives went to the public worship of God. Now there are many houses of God, places for the public worship of God, but yet through the corruption of our times, the ministry of the Word (the most important means of spiritual edification) is not everywhere to be enjoyed. Therefore such ought a husband's care for his wife in this respect to be, as to dwell where she may have the benefit of the preaching of the Word, or else so to provide for her, as she may weekly go where it may be had.

If men of wisdom and ability purchase or build a house for their residence, they will be sure it shall be where sweet rivers and waters are, and good pasture ground, and where all necessary provision may be had. God's Word preached is a spring of water of life; the place where it is preached a pleasant, profitable pasture; all necessary provision for the soul may there be had. Let this therefore be most of all sought after, and no residence settled but where this may be had.

Neglecting Their Wife's Edification

Their practice is opposed, who having their vocation in places where the Word is plentiful, yet upon outward respects of pleasure, delight, ease, and profit, move their families into remote places where preaching is scarce, if at all, and there leave their wives to govern the family, not regarding their lack of the Word, for as much as they themselves often coming to London or other similar places by reason of their vocation, enjoy the Word themselves. Many businessmen, lawyers, and others are guilty of great neglect of their wives in this respect.

So also are those who abandon all religious exercise in their houses, making their houses more like hothouses of the devil than churches of God. If for lack of means, either public or private, a wife lives and dies in ignorance, profaneness, unbelief, and unrepentance, which cause eternal damnation, surely her blood shall be required at his hands, for a husband is God's watchman to his wife (Ezek. 3:18).

A Husband's Providing Things Needful for His Wife's Body

A husband's provident care of his wife must extend also to the body, both in health and sickness. In health by providing such things as are needed to preserve health, as sufficient food, clothing, and similar necessities. Where the prophet, to show how bad will be the misery of the people, says, "Seven women shall take hold of one man, saying, We will eat our own bread, and wear our own apparel, only let us be called by thy name" (Isa. 4:1), he implies that it was a husband's duty to provide food and clothing, that is, all necessities for his wife; which the law of Moses also implies, where it commands him that takes a second wife not to diminish the food and clothing of the former (Ex. 21:10). In sickness such things are to be provided as are needed either to restore her health, or to comfort, cherish, and refresh her in her sickness.

A Husband's Provident Care for His Wife about Her Child-Bearing

Most proper to this place is that provident care which husbands ought to have of their wives both before and in the time of their labor and childbirth, in two things especially.

First, in obtaining for their wives to the utmost of their power and ability, such things as may satisfy their cravings, in case they do crave some food (as in all ages women in the time of breeding and bearing children have been subject to). For it is well known, that it is very dangerous both for mother and child to lack what she craves. The death, sometimes of the one, sometimes of the other, sometimes of both, has followed as a result.[2]

Secondly, in providing such things as are needed for their labor and childbirth. This time is especially to be provided for, in many respects.

1. Because it is a time of weakness, in which the woman cannot well provide for herself.

2. Because her weakness is joined with much pain. The pain of a woman in labor is the greatest pain that ordinarily is endured by any for the time. None know it so well as they that feel it, and many husbands, because they are not so subject, think little of it. If we duly weigh that the Holy Spirit, when He would set forth the extremity of any pains and sufferings, compares them to the pains of a woman in

---

2. In the seventeenth century, people recognized the serious effects of a mother's diet upon her unborn child, and it was believed that the unmet cravings of a pregnant woman could harm her baby.

labor, we may well deduce, that of all they are the greatest (Ps. 48:6; Isa. 13:8; 21:3; Jer. 4:31; 30:6; Mic. 4:9). This is further shown by the screams and cries which not only weak and faint-hearted women utter in the time of their labor, but also are forced from the strongest and toughest women that are, and that though beforehand they resolve to the contrary.

Neither should we be surprised at this, for their body is as it were set on a rack (at least if the labor is sharp) and all their parts so stretched, as a wonder it is they should ever recover their health and strength again, or that they should endure the shock of it, and not die with their labor, as Rachel (Gen. 35:16), and the wife of Phinehas (1 Sam. 4:19–20), and many in all ages have done.[3] Surely among ordinary deliverances I know none so near a miracle, none in which the Almighty does so evidently manifest His great power and good providence, as in the safe delivery of women.

Besides the great pains of labor, women are also after their delivery subject to many agonies which are very painful. From all these pains and great weakness which happen to women in childbirth, especially if they nurse their children, men are freed by reason of their sex. To apply this point, seeing women are brought to such pains and weakness in bringing forth those children which are the man's as well as hers, and he freed from all, is it not very just and fitting that he should provide all things needed for her well-being, rest, and recovery of strength?

3. Because the lack of things needed is at that time very dangerous, dangerous to the health and life of the woman and child also.

---

3. Today in the United States the maternal death rate is about 1 in 10,000, but in early modern England it may have been around 1 in 100. Since many women had several children, a significant number of women died in childbirth.

Neglecting Wives in Their Weakness

Against a husband's provident care in general are those vices which were covered in a previous chapter on mutual duties, such as resenting the responsibilities placed on a wife, greed, extravagant spending, and laziness.[4]

But working against a husband's care for his wife in childbirth in particular, is the inhumane and more than barbarous unkindness of many husbands, who do not consider the weakness of their wives in this case, to help, rest, and comfort them, but rather make their burden much heavier. For some through greed refuse beforehand to give means to their wife to provide such things as are needed for herself and the child, and when the time comes, if their wife desires a midwife[5] that charges somewhat more than the next, she shall have none if she will not have the next. And as for a nurse to tend her, they think their maid will serve well enough; they need not pay the charges to bring a nurse into the house. Regarding convenient lodging some will say, "Cannot my wife be put in a bed in a room without a chimney[6] as well as the virgin Mary? Why should my wife need more things than she did?" Furthermore, there are many that when the time that their wife should be delivered approaches, carry her from all her friends into a place where she is not known, lest her friends should beg him to spend and lay out more upon his wife than he is willing. In the time while their wife is weak in childbirth, many hate to allow them any other diet than is for themselves and children provided in the house, not considering that her stomach cannot be like theirs.

---

4. See chapter 6, "Guarding Each Other's Health, Reputation, and Property."

5. Births took place at home attended by a midwife, not in a hospital attended by a doctor.

6. *Room without a chimney*: without central heating and insulation, a room with no fireplace got very cold in winter.

Many other such bitter fruits of unkind husbands arising from covetousness might be reckoned up, by which husbands plainly show that they love their wealth better than their wives; they had rather lose *them* than part with *that*.

Others, through jealous suspicion, do not refrain even in the time of their wives' pain and weakness, to accuse them with foolish words, and say that the child is not theirs. To accuse a wife of this unjustly is at any time a most shameful and hateful disgrace, but in the time of childbirth, whether just or unjust, a thing too bitter and vengeful. Some wives are so far overcome (especially in the time of their weakness) that they are not able to bear it, but even faint and die under the disgrace. Others of stronger constitution vow never to know their husbands again. Many similar troubles follow from such unkindness.

A Husband's Providing for His Wife According to His Estate and Ability

In a husband's providing for the body of his wife consideration must be given to the measure, and to the manner.

The *measure* must match his ability, for a husband ought to support his wife in as good an estate and fashion as himself. By marriage she is advanced to as high an estate and dignity in relation to others as he is, and for her own use she is made a partner of all his goods, and accordingly should share in them.

For the *manner*, he must allow her (if at least he observes her to have any sufficient wisdom) to order such things as needed for herself according to her best liking.

Both in the measure and in the manner of providing, there must be a difference made between a wife and servants or children. These may have their portions of food, clothing, and similar necessities proportioned and limited to them, which is unfitting to be done to a wife. Neither is it necessary that so plentiful a provision be made for them as for her.

A Husband's Stinginess to His Wife

A husband's stingy dealing with his wife is against his duty of providing for her, when the allowance she has is both far under his estate, and also given her only a little bit at a time, as if she were a child. Many husbands make their wives slave away at home, eat sparingly, and dress poorly; who are themselves showy in clothing, party and feast away from home, and so exceed their wives that they are ashamed to be seen in company with them. They who marry their maids, or others of lower rank than themselves, often so deal with them, esteeming them but as servants and low persons though they be their wives. But it has been before shown that wives by marriage are advanced to their husband's dignity, however low they were before.

Husbands Allowing Their Wife to Give to Others As They See Good Reason

So far ought the provident care of a husband for his wife to extend, as she may have (beside things necessary to herself) to give to those to whom it is required for her to give, such as children and servants in the house, and others also out of the house. This is noted in Solomon's description of a good wife, "She...giveth meat to her household, and a portion to her maidens" (Prov. 31:15), and "all her household is clothed with scarlet"—that is, by her planning and managing the matter (v. 21). "Her children arise up, and call her blessed" (v. 28) for her general conduct in the family, as for her particular favors given to them. As for others outside of the household, it is also noted that "she stretcheth out her hand to the poor; yea, she reacheth forth her hands to the needy" (v. 20). These things she did by virtue of that power and liberty which her husband gave her, as appears by two points noted there:

1. In that before any mention is made of those things which she did, it is said, "The heart of her husband doth safely trust in her" (v. 11).

2. In that, after all her good deeds are reckoned up, it is said, "Her husband praiseth her" (v. 28).

It is good that other husbands (whose wives are wise and faithful) should deal with their wives according to this pattern, that in the house they might have more honor from children and servants, and that outside of the house they might give better testimony of their charity.

For consider the many excellent promises that are made to works of mercy and charity, and the many terrible threats that are pronounced not only against those who exercise cruelty, but also against those who show no mercy. Considering also that wives together with their husbands, are "heirs of the grace of life" (1 Peter 3:7), it is very necessary that they should manifest their faith by some work of mercy and charity. Now unless her husband gives her something at her own discretion to give to others, true and thorough trial of her merciful and charitable mind cannot be made. If she gives of that which her husband has reserved to himself, as her giving is against God's law, so she may be thought generous but actually is not merciful because despite her generous giving she gives up nothing of her own. Even though she has a general consent to give as she sees cause of the common possessions of the family, that is not so sure and sound a test of her charity, and mercifulness, as if she had something of her own which she might keep or give away as pleases herself; and what she does not give away, lay up as her own savings belonging to herself. There is naturally such a self-love in man, and a desire to keep that which belongs to one's self, that he really hates to let go of any of it, unless conscience and grace alter this corruption of nature, and so move him willingly to give out something for charitable uses. But otherwise of that which in whole or in part belongs to another (be that other, husband, parent, master, friend, or any else) he is easily moved to be generous and bountiful. A man will gladly cut a large piece (as we speak) out of someone else's leather.

It is known that many children and servants who have been generous of their parents' and masters' possessions to the poor, when they come to be owners of their own, are very stingy and miserly. Those who share in savings will be much more eager in giving away that which is common with another than that which belongs to each of them. The truest test of a merciful and charitable heart lies in the distribution of what is one's own property.

It is therefore fitting upon this very ground, that a husband should, according to his ability, let his wife have some savings and portion of her own, free to dispose of as she sees good, telling her that the most important reason why he provides so plentifully for her is that she may show forth the fruits of her faith by some works of charity, and exhorting her so to do. Many religious, wise, kind husbands thus do, some giving quarterly allowance in money to their wives, others giving their wives power to receive a certain portion of rent out of certain lands or houses, others granting their wives an absolute ownership of some inheritance, and allowing them to receive the profits and revenues of it, others giving them certain fees of their offices, or of their trade; others, that are poor, allowing them to work for themselves, and manage their earnings as they see cause, some one way, some another. Everyone in his position best knows the means how to gratify his wife in this way. It shall be sufficient for me to have laid down the general rule.

Husbands' too Great Strictness over Their Wives

Against this is the tight-fistedness to their wives of those who allow them no more than may be for their own personal use. They think it a great matter and as much as a husband is bound to do, to let her have clothing, food, and drink, and such necessities as are appropriate for her rank, but all other additions they think unnecessary. Thus their wives are not only deprived of means to gain respect from their children and servants at home, and to reward those who are obedient and ready to do service to them, but also to perform such works of mercy as both opportunity requires, and also their conscience moves them to do. Yes, many wives of rich husbands are brought to great shame by this, being in places where there is a good opportunity to contribute to some charitable cause, and by reason of their rich and costly clothing it is expected they should be bountiful, but they have nothing at all to give. The fault of some husbands in this respect is great in many ways. They bring shame and grief to their wives, to whom they should show consideration with all tenderness. They dishonor their own positions: for they who take notice of this strictness to their wives, will be ready to judge them both greedy and unkind. They will be held responsible for the omitting of that work of mercy which their wives should have done. They shall hear that dreadful doom, "Depart from me, ye cursed, into everlasting fire, prepared for the devil and his angels: for I was an hungred, and ye gave me no meat" (Matt. 25:41–42), and if they answer, "When did we see Thee hungry?," it shall be replied, "In that you did not allow your wives to do it, you did it not."

This ends the extent of a husband's provident care for the good of his wife. It follows to speak of the duration of it.

A Husband's Care to Provide for His Wife so Long as She Shall Live

The *duration* of a husband's provident care for his wife must be so long as she lives, even though she outlives him, not that he can actually when he is dead provide for her, but that he may before his death so provide for her, as she may have the means to support herself, and to live according to that position where he advanced her. At least that he should leave her not only so much as he had with her, but something more also in testimony of his love to her and care for her. Husbands have the example of Christ to press this duty upon them, for when He went away from His church here on earth, He left His Spirit, which provided it with gifts as plentifully as if Christ had still remained with her, if not more abundantly (Eph. 4:8).

To better perform this duty, husbands who die before their wife must observe among other things two especially.

1. That plainly and explictly they declare their mind and will before they die, lest their wife should be taken advantage of and cheated of that which they intended them. Thus did David upon the motion of Bathsheba; he settled his estate and caused Bathsheba's son to be actually crowned before he himself died, which he did, as for other weighty reasons, so in particular for his wife's good, as may be gathered from that reason she gave to the king in these words, "Otherwise it shall come to pass, when my lord the king shall sleep with his fathers, that I and my son Solomon shall be counted offenders" (1 Kings 1:21).

2. That he request some faithful friend in his place to be a helper to her as Christ commended His mother to His disciple John (John 19:16, 27), which will be necessary regarding her weakness and lack of experience to manage such affairs especially as are outside of the household.

At the time of a man's departure out of this world from his wife, will the truest test of his affection to his wife be given, for many that provide for their wives while they live with them, at their death show that there was no soundness of affection in their heart towards them. All was but a mere show for some hidden agenda.

Husbands' Neglect of Their Wife's Future Estate
The various practices of unkind husbands are against this.

1. Some through lack of planning or extravagant spending make themselves unable to do good to their wives after their death, and so leave their wives nothing, or (that which is worse than nothing) in debt, and with a great responsibility for the children. That care which husbands ought to have of their wives should make them think beforehand of the time to come, and even for their wives' sake be somewhat the more diligent, thrifty, and prepared, and cut off many unnecessary expenses, or their sin is doubled first by a needless wasting of their estate, and second by neglecting their wives.

2. Others by flattering or forceful means draw their wives to give up the rights they have in money, possessions, house, or land by jointure,[7] inheritance, or any other way, and yet make them no sufficient payment in another way, but at their death leave their wives in a far worse estate than they were in before marriage, beside a greater charge than they had before. As this is a great part of unkindness, so also a main point of injustice.

3. Others resenting the laws under which they live for providing for a wife a third[8] of his estate or otherwise, use all the fraudulent means they can to deprive her of that which

---

7. *Jointure*: arrangement for a wife's financial provision after her husband dies.

8. *Third*: English common law assigned a third of the inheritance to the widow, and two-thirds to the heirs.

otherwise the law would lay upon her. The civil laws of the place where we live ought to be the rule of our civil actions (so far as they are not contrary to God's Word) and we ought for conscience sake to be subject to them (Rom. 13:5). Besides, a husband ought (though the law does not force him) to leave at least a third to his wife, as a testimony of his love to her, and care for her. This also is a double fault, both a transgression of the law and a note of unkindness.

4. Others having aged and sickly wives, or otherwise thinking that their wives may, or rather hoping that their wives will die before themselves, put off the making of their wills with the purpose that they might not put in their wives' third, but use them some other way. Besides the fact that these husbands show no good affection towards their wives, they provoke God to disappoint them of their hopes, as He often does, for He takes them away before their wives, and so takes them away, as having not time to make their will, not only their wives enjoy their third (which they so much desired to avoid) but also some others (whom of all in their lifetime they disliked) seize upon the other two parts.

A Husband's Protecting His Wife from Danger

Having showed how a husband is to provide things necessary for his wife, it remains to show how he is to protect her from things harmful to her. Regarding that protection which a husband owes his wife, he is called "a covering of the eyes" (Gen. 20:16), which phrase implies submission on the wife's part, and also protection on the husband's. To protect one, is, as it were, to cover them, namely, from danger; to be negligent and careless of them, is, as it were, to lay them open to danger. The same duty is implied under another phrase of "spreading his wing" over his wife (Ruth 3:9).[9] The metaphor

9. The KJV of Ruth 3:9 reads, "spread therefore thy skirt over thine handmaid," but the Hebrew is "thy wing."

is taken from winged fowls, which to keep their young ones from hurt, use to spread their wings over them. This phrase and metaphor is also attributed to God, to set forth His protection (Ruth 2:12). But most pertinent to this purpose is the title, "saviour," given to a husband in relation to his wife (Eph. 5:23). For this end the Lord, who subjected a woman to her husband, gave to his sex greater strength, courage, and boldness than to hers, that he might protect her who is the weaker vessel. In this duty of protection Christ shows Himself an excellent pattern and example for husbands.

To better perform this duty, a husband must be careful to prevent, as much as he may, such dangers as his wife is likely to fall into, and to rescue her out of those which she falls into. For this purpose David took his wives into Gath lest, if they were left in Israel, Saul should cause them some trouble (1 Sam. 27:3), and again, when they were taken by the Amalekites, he rescued them (1 Sam. 30:18). According to that danger to which wives are subject must a husband's care of protecting his wife be shown.

1. If she is in danger of being seduced and enticed, as Eve was, by any evil instruments of the devil, as Jesuits, priests, friars,[10] profane, blasphemous, immoral, or out-of-control persons, his care must be either to keep them away that they do not come to her, or to get them away from her so soon as he can. He may not tolerate them to stay in his house.

2. If by any trick she is drawn from his house, he must seek her, and get her again, as the Levite did his wife (Judg. 19:2), or cause her (if he can) to be brought home again, as David caused Michal to be brought (2 Sam. 3:13–14), especially if they are taken away by force, as Ahinoam, and Abigail, David's wives, were (1 Sam. 30:18).

---

10. *Jesuits…friars*: members of Roman Catholic orders operating in England to undermine the Reformation.

3. If she is unjustly slandered, he is to maintain her honor and reputation as much as his own, as Christ counts Himself despised when His church is, so must he (Luke 10:16). This concern he must have of his wife's credit, even after her death, as well as while she lives.

4. Whatever other trouble is intended or practiced against her, he must be a tower of defense to protect her, as Ahasuerus was to Esther against Haman (Est. 7:7–8), and not only against strangers outside the house, but also against children and servants in the house. Children grown older, that are proud and stubborn, will be ready to rise up against their mother, especially if she is a step-mother, because she is the weaker sex. The presence of a father is most effective generally speaking to maintain respect in the home. Therefore the husband must be a help to his wife, and maintain her honor against them, even though they are children of a former wife.

A Husband's Supporting His Wife against Children of a Previous Relationship, and Servants

Objection: Step-mothers often prove unkind and unjust mothers, and deal unmercifully with their husband's children. Must a husband in such cases assist his wife against his children?

Answer: The protection I speak of, is if in case a wife is wronged, then her husband is to do what he can to defend her rights. But if she is the wrong-doer, he may by no means support her against his children, and so make their wrong the greater. Yet so far ought he to respect his wife, as by all the fair means he can, to labor to pacify her mind, and turn her heart towards them, and if he observes her heart to be completely alienated from them, then to send them out to be brought up in some other place, and so to take away from her the object of her displeasure, that he and she may live more quietly together. For if a man must forsake father and mother, he must also forsake children and cleave to his wife. Peace and unity between husband and wife must be kept sacred. "Though you cast away all, nothing more troublesome can happen to you than not to have a quiet wife at home. You cannot find sin more grievous than to have fights with your wife."[11]

If a wife must be supported against the stubbornness of children, much more against the insolence of servants, for which purpose the example of Abraham is recorded, whose servant might have privilege above other, because he had slept with her. Yet when she grew insolent against her mistress, first he put her into her mistress's hand to do to her as it pleased her, and afterwards he cast her out of his house (Gen. 16:6; 21:14).

Neglecting to Maintain Their Wife

The lawless carelessness of husbands, who care no more to help and assist their wives than any other person, works against this.

1. Some more fear to offend their wives than they care to do them good, and in that respect they let any sort of people come to their wives that are welcome to them. If magistrates in a nation shall answer for allowing seditious men to come into their dominions to deceive their people, much more shall husbands answer for allowing them to come and deceive their wives, for several reasons. First, they have a greater responsibility for their wives than magistrates for their people. Secondly, wives ought to be dearer to husbands than people to magistrates. Thirdly, because they may sooner see them in their house than magistrates in the nation. Fourthly, because they may be much more easily kept out of a house than out of a nation or a city.

2. Others do not care where their wives wander, and if they do go out of their house, they shall never be sought

---

11. Gouge again cites Chrysostom's 26th homily on 1 Corinthians.

after by their husbands. Though this may be a just punishment on wandering wives, yet it is not just for husbands so to deal with them. If Christ our Husband should so deal with us, we should soon be lost, for we often go astray like wandering sheep, but He is that good shepherd, who seeks after the lost sheep until He finds it (Luke 15:4).

3. No wonder then that many husbands are no more affected with the bad reports and rumors raised against their wives, when they so little regard who come to them, or where they go. Assuredly the dishonor of a wife will turn to the man's dishonor, for as "a virtuous wife is a crown to her husband," so by the rule of contraries, an infamous wife is a shame to her husband (Prov. 12:4). If therefore not for his wife's sake, for his own sake a man ought not to carelessly pass over the bad reports which are raised against his wife.

4. There are such unkind husbands that are moved with no bad treatment given to their wives, nor will hear any complaint that they make to them. Even if they see them mistreated, they will either not seem to see it, or but smile at it, and so go their way, and allow their wives to defend themselves as well as they can. As it fits no Christian to allow his neighbor to be wronged—for it is noted as a commendable matter in Moses, that when he saw two Hebrews striving together, he took his part that had wrong done to him, and reproved the other (Ex. 2:13)—so much less a husband, to whose safe-keeping his wife is committed. Nature teaches us that the head is as much affected with a wrong done to the body as to itself; so ought a husband be.

5. As the wrong which is done by those who are in submission in the house under the wife is greater than that which is done by strangers, so the husband's fault is the greater in allowing it. He has more power over them in his house than over others. What then may we think of such, as either by their turning a blind eye, or by taking sides against

their wives, allow both children and servants to jump all over them? Surely those husbands themselves will find some taste of the bitter and evil fruit of it, and that not only by that great unhappiness which their wives must take, but also by that contempt which will come on their own persons, both by their wives (who cannot think them good heads to govern others), but also by their children and servants, who will take the opportunity to grow proud and presumptuous against him. By despising the weaker, men grow by little and little to despise the stronger. This men of wisdom and experience well know, so that in nations and states governed by wise men, the authority of subordinate magistrates is upheld and maintained. Superior magistrates will not tolerate those who are in authority under them to be despised, for it is well known that it tends not only to the honor and peace, but also to the safety of the supreme magistrate to have the power and authority of subordinate magistrates respected and not trampled under feet. It proves therefore both lack of affection and of discretion and understanding in husbands to allow a child, servant, or any other in the household to insult their wives, who are joint governors with them over the house.

18

A Husband's Sincere and Steady Love for His Wife

The general *matter* together with the particular kinds of husbands' duties being handled so far, the *manner* also of performing them is to be delivered.

To instruct a husband in the manner of performing his duties to his wife, the apostle lays down two patterns, both Christ and ourselves. As Christ loves His church, and as we love ourselves, so must men love their wives. That we may the better follow these patterns we must distinctly note how Christ loves His church, and how we love ourselves.

The love of Christ to His church is commended to us in six distinct points, which are the order, the truth, the cause, the quality, the quantity, and the duration of it.

For the *order*, Christ began to love His church. He showed His love to her before she loved Him. As the air heated by the sun is hot, and a wall on which the sunbeams shine gives a reflection of heat back again, so the church, as it was heated and warmed in heart by the sense of Christ's love, loved Him, as the apostle plainly notes, "We love him, because he loved us first" (1 John 4:19), and the church herself acknowledges, saying, "Because of the savour of thy good ointments" (by which we are revived and cheered) "the virgins love thee" (Song 1:3).

There is in us by nature no spark of love at all. If Christ by His loving of us first did not instill love into us, we could no more love Him than a living bird rise out of a cold egg, if it were not kept warm by the mother's sitting upon it.

Thus must a husband first begin to love his wife. His place of high rank and authority requires that he should be to his wife, "a guide" (Prov. 2:17), which title is plainly given to him by the Holy Spirit to teach him to go before her, and by his example to instruct and encourage her to do her duty. What a shame would it be for a man who is the image and glory of God, the head of his wife, in the same position to her that Christ is to His church, to be prompted to love his wife by her conduct (she being the weaker vessel, under him, to learn of him)? There are reasons to stir up a wife to try to go ahead of her husband in doing her duty, which if she does, it is the greater glory to her; but this pattern of Christ should stir him much more to strive to go before her.

Husbands Repaying Unkindness for Love

Their disposition is contrary, who, having loving and faithful wives, are notwithstanding not moved to love them again, but are as unkind and rude as if they had the most irritable and perverse wives that could be. But what shall we say of those who love their wives the less, and even hate them for their eagerness to love, and (in testimony of true love) to perform all good duty? What shall we say but that they are truly devils in the flesh? For it is the devil's property to overcome good with evil. These make the doctrine of a wife's submission to seem harsh, and a careful performance of it, a heavy burden. Never shall they partake of Christ's love, who in their position show themselves so unlike to Christ.

The Truth of Husbands' Love

The *truth* of Christ's love was manifested by the fruits of it to His church. He gave Himself for it. It was therefore not in word only, no, nor only in heart, but in action also. Thus His love proved profitable and beneficial to His church, which by it was cleansed, and made a glorious church (Eph. 5:26–27). Had He only had a tender compassion and feeling of pity towards it, or labored only with comfortable and sweet words to uphold and assist it, it would still lay filthy with sin, in the power of the devil, and under God's wrath, and so receive no profit and benefit at all.

So must husbands love their wives in truth and in action. Such a love is required of a man to his brother (1 John 3:18), much more therefore to his wife, who is not only a sister as the apostle expressly calls her (1 Cor. 9:5), but nearer than sister, mother, daughter, friend, or any other whoever. This therefore serves to press the practice of all the duties pertaining to a husband.

Husbands' Disguise

Contrary is their disguise and hypocrisy, who make great show of much love, and outward shows of earnest affection, using many outward compliments, but fail when they come to the truest test, the *action*. Some, like men coming to court and woo a woman, will promise mountains, but not perform mole hills. Others will snuggle and kiss their wives much, but trust them with nothing, nor provide for them things required. Some will weep much when their wives are sick, yet not give medicine for their recovery. Many will carry a fair face their whole life towards their wives, and at their death leave them nothing to live by.

For this reason many, who by others are counted to be very kind husbands, are by their wives found to be far otherwise. If a test is made of husbands' love by their practice and performance of their duties, it will be found that they for the most part come as far short in love, as wives in submission.

The Freeness of Husbands' Love

The cause of Christ's love was His love, as Moses notes that God "set his love upon you...because the LORD loved you" (Deut. 7:7–8). His love arose only and wholly from Himself, and was free in every way. As there was nothing in the church before Christ loved her to move Him to love her, so can there be nothing that He could hope for afterwards, but what He gave. Indeed He delights in that righteousness by which, as with a glorious robe, she is clothed; and with those heavenly graces, by which, as with precious jewels, she is adorned. But that righteousness and those graces are His own, and of His free gift, "that he might present it to himself a glorious church" (Eph. 5:27).

In imitation of Christ husbands should love their wives, even if there is nothing in wives to move them so to do, but only because they are their wives, even though no future benefit could after be expected from them. True love gives its attention to the person which is loved, and the good love may do to her, rather than to the person who loves, and the good that he may receive. For love "seeketh not her own" (1 Cor. 13:5).

Christ's love in this branch of it should further move husbands to do what is in their power, to make their wives worthy of love. Thus will it be said in truth, that they "dwell with their wives according to knowledge" (1 Peter 3:7), and thus will their love appear to be as Christ's love, *free*.

Husbands Loving for Their Advantage

Those who love only for their own happiness and advantage are against this. Many can love no further than they may have some bait to attract their affections, as beauty, wealth, honor, or similar reasons, or at least hope of some inheritance or portion above that which they have, or of some favor that they expect from their wife's friends. This cannot be a true sound love. Such a man may be thought to love his wife's beauty, inheritance, and friends rather than his wife. This love cannot last.

The Purity of Husbands' Love

Christ's love for its *quality* is an holy, pure, chaste love. As He is, so is His love, as is evident by the effect of it. It moved Him to sanctify and cleanse his church, to make it a glorious church without spot (Eph. 5:26–27). He did not therefore make His spouse dirty or unclean, and so that His love might more clearly appear to be chaste love, cast only upon one spouse and not many, He united all His saints together by the bond of His Spirit, and made them all one body (1 Cor. 12:12–13).

By this husbands must learn so to have such affection towards their wives as may be consistent with holiness, and chastity. Though much love be required, it may not overflow those banks. "Marriage is honourable in all and the bed undefiled" (Heb. 13:4). It must therefore be used in purity. This indeed pertains to the wife as well as to the husband. But because he is the head, and guide of his wife, and ought to be as a pattern and example before her, as Christ is before him, therefore is it more especially applied to him. The purity of a husband's love here spoken of, has a double use,

1. It limits a husband's love to his own wife. There is a general Christian love by which all occasions of doing good are taken, with which a husband may, and ought to love others, and a particular matrimonial love, by which he is moved to prefer his wife before all, and to have his heart set and fixed on her, and so proper and particular to her.

2. It orders and moderates his love, so that it turns not into sinful lust, by which that estate (which in itself by virtue of God's ordinance, is holy), is made dirty.

Husbands' Lightness

Against this purity, is not only adultery, but also immorality, lewdness, and uncleanness with his wife. For many husbands without self-discipline or purity, giving the reins[1] to their uncontrolled lusts, show as much indecency and plain filthiness in their words, gestures, and actions (to say nothing of their thoughts which are not seen) to their wives, as others do to prostitutes and harlots. This is a most shameless thing, and I am even ashamed to mention, but because it is mentioned, let such know, that they shall be accounted among such "whoremongers[2] and adulterers as God will judge" (Heb. 13:4).

Husbands Loving Their Wife More Than Themselves

The *quantity* of Christ's love cannot be expressed, for the measure of it was above measure. Christ "gave himself" for the church (Eph. 5:25), and in that respect He calls Himself that good shepherd that gave His life for His sheep (John. 10:11). "Greater love hath no man than this" (John 15:13). What will He not do for His spouse, that gave His life for her?

This may seem to be too high a stretch and level of love for a husband to attain to—a matter in which he is to leave his pattern, and not to follow Christ. But John writes that the love of our brethren should reach even this degree, "We ought to lay down our lives for the brethren" (1 John 3:16), therefore, by just consequence, for our wives.

But that this degree of love is not stretched too far, and husbands cast into a pit of unnecessary danger, two cautions must be noted. First, there must be an absolute necessity to bring us to this difficult demand of parting with our life, which is, when the good we aim at in the behalf

---

1. *Giving the reins*: letting go of the reins of a horse, an image of letting something run as it pleases.
2. *Whoremongers*: people guilty of the sin of sexual immorality.

of our wives cannot any other way be brought to pass but by risking our life. There was no other way to redeem the church, but by the blood of Christ. Secondly, that the good we intend in this case to our wives be of greater value than our temporal life, as is the good of saving her soul. Thus the apostle says, "And I will very gladly spend and be spent for you" (2 Cor. 12:15). This attitude men must carry much more towards their wives. It was for our salvation that Christ gave Himself.

Husbands' Unkindness

Those unkind who prefer every little thing of their own before the good of their wives work contrary to this. Their profit, their pleasure, their promotion, completely draw away their hearts and affections from their wives. If any extraordinary responsibility must be laid out or labors taken for their wives' good, little love will then appear, by which it appears that there was no true and sound love settled in their hearts towards their wives. As gold and other similar metals are tested by the fire, so love by afflictions and crosses.

Fighting for Wives' Honor

The other extreme is the too bold and rash show of manhood of such husbands that upon every jealous suspicion and small report, are ready to challenge someone to a fight, and to enter into single combat and duels, for maintaining their wife's honor. This being no authorized course of righting a wrong, no honor can return to the wife by it, but much dishonor and danger to the husband. If he prevails over his adversary and kills him, he is made guilty of murder, and so disgrace and shame must come to himself, wife, and his whole family. If he is overcome and slain, she may be counted guiltier than she was before. Often it happens that God in just judgment gives over the challenger into his adversary's hand, because he has undertaken such a poorly chosen course.

Husbands' Perseverance in Love

The duration of Christ's love was without end, "Having loved his own…he loved them unto the end" (John 13:1). His love was constant, not by fits and starts, now loving, then hating, and everlasting (Hos. 2:19), never regretting it, never changing or altering his mind. No provocations, no transgressions could ever make Him forget to love, and cease to do that good which He intended for His church. Note what He said to her even when she turned away from Him, "Thou hast played the harlot with many lovers, yet return again to me" (Jer. 3:1), and again, "My mercy shall not depart away" (2 Sam. 7:15).

His love is based not on what His church deserves, but on the unchangeableness of His own will. As this manifested Christ's love to be true sound love, so it made it profitable and beneficial to the church, which, despite her many frailties, by virtue of this is glorified.

This last branch must be added to all the former branches of a husband's love, or else they will be all in vain and to no purpose. This gives the truest test of sound love. Such was the love between David and Jonathan, the soundest love that ever was between parties. This brings the greatest glory to the party which loves, and the greatest benefit to the party which is loved. That a man's love may thus remain firm and sacred,

1. He must be sure to lay a good foundation. He must ground his love on God's ordinance, and love his wife regarding the matrimonial bond which knits them together, and that close union which arises from it, and so it will last so long as that knot lasts.

2. He must further support and strengthen it with an sacred resolution to be changed and altered with no

provocation, but rather to pass by all weaknesses; working in love to fix them if he possibly can; if not, to bear with them.

Husbands' Fickleness

Against this is their fickleness, whose love is ready to turn as a weather vane with every blast of a contrary wind, now tender-hearted, then again hard-hearted, now smiling, then pouting, now giving this and that favor, then denying everything, even such things as are needed.

Many whose love was as hot as fire while their wives were young, or their friends lived, or while they pleased them, when those causes are taken away, prove in their love as cold as ice. Again others, after some time in doing good to their wives, think it a burden, and growing weary completely leave their former good course, which plainly shows that they never truly and entirely loved their wives.

By this pattern of Christ proposed to husbands, we have on the one side a good direction to teach us how to love our wives, as has been particularly declared; and on the other side, matter of humiliation, in that it shows us how far short we come of our binding duty. However, wives may most complain of their burden, because it is a submission to which by nature we all hate to yield. Yet I am sure the heaviest burden is laid upon the husband's shoulders, and much it is easier to perform the part of a good wife than of a good husband.

Husbands Loving Their Wife as Themselves

To the example of Christ the apostle adds the pattern of one's self, in these words, "So ought men to love their wives as their own bodies" (Eph. 5:28).

Question: Is not the former pattern sufficient? Is this latter more excellent, more perfect?

Answer: Christ's example is a full, complete, perfect, and all sufficient pattern, far more excellent than of a man's self.

This is not attached to add anything to that, or regarding the excellence, but only because of our slowness, to make the point somewhat more plain and clear. For this pattern is more tangible and more easily discerned. Everyone knows how he loves his own body, but few or none know how Christ loves His church. Besides, that example of Christ may seem too high and excellent for any to attain to, even beyond imitation; therefore to show that he requires no more than a man may perform, if he will set himself with care and conscience to do his duty, he adds the pattern of one's self. That which one does to his body, if he will, he may do to his wife.

No direction can be taken from this latter pattern, but might be referred to the former, as most of the former example (though in a far lesser manner) may be referred to the latter. For the love which a man bears to himself is true, and entire without any hypocrisy: the most hypocritical wretch in the world (who in his dealings with other men does nothing uprightly) nor will nor can play the hypocrite with himself; though other men shall never know the depth of his heart, yet the spirit which is in him, even himself, knows it (1 Cor. 2:11).

This pattern also presses truth and sincerity on husbands in their affection towards their wives. Of all others they may not conceal and be two-faced with them, but let them know their complete affection towards them, and see they neither merely seek their favor, nor flatter them. They which pretend great love to their wives in show only, sin against nature itself. As the love of a man's own self is in its manner complete and true, so also it is free, not forced, and for measure as great as it possibly can be, and for perseverance, constant, and so similar to Christ's love. But there are two points especially to be considered in the love of one's self which above others are most plainly discerned in this pattern: tenderness and cheerfulness.

No other man will or can so tenderly handle a man's hand, arm, leg, or any other part of his body, as himself. He is very aware of his own pain.

The metaphors which the apostle uses in these words, he "nourisheth and cherisheth it," vividly set forth this tenderness (Eph. 5:29), for they are taken from fowls and birds which very cautiously and tenderly hover over their young ones, covering them with their wings and feathers, but so bearing up their bodies as no weight lies upon them.

Thus ought husbands with all tenderness, and gentleness to deal with their wives, as we have before noted in many particulars. Only this example of a man's self I thought good to set before husbands, as a vivid pattern in which they might behold an example without exception, going before them, and by which they might receive excellent direction for the better performing of the particulars before noted.

Again, no friend, no parent, no other party will or can so willingly and cheerfully do any kindness for one, as a man for himself. This among other is one especial point which the law aims at when it enjoins a man to love his neighbor as himself, namely, as willingly and eagerly as himself (Lev. 19:18). Whatever a man does for himself he does much more cheerfully than for another. No other proof than experience is needed. Let men take notice of their own mind and disposition when they do things for themselves, and this will be as clear as the light when the sun shines forth at noon day.

Such affection ought husbands to have to their wives. They ought more willingly and cheerfully to do anything for their wives than for parents, children, friends, or any others. Though this cheerfulness is an inward disposition of the heart, it may be manifested by a man's eagerness and readiness to do his wife good, when his wife shall no sooner desire a kindness, than he will be ready to grant it. Boaz says to Ruth, "I will do to thee all that thou requirest" (Ruth 3:11).

If by any means he may know that this or that will benefit her, though she desire it not, yet to make it happen for her, this was the mindset of Boaz to Ruth.

Contrary is the disposition of those husbands who so resentfully and unhappily do those things which they do for their wives, so that their wives would prefer they were not done at all. The manner of doing them causes more grief to tender-hearted wives, than the things themselves can do good.

Thus ends the manner which husbands ought to observe in performing their duties. The reasons to enforce the same remain to be handled.

Christ's Example, a Motive to Provoke Husbands to Love Their Wife

The examples of Christ and of ourselves as they are patterns for our direction, are general motives to provoke and stir us up to perform all these duties after the manner required. A greater and stronger motive cannot be given than the example of Christ. Example in itself is of great force to motivate us to do anything, especially if it is the example of some great one, a man of position and fame. Who is greater than Christ? What more worthy pattern is there? If the example of the church be of great force to move wives to be subject to their husbands, the example of Christ must be of much greater force to move husbands to love their wives. It is a great honor to be similar to Christ, and His example is a perfect pattern.

There are two things in Christ's example which are especially to be noticed to move husbands to love their wives, both that great inequality which is between Him and His spouse, and that small benefit which He reaps by loving her.

To better discern that inequality, the greatness of Christ on the one side, and the lowness of the church on the other, are duly to be weighed. Christ's greatness is set forth in Scripture by comparing Him with creatures and the Creator.

Compared with creatures He is far more excellent than the most excellent, as the apostle by many arguments proves in the first chapter to Hebrews; that whole chapter is spent in proof of this point. In another place it is said that He is set "far above all principality, and power, and might, and dominion, and every name that is named not only in this world, but also in that which is to come" (Eph. 1:21).

Compared with the Creator He is not subordinate to Him, but *equal* (Phil. 2:6). He is "the brightness of glory, and the express image of his person" (Heb. 1:3) and that Word of whom it is said, "In the beginning was the Word, and the Word was with God, and the Word was God.... All things were made by him" (John 1:1,3). So He is the very Creator himself, eternal, infinite, incomprehensible. Thus is Christ's greatness beyond our understanding.

The lowness of the church is as low on the other side. She is a creature, fashioned out of the earth, proceeding from the loins of corrupt Adam, not only finite, but in itself of low and little value. The prophet Ezekiel sets her forth in vivid colors as she is in herself (Ezek. 16:1–6). Compared therefore to Christ she is "nothing," "less than nothing" (Isa. 40:17). What equality, what proportion can there then be between Christ and her?

But if man and woman be compared together, we shall find a close equality, both in the points of their humiliation and also of their exaltation. Regarding the former, they are both of the same mold, of the same corrupt nature, subject to the same weaknesses, at length brought to the same end. Regarding the latter the best and greatest privileges are common to both of them. They are both made after the same image, redeemed by the same price, partakers of the same grace, and heirs together of the same inheritance.

Question: What is then the higher rank of the male kind? What is the excellence of a husband?

Answer: Only outward and momentary. Outward, in the things of this world only, for in Christ Jesus they are both one (Gal. 3:28). Momentary, for the time of this life only, for "in the resurrection they neither marry, nor are given in marriage, but are as the angels of God in heaven" (Matt. 22:30); then all submission of wives to husbands ceases.

To conclude this point, the inequality between Christ and the church, and equality between husband and wife being such as has been declared, seeing Christ grants love to His church, should not man by this be moved to love his wife?

The other point concerning the small benefit which Christ reaps by His church, will yet further enforce the point. To illustrate this we will notice the great benefit which man reaps by his wife.

The benefit which Christ reaps from the church is in one word *nothing*, for Christ is in himself *all-sufficient*. He neither needs anything, nor can receive anything. "If thou be righteous, what givest thou him? Or what receiveth he of thine hand?" (Job 35:7). Yet abundantly He gives all kinds of gifts: temporal and spiritual, earthly and heavenly. It was not therefore His own good that He considered in loving the church, but her good, for He being God became man (1 Tim. 3:16). Being Lord of heaven and earth, He took upon Himself the form of a servant (Phil. 2:6–7). Being rich He became poor (2 Cor. 8:9). Having the keys of hell and of death (Rev. 1:18), and being the Lord of life (Acts 3:15), "he humbled himself, and became obedient unto the death" (Phil. 2:8). Thus, to show love to His church, He left much for her sake, but received nothing from her.

But the benefit which man reaps from a wife is very great, for "it is not good that the man should be alone" (Gen. 2:18). "He who findeth a wife findeth a good thing" (Prov. 18:22), and that in all the points of goodness, a profitable thing, a comfortable thing, a delightful thing. They do know the benefit of the married state, who prefer single life above it, especially if the married state be ordered by God's Word, and husband and wife careful to perform their own duty each to other.

To apply this point also, and to bring it to the conclusion, if Christ who can receive nothing from the church still loves her, should not men much more love their wives, who in many ways receive much good from them, and without whom they cannot be well?

This example of Christ is to be noticed because it completely wipes away all those false colors, and vain pretenses which many assert as reasons to show that there is little reason they should love their wives. Some of their claims are these:

1. Their wives are of a far lower rank than themselves. Should they perform duty to their subordinates? Commonly they who marry their kitchen maids, or others far under their degree, assert this claim.

Answer: I might reply that marriage advances a wife to the degree of her husband: and that it was his own folly to marry one so low, but for the purpose and point in hand, let any tell me, whether the supposed difference between them and their wives is in any degree comparable to that which is between Christ and the church. Yet Christ thinks it not much to do duties of love to His church.

2. There is nothing in their wives worthy to be loved.

Answer: The simple fact that she is your wife is cause enough to make her worthy of love. But what was there in the church to make her worthy of Christ's love? If it be said that she is endued with many excellent graces which make her lovely in Christ's sight, I answer, that of herself she has none of those graces, Christ has given them to her, and so made her lovely, and thus should you work by using all good means you can to make your wife match your love, but in ancy case to love her.

3. Their wives give good reason to be hated by reason of their irritability, stubbornness, pride, and other intolerable vices.

Answer: There is no good reason to move a husband to hate his wife, nor any vice that should seem intolerable to him. With goodness he ought to overcome evil. If scandalous sins seemed intolerable to Christ, or that He thought there was a good reason to cause hatred, many that are of His church would often draw His hatred upon them, but Christ never hates a member of His church.

4. There is no hope that I shall ever receive any help of my wife, or benefit from her.

Answer: There is little love in those who can conceive no hope, for love "hopeth all things" (1 Cor. 13:7). Yet this is the case with Christ. The church is so utterly unable to help or benefit Him, that He may justly say He cannot hope to receive anything from her. Christ loves the church for her own good, not for His; so ought husbands. Thus if Christ's example be well weighed and observed by husbands, it will give matter enough to remove every doubt or objection raised to alienate their affections from their wives. Wisely therefore has the apostle set it before husbands, both to direct them how to love their wives, and also to move them so to do.

A Man's Love to Himself, a Motive to Provoke Him to Love His Wife

To the same purpose that Christ's example tends, tends also the pattern of a man's self. Great is the affection that a man bears to himself, to his own flesh, his own body. He never hates, but ever loves himself. No sore, no disease, no pain, no stench that the flesh brings to a man can make him hate it, but rather all manner of weaknesses do make him the more to pity, treat it tenderly, and cherish it. This is a work of nature; the most pagan barbarians that ever were, do it.

Now a wife, being to a man as his body and his flesh, and God having commanded men to love their wives as their own bodies, these conclusions will necessarily follow from this motive:

1. He that does not love his wife is more carried with the instinct of nature, than with the plain command of the God of nature. Nature's instinct moves him to love his body. But God's plain command does not move him to love his wife.

2. He that does not love his wife is worse than an unbeliever and a barbarian, even than a very beast, for all these love their own bodies, and their own flesh, but a wife (by God's ordinance) is as one's body, and his flesh.

3. He that loves his wife loves himself. The apostle himself in these very words lays down this conclusion, from which by the rule of contraries this also will follow: he that does not love his wife, does not loves himself.

4. He that does not love his wife cannot avoid bringing sadness and trouble upon himself. For the damage and trouble which results a wife through any neglect of duty on her husband's part, comes also on him, since the trouble which results on the body through any negligence of the head, comes also on the head.

If these are not sufficient motives to motivate a husband to love his wife, I do not know what can be sufficient.